THE
TAX
GUIDE FOR
TRADERS

ROBERT A. GREEN, CPA

McGraw·Hill

New York   Chicago   San Francisco   Lisbon   London   Madrid   Mexico City
Milan   New Delhi   San Juan   Seoul   Singapore   Sydney   Toronto

Library of Congress Cataloging-in-Publication Data

Green, Robert A., 1955–
    The tax guide for traders / by Robert A. Green.
        p.   cm.
    ISBN 0-07-144139-5 (hardcover: alk. paper)
        1. Securities—Taxation—Law and legislation—United States.   2. Floor traders (Finance)—
    Taxation—Law and legislation—United States.   3. Tax planning—United States.   I. Title.

    KF6415.Z9 G68   2004
    336.24′24—dc22   2004012344

4 5 6 7 8 9 0   DOC/DOC   0 9 8

ISBN 0-07-144139-5

McGraw-Hill books are available at special quantity discounts to use as premiums and sales promotions or for use in corporate training programs. For more information, please write to the Director of Special Sales, Professional Publishing, McGraw-Hill, Two Penn Plaza, New York, NY 10121-2298. Or contact your local bookstore.

This book is printed on acid-free paper.

Contents

CHAPTER 4

Retirement Plans   89

CHAPTER 9

Proprietary Trading   261

Look Closely at Agreements
*Employment Contracts or Deals Without Signed Contracts •
Independent Contractor Agreements or Deals Without Signed
Agreements • LLC Operating Agreements*
Important Tax Matters for Proprietary Traders
*Independent Contractors Receiving a Form 1099-Misc •
LLC Members Receiving a Form K-1 • Employees Receiving
W-2s • Deposits and How to Write Them Off on Tax Returns •
Nonresident Proprietary Traders*
State Rules for Registered Investment Advisors
Chapter Summary

CHAPTER 10

IRS Exams   275

Turning Up the Heat on Taxpayers
*Case 1: NYC Trader Exam • Case 2: Part-Time Trader Exam •
Case 3: Full-Time California Trader Exam*
Do Schedule Cs Cause IRS Troubles for Traders?
Chapter Summary

CHAPTER 11

Tax Law Changes for Traders   289

How the 2003 Tax Act Affects Business Traders
Dividends • Investment Income
Miscellaneous Rules for Traders
*Short-Sale Expenses and Substitute Payments in
Lieu of Dividends • Short-Sale Expenses • Substitute
Payments in Lieu of Dividends*

Conclusion   295

Index   301

Why You
Need This Book

Are you a *business trader*? If you actively trade financial products (securities, commodities, futures, and currencies) with the intention of making a living, you may qualify for business treatment with trader tax status.

It is well worth your time and effort to learn about trader tax laws and benefits. Learn how to deduct every business-related expense possible including home office, education, and much more, generating average savings well over $10,000 per year. Learn how to elect mark-to-market accounting on time so you can get immediate tax refunds on all your trading losses, without limitation (tax loss insurance); otherwise you are stuck with capital loss limitations and wash sale rule deferrals. Learn how to use entities for added tax savings on retirement and fringe benefit plans. Investors get the shaft in the tax laws, but traders get the golden goose. The only problem is that you must learn about these laws and make key elections and filings on time. Most traders miss the boat, but you just caught it by finding this book. Read on and prosper.

Traders can save a fortune with legal means. This book is not for tax avoidance schemes or tax cheats. Taxpayers are keen on using every legal and ethical means to lower their tax bills. Some go too far over the gray line chasing tax avoidance schemes; others are plain tax cheats.

If you are looking for tax avoidance schemes, this book is not right for you. It is for the legitimate and significant tax savings you can realize by unlocking all the tax benefits related to trader tax status. Most traders still have not tapped into the minefield of benefits, so why chase fool's gold when you can tap into this trader tax gold?

If you are a business trader or active investor, you need this book; you can't find this information anywhere else and without it, you will most likely miss out on many trader tax benefits. Or, you will find some of this information elsewhere but skewed in the wrong direction, and you may be pushed into complex entities and trader tax schemes you don't need. The boom needs to be lowered on the trader tax scam providers, and you will want the necessary alerts. Trader tax success is as much about trusted judgment as it is about information, and both are clearly lacking in the marketplace today.

We start with showing you every possible way to save taxes as a trader and focus on helping you determine whether you qualify for these benefits in the first place. If you fall short of qualification, we show you the next best things you can do as investors to save as much in taxes as possible.

Tax cheating and avoidance were always against the law. In the current environment of corporate, accounting, and tax scandals, it's just plain foolish to pursue such options. Yesterday's recipe for success using tax avoidance schemes—many promoted by premiere names in the law and accounting fields, Wall Street, and big money center banks—are tomorrow's recipe for fines, penalties, interest, and possibly even jail time.

Use your common sense when evaluating tax strategies; if it seems "too good to be true" and it makes little or no economic sense, and it costs plenty of money with the professionals advocating it, then you should figure it is trouble and walk the other way.

Taxes are like a long-term investment over many years. It often takes the Internal Revenue Service (IRS) a few years to catch up and once they do, they are entitled to go back three tax years for most items and as far back as they like for fraud. Throw those wishes of "no tax" nirvana out the window and get real. This book will show you all the trader tax benefits.

The focus falls first on trader tax benefits, high net-worth family tax planning comes later. High net-worth taxpayers (with millions of dollars) should also be interested in estate, gift, and family tax planning. No sense giving half your estate to Uncle Sam and depleting what you pass on to your heirs.

Trader tax law benefits are fully legal but still widely unknown and underutilized.

Because trader tax laws are beneficial, our mission in this book is to deliver the secrets to tax success for traders, while keeping traders out of tax trouble, for a winning long-term tax position.

Most trader tax benefits are still widely unused by traders, and our mission is to get the word out. This book is unique. Not only do we give you the information you need, which is scarce, but we give you our best ideas, strategies, and judgment, which are all keys to trader tax success.

Walk into any national chain of tax offices and ask about "trader tax status," "mark-to-market accounting," "net operating losses," or anything else in this book and in almost every instance you will get a blank stare from a tax preparer who does not have a clue about these laws and benefits.

Ask your local CPA or tax attorney and they may know a little about it, but probably not much. Too many business traders missed out on mark-to-market (MTM) accounting—their trading house burned down and they did not have tax loss insurance—because their trusted long-time CPA or tax attorney missed the boat on MTM. Or they said okay, let's elect MTM, but they then missed the election deadline. Or they elected MTM on time but then botched the necessary filing deadline or form entries to Form 3115 (Change of Accounting Method) required to complete the MTM election process.

Big law and accounting firms have not shown much interest in the small business trader. The larger firms prefer to cater to the interests, research, and practices of large corporations and public companies.

Trader tax laws are complex and vague, with many nuances, most of which require good judgment based on many years of dedicated experience. Unless a CPA or tax attorney handles dozens of traders, they probably will come up short in their advice to you.

Everything we know about the trader tax laws, delivering tax benefits to thousands of traders for more than twenty years, is included in this book. We give you our best advice. If you were to pay us our hourly rates for delivering this advice, it would cost you tens of thousands of dollars. The price of this book, if you read and use it, will be the best investment you make this year in your trading business. Plus, it's a business deduction if you have trader tax status, or an itemized deduction if you don't.

General tax help guides and software are good, but you still need this book. General all purpose tax guides are helpful for most taxpayers, but they do not cover special trader tax laws, benefits, and strategies.

The IRS website at www.irs.gov is excellent for tax information and includes information for business traders, but don't rely on the IRS for the best tax strategies and everything you need to know—you will come up short. Do you really want the IRS to prepare your tax returns and do you want to rely on the IRS as your trusted source to deliver the most savings possible? Bad move, as you will see in this book. Some of their "unofficial" website information is not correct and damaging to traders.

Consumer tax preparation software programs and online services are excellent for many Americans, but they don't include trader tax content, questions, or resources that are a must for business traders. Some lack a few key trader tax forms.

Most importantly, tax guides and software are geared for after-the-fact tax preparation, after year-end. You need our book to make vital elections, determinations, and tax plans early in the tax year, which is where the money is! These other products are not geared for tax planning, especially not trader tax planning.

A business trader tax return can generate IRS questions unless it includes special footnotes and other strategies to reduce red flags. General tax guides and preparation programs and services don't include what you need in this regard, but our book does.

This book comes with free updates at www.greencompany.com/Book/ index.shtml, user name: greentaxbook and password: mh04x729.

CHAPTER 1

Are You a Business Trader?

Active traders who rise to the level of "trading as a business" (as a sole proprietor or in an entity) qualify (in the eyes of the IRS) for trader tax status. These traders have two principal tax benefits over investors. The first is that traders may consider their trading losses (if mark-to-market) and business expenses as "ordinary" deductions from gross income, and they can be deducted without any kind of limitations. Investors are severely limited under the tax code from deducting their trading losses and expenses. They are subject to capital loss limitations, wash sale loss deferral rules, and limitations on deducting their investment interest expenses and investment expenses as itemized deductions. Investors have no tax benefits over traders, although both may benefit from long-term capital gains rate relief.

The first part of trader tax status, ordinary business expenses, is mandatory and always beneficial taxwise. It provides a lot of leeway. Trader tax status may be applied (claimed) to a trader's tax returns after the fact, which means that you may take this trader tax status benefit for all "open year" tax returns. Open years include the current tax year, the tax year just ended (for which you may or may not have filed a tax return already), and filing amended tax returns limited to the prior three tax years. In other words, you can read this book, determine whether you qualified for trader tax status, and then file amended tax returns to claim tax refunds for your trading business expenses.

The average trader saves significant taxes each year by using the first part of trader tax status: ordinary business expenses. The average trader is able to deduct computer hardware and software costs, home office expenses, margin interest expenses, Internet services, and other traditional trading expenses (such as research, books, periodicals, online subscription services, chat room services, seminars, travel to conventions, meals and entertainment with other traders, professional tax service and guide expenses, phone, furniture, fixtures, and more). Remember, investors may only deduct a fraction of these types of expenses, and the amounts they can deduct are severely limited, due to an itemized deduction phase-out, a 2 percent AGI miscellaneous expense floor, and no deduction for the alternative minimum tax calculation.

The second part of trader tax status is mark-to-market accounting. The details of mark-to-market will be discussed in Chapter 2.

HOW TO QUALIFY FOR TRADER TAX STATUS

Qualification: The First Step

Before you are able to use trader tax status benefits (i.e., business expenses and the opportunity to elect mark-to-market accounting), you first must qualify as a trader in the eyes of the IRS. Even if you don't choose mark-to-market accounting, gaining trader tax status is beneficial in all instances. It allows you to report your trading expenses on an individual tax return, Schedule C, and you may amend past tax returns after the fact (up to three years prior) if you qualify as a trader for those years. MTM accounting may not be taken after the fact.

The Tax Laws for Qualification

Unfortunately, no objective tests establish qualification. It is dependent on existing tax court cases, most of which happened well before the online trading revolution. The tax court developed a two-part test, and both parts must be satisfied for a trader to qualify for trader tax status. As you will see, however, both parts are ambiguous and leave plenty of room for interpretation:

1. The taxpayer's trading must be substantial, regular, frequent, and continuous. Sporadic trading won't be a trade or business.
2. The taxpayer seeks to catch the swings in the daily market movements and profit from these short-term changes rather than profiting from long-term holding of investments.

Many traders need more help in determining whether they qualify. The following scenarios are situations our firm encountered over the years, but they are hypothetical and you are not automatically disqualified if you do not fit into one of the categories. Your best bet is to consult a trader tax professional.

If you are a full-time trader (and you have no other major sources of income to pay your living) and you spend all day, every day trading, you qualify without question (unless you lose money every year).

If you are a part-time trader because you have another business activity (a business or a job), the IRS will scrutinize your qualification for trader tax status, especially if you elect mark-to-market accounting and carry back a huge net operating loss (NOL), which will be described in detail later on in the book. You can still qualify as a part-time trader if you can prove to the IRS that you spend more than three hours per day in your trading business. If you trade less than once per day, the IRS may reject your trader tax status.

If you qualify as a pattern day trader (PDT) under the rules implemented by the Securities and Exchange Commission (SEC) in 2001 (i.e., you make more than four day trades in a five-day period), it is a big plus if you are being questioned by the IRS. However, if you are not a PDT, it does not automatically mean you will not qualify.

IRS PUBLICATION 550:
SPECIAL RULES FOR TRADERS IN SECURITIES

What follows is an excerpt of the special rules for traders from IRS Publication 550. We add our observations in italics.

> Special rules apply if you are a trader in securities in the business of buying and selling securities for your own account. To be engaged in business as a trader in securities, you must meet all the following conditions.

> ■ You must seek to profit from daily market movements in the prices of securities and not from dividends, interest, or capital appreciation.

> *Observation: Most active securities traders easily meet this condition; their dividends received are a tiny fraction of their sales proceeds.*

> ■ Your activity must be substantial.

> *Observation: Most active traders easily meet this condition. They have one or more active online or direct-access brokerage accounts, they spend countless hours watching and reading business news, they buy trading books and online services, they buy computers and software just for their trading business, and they generate millions of dollars in sales proceeds from "churning" their own accounts.*

> ■ You must carry on the activity with continuity and regularity.

> *Observation: Most active traders easily meet this condition, although part-time traders may have a difficult time. Full-time traders are busy in the markets throughout every trading day. However, certain other traders are not able to trade every trading day or throughout the trading day— traders such as part-time traders who have other jobs or business activities.*

The following facts and circumstances should be considered in determining if your activity is a securities trading business:

■ Typical holding periods for securities bought and sold.

Observation: Most active traders easily meet this condition. They don't hold positions open for longer than a few weeks, and in the case they do, they usually are trading around that position as part of a hedge. Some traders hold positions for a day (day traders), others for a few days, and still others for a few weeks to a month (swing traders).

All of these types of traders may qualify. The longest holding periods are with swing traders. One site on the Internet describes swing trading as follows: "Taking advantage of brief price swings in stocks lasting anywhere from one day to a month and using technical analysis to pinpoint entry and exit points." It is not high-speed day trading or scalp trading. Nor is it buy, hold, and pray (otherwise known as investing). Some people call it momentum investing, because you only hold positions that are making major moves. By rolling your money over rapidly through short-term gains you can quickly build up a great deal of equity.

■ The frequency and dollar amount of your trades during the year.

Observation: Most active traders easily meet this condition, because they trade daily and their sales proceeds total more than several million dollars per year. The IRS receives a copy of a trader's Form 1099 from the trader's broker showing each and every stock sale transaction and the total amount of sales proceeds. If you have pages and pages of sales, and one almost every day, the IRS will conclude on its own that you qualify. If the opposite is the case, the IRS may ask you questions.

Equity options are not listed in the front part of the Form 1099 (the part the IRS gets); they don't get the Supplemental Information. Options are only given in totals by most online and direct-access brokers.

Commodities are also not reported in detail per transaction. Instead, they are only listed by "aggregate profit and loss." As a result, the IRS can't see your frequency and dollar amount of proceeds on commodities. As a rule of thumb, qualified traders need at least one trade per day, whether they are trading full-time or part-time. See more rules of thumb that follow.

■ The extent to which you pursue the activity to produce income for a livelihood.

Observation: Most active traders can meet this condition. However, this IRS requirement is the one that may provide the most trouble to some traders in their pursuit of trader tax status qualification.

This "livelihood" requirement is rather vague when applied to the trading business. Most traders may only enter the trading business if they have sufficient capital to trade with; after all, "it takes money to lose money." Some traders have more than sufficient capital to cover their future "livelihood" and the risk of trading. The following types of traders fall into this category: Retired persons who are not ready to clip coupons and play bridge all day, and who would rather operate a trading business, while enjoying retirement activities on weekends; downsized Wall Streeters and other corporate executives who leave employment with a huge nest egg, can't find other work, and decide to hire themselves in their own trading business.

Other traders already have a job or business activity that "produces income for a livelihood." Nothing in this requirement mentions anything about not being able to have two or more "activities to produce income for a livelihood." Isn't that what a second job is all about—providing more income to support your family? See the section on part-time traders. The IRS website says, "Your day trading activity . . . is expected to be your primary income for meeting your personal living expenses" and "you do not have another regular job." Notice how the IRS slipped in that part about not having another regular job. However, their website is older than the IRS Publication 550 section, and the latter is official, whereas the website is not, which is good news for part-time traders.

Before entering a trading business, most traders are aware of the inherent risk of losing all their capital. Most traders manage this business risk by first learning the business (reading trading business books, attending trading seminars, and subscribing to trading business services). The majority of traders enter the business because they are hungry to "produce income for a livelihood."

■ The amount of time you devote to the activity.

Observation: Most active traders easily meet this condition. They spend way too much time (according to their spouses) on the computer in their trading business. Do yourself a favor: Log that time and save your cache, and/or keep a diary. If you get examined, the IRS will be overwhelmed when they see how much time you actually spent trading.

As a rule of thumb, you should spend at least three hours per day in your trading business. Although it is a significant amount of time, it is feasible for part-time traders.

Part-time trader tax status should remain a focal point in IRS exams and tax court cases for traders. You should check for free updates at www.greencompany.com/Book/index.shtml (user: greentaxbook and password: mh04x729).

If your trading activities are not a business, you are considered an investor, and not a trader. It does not matter whether you call yourself a trader or a day trader.

What About Commodities?

Notice that IRS Publication 550 states "special rules for traders in securities." It does not mention commodities. Don't worry, all the new mark-to-market trader tax laws are written for "traders in securities or commodities."

It may be easier for commodities traders to qualify as being in the business of trading than securities traders. Consider the special rules for securities traders in Publication 550. Few commodities traders seek capital appreciation, and you cannot receive interest or dividend income on commodities.

The nature of commodities trading is short-term trading. Not too many tax-payers "invest" in commodities, so the IRS may not scrutinize commodities traders as much as they will scrutinize securities traders, who are not as active. However, a commodities trader needs to meet all the conditions of IRS Publication 550.

Securities and commodities trading businesses are normally separate businesses, although at times they can be one.

It is not written in the law, but an analysis of the law indicates that securities trading and commodities trading are two separate businesses. You may actively trade in tech stocks for your securities trading business and actively trade in currency futures for your commodities trading business. Your currency futures trading has nothing to do with your tech stocks.

On the other hand, you may have one trading program that requires side-by-side trading in securities and commodities. For example, one of your trading plans could be to trade tech stocks and tech stock indexes (indexes that are treated as commodities). You might hedge your tech stocks with the indexes.

If you need to address securities and commodities trading as two separate businesses, then you need to qualify for each separately. If you can combine the businesses per the preceding example, then you can qualify for the trading business of securities and commodities together. Combining can be helpful if the following scenario applies: You trade securities 200 round-trips per year and commodities 200 round-trips per year. Each alone is perhaps not enough to qualify. Together, though, they are enough to qualify.

Many types of traders may not qualify for trader tax status. Let's look at a few different types.

Part-Time Traders

The definition of trader tax status is vague. It is based on tax court cases rather than tax law. Part-time traders need to proceed with caution. They should be prepared for the IRS to question or challenge their trader tax status. However, we strongly believe that many part-time traders qualify for trader tax status and they should not be scared off from using it.

Here are three reasons why we believe the IRS may challenge a part-time trader's use of trader tax status.

1. Our firm has been engaged by a few part-time traders to represent them in an IRS exam. The IRS denied a commercial airline pilot trader tax status because they could not understand how she could both fly a plane as her full-time occupation and operate a trading business. We had to fight hard to explain to the IRS that while the pilot flew the plane, her trading business was on auto-pilot (using "stop" and "stop limit" orders, monitoring software, beepers, phone and laptops, etc.), and on the many days she was required by law not to fly, she operated her trading business full-time.

2. The IRS website specifically states problems for part-time traders. It states that trading is "expected to be your primary income for meeting your personal living expenses, i.e., if you do not have another regular job, your trading activity might be a business."

3. IRS Publication 550 section "Special Rules for Traders in Securities" also states "the extent to which you pursue the activity to produce income for a livelihood." This requirement is vague.

The good news is that the IRS does not mention anything about "part-time" or "another regular job" in IRS Publication 550. This publication was completed after the IRS website section. Also, IRS Publication 550 is an official position, whereas the IRS website is not.

The IRS website indicates you can't use trader tax status if you have another job. It states the following:

A business is generally an activity carried on for a livelihood or in good faith to make a profit. Rather than defined in the tax code, exactly what activities are considered business activities has long been the subject of court cases. The facts and circumstances of each case determine whether or not an activity is a trade or business. Basically, if your day trading activity goal is to profit from short-term swings in the market rather than from long-term capital appreciation of investments, and is expected to be your primary income for meeting your personal living expenses, i.e., you do not have another regular job, your trading activity might be a business.

Notice the two problematic statements: "your day trading activity . . . is expected to be your primary income for meeting your personal living expenses" and "you do not have another regular job." Don't panic. As we pointed out previously, IRS Publication 550 is more current than the IRS website (as of this search) and IRS Publication 550 is official, whereas the website is "unofficial" (according to an IRS agent and a person in charge of writing the new trader tax mark-to-market laws).

The preceding IRS statement says "another job." It does not say "another business." The fact is that many people do operate more than one business (or even more than one job) at any given time. Nowhere in the tax code does it say a taxpayer is allowed employee tax status for only one job at a time, or business tax status for one business at a time. For example, one might have a full-time job, but also be partners with their spouse in a family business. They spend time at work, but they spend nights and weekends running the business (or handling their particular area of the business). As another example, consider certain people you know who operate many businesses at one time, such as real estate, law, or a new Internet business.

The bottom line is that nothing in the tax law states a business can only receive business tax treatment if it's the exclusive business operated by the taxpayer. It is probably why the IRS was not able to unequivocally point this out in IRS Publication 550.

Needless to say, the IRS will not be happy about active investors claiming trader tax status and using mark-to-market accounting to carry back hundreds of thousands of dollars in NOLs for six-figure refund checks. So, if your case is not solid, proceed with caution and perhaps contact our firm for more help. We have important updates on part-time trader tax status at www.greencompany/Book/index.shtml.

Why a Part-Time Trader with Another Job Can Qualify

In these times, given today's advances in technology and ability to virtually (i.e., through the Internet) be in more than one place at one time, it is possible for taxpayers to operate more than one job or business. A person can operate two jobs at once, each for 30 hours per week. One could consider each a "full-time" job.

Trading is a job that can be done easily while operating another business or job. For example, we have many clients in California who have jobs in Silicon Valley and operate active trading businesses. These clients qualify for trader tax status.

Example: Here is a composite example of how many part-time, qualified traders spend their week timewise. They actively trade in the markets from 6:30 A.M to 9 A.M. PST, which is 9:30 A.M to noon EST, prime time in the markets. They leave for work at 9 A.M PST and, while in their office from noon to 6:30 P.M EST, monitor their positions, make some trades, and do some research during breaks. After dinner at home, they spend the evening in their trading business, doing administration, accounting, research, and planning trades for the next morning. At the end of the week, they made several round-trip trades every trading day, they held trades open only for minutes, their entire strategy was to look for short price swings, they spent six hours per day in the trading business, and they ended the week with more profits from trading than from their salary. The IRS would be hard-pressed to deny them trader tax status. If our firm prepared their returns, we are highly confident we would successfully prevent the IRS from making any changes to their taxes as far as trader tax status is concerned. In fact, we already won a few similar IRS exams.

Example of the IRS Partially Ruling Against a Part-Time Trader

We did have a difficult time with the exam for the pilot mentioned previously. We did not prepare her tax return—she engaged us to help defend her trader tax status after she received an IRS exam notice. She traded less than once per trading day and had fewer than 200 round-trip trades for the year. She also held some positions for a month or more. She was serious about trading, but her factors just did not add up and she was a close call. The IRS initially said no, because they did not even understand trader tax status. After we educated them on trader tax status, they still wanted to say no, but settled by allowing trader tax status for one year and denying it for another. It was not worth going to IRS appeals.

Rules of Thumb for Part-Time Traders

As a general rule of thumb, we think a part-time trader should have at least one round trip per day (preferably three or more per day), every trading day (with some exceptions allowed); they should hold securities for no longer than a few days; they should have total proceeds at year-end in the millions of dollars; they should spend at least three hours per day, every day, in their trading business; they should have serious trading business expenses and services; and they should not rely on others for trading decisions.

Perennial Money-Losing (or Not-for-Profit) Traders

The IRS has its "not-for-profit activity" rules to prevent taxpayers from deducting tax losses in certain business activities that produce losses every year. The IRS considers these activities to be either "hobbies," continual losing activities, or not serious businesses. The IRS utilizes application of these rules to deny a taxpayer normal business tax treatment, which would entitle that taxpayer to unlimited ordinary business losses.

Ordinary trading business losses can be the focus of the not-for-profit activity rules. Not-for-profit activity rules can be a problem for traders, especially if they lost money in their trading business for many years in a row (some traders never show a profit). Trading business losses—the potential focus of these rules—come from trading business expenses (reported on Schedule C for individuals) and ordinary trading losses (if the trader elected and uses mark-to-market accounting). If a trader has capital losses (i.e., doesn't use MTM), that part of their losses is not subject to application of the not-for-profit activity rules, because the taxpayer could resort to investor treatment, where these rules cannot be applied.

Mention of These Rules on the IRS Website

On the IRS website, one of their answers about traders mentions the following: "For details about not-for-profit activities, refer to Chapter 1 in Publication 535, Business Expenses. That chapter explains how to determine whether your activity is carried on to make a profit and how to figure the amount of loss you can deduct." This mention by the IRS indicates that the IRS believes these rules can be applicable to traders.

To date, we have not yet heard of the IRS deeming a trading business a "hobby," or a business that is not serious in nature. The problem is that a trading business is similar to an investing activity, and the difference is just in the degree of volume (time spent, number of trades, holding periods, etc.).

The good news is that these rules are not specifically mentioned in the section on traders in IRS Publication 550. We analyzed the actual rules and believe traders can win on this issue.

How to Avoid the Hobby Loss Rules

The hobby loss rules were created to take the subjective assessment out of the equation and to have a benchmark objective test to determine whether the taxpayer has a profit-making intent. This objective test is summarized in an excerpt from the IRS website. [A more detailed and informative listing should be read at IRS Reg § 1.183-2. "Activity not engaged in for profit": paragraph (b) Relevant factors.] After reading the relevant factors in detail in IRS Reg § 1.183-2, we believe most qualified traders will easily avoid the hobby loss rules based on meeting the profit-making intent test.

A trader can use two ways to avoid the hobby loss rules. The first is to meet the profit-making intent test. The IRS regs themselves say that the hobby loss rules won't apply if the facts and circumstances show that you have a profit-making objective.

The second way is to show a profit in at least three out of five consecutive years (two out of seven years for breeding, training, showing, or racing horses). The key point here for traders, is that you can avoid hobby loss rules just based on the profit-making intent test.

This point is key for traders. It is this writer's opinion that traditional hobby businesses can more easily fail the profit-making intent test, and they are then forced through the hoops and elections of the 3-out-of-5-years profit-making test. Be strong and don't fail the first test.

Relevant Factors for the Profit-Making Intent Test

Is it a business or a hobby? (excerpt from www.irs.gov)

It is generally accepted that people prefer to make a living doing something they like. If you are thinking of starting a business but it does not provide you with "a living," or make a profit, your expenses may not be deductible. Expenses connected with your business activities may be tax deductible or limited to the rules for hobby expenses. The limit on not-for-profit (hobby) losses applies to individuals, partnerships, estates, trusts, and S corporations. It does not apply to corporations other than S corporations.

In determining whether you are carrying on an activity for profit, all the facts should be taken into account. No one factor alone is decisive. Among the factors to consider (*this is the profit-making intent test*) are whether:

- You carry on the activity in a businesslike manner.
- The time and effort you put into the activity indicate you intend to make it profitable.
- You depend on income from the activity for your livelihood.
- Your losses are due to circumstances beyond your control (or are normal in the start-up phase of your type of business).

- You change your methods of operation in an attempt to improve profitability.
- You, or your advisors, have the knowledge needed to carry on the activity as a successful business.
- You were successful in making a profit in similar activities in the past.
- The activity makes a profit in some years.
- You can expect to make a future profit from the appreciation of the assets used in the activity.

The IRS is increasing its examination of traders and has indicated a willingness to apply the hobby loss rules to traders. Congress and the IRS were right to create the hobby loss rules to combat the types of tax shelter abuse mentioned previously. But the IRS will be wrong to apply the hobby loss rules to traders.

The online trading revolution is new to the IRS; it just got into full swing in the late 1990s. IRS agents are beginning to examine trader tax status tax returns, and some IRS agents have expressed concern about the IRS paying six-figure refund checks to traders who lost money trading year after year.

IRS agents are mostly inexperienced with the new trader tax laws. IRS agents can be expected to question trader tax reporting (Schedule C and Form 4797), qualification for trader tax status, and application of the hobby loss rules in the case of losses.

At www.irs.gov under the "Tax Topic" for "Day Trader" the following is stated:

> A business is generally an activity carried on for a livelihood or in good faith to make a profit. Rather than defined in the tax code, exactly what activities are considered business activities has long been the subject of court cases. The facts and circumstances of each case determine whether or not an activity is a trade or business. Basically, if your day trading activity goal is to profit from short-term swings in the market rather than from long-term capital appreciation of investments, and is expected to be your

primary income for meeting your personal living expenses, i.e., you do not have another regular job, your trading activity might be a business.

This page further states,

"For details about not-for-profit activities, refer to Chapter 1 in Publication 535, Business Expenses. That chapter explains how to determine whether your activity is carried on to make a profit and how to figure the amount of loss you can deduct."

This page implies that the IRS might want to apply the hobby loss rules (otherwise known as the not-for-profit activity rules).

Recently, during our representation of a trader client in his IRS exam (his return was prepared by another preparer who botched many things), the agent stated she wanted to apply the hobby loss rules to disallow this client's large ordinary trading losses. We strongly objected and said our trader client clearly met the profit-making intent test and that the IRS would never prevail on applying hobby losses to traders. To date, the agent has not presented a formal application of the hobby loss rules to that case, but the case is ongoing as of the time of this writing. The agent mentioned the IRS may want to pursue hobby loss rules against traders to set a precedent in a court case.

A Good Case to Overcome the Hobby Loss Rules

Trading businesses differ from traditional hobby/businesses such as farming or sports activities. Traditional hobby/businesses have a hard time showing a profit-making intent and the IRS has grounds to be skeptical. When in doubt, the IRS strong-arms no profit-making intent and forces the taxpayer to show a profit under the 3-out-of-5-years test. The IRS likes to take the easy road on these matters. The IRS prefers this second test because it is easy to apply; the taxpayer either has a profit in 3 out of 5 years, yes or no.

Traders should not give up on the profit making intent test for two reasons. First the 3-out-of-5-years test is a hassle and requires an election to be filed to presume profitability.

Second and more importantly, a trader cannot concede the profit-making intent test, because that would also inadvertently concede their qualification for trader tax status. It also hinges on your intent to profit from quick swings in market price (rather then merely investing for long-term profit appreciation).

The Bottom Line: If you have large trading losses in 3 out of 5 years or even in your first year or two trading, you need to learn about the hobby loss rules and how they relate to trading businesses. If you get examined by the IRS and have trading losses, you should immediately contact a trader tax expert to review how you can avoid application of the hobby loss rules and defend your trader tax status and reporting. IRS agents make their hay on strong-arming taxpayers directly; you need a trader tax expert in your corner.

Non-U.S. Resident Traders

Many international taxpayers, who otherwise do not pay U.S. taxes, have opened U.S.-based brokerage accounts and they have questions about what U.S. taxes they owe in the United States. We provide a full set of resources for international investors, traders, and proprietary traders.

If the nonresident is a member of a U.S.-based pass-through taxable entity (like a partnership or LLC) in the business of trading securities or commodities, then that person has "effectively connected income" (ECI). That person must file a nonresident tax return, U.S. Form 1040NR, to report any ECI income and pay U.S. taxes on that income.

Here is a composite of the typical questions that come from foreign-based traders:

In 2003, I lived outside the United States, but my business was trading in U.S.-based securities with a U.S.-based "direct-access" brokerage firm. In addition to that trading account, I also joined a U.S.-based "proprietary trading firm," which is organized as a U.S.-based Limited Liability Company and taxed as a partnership.

When I opened my direct-access brokerage account, I notified the broker that, for tax purposes, I was not a U.S. resident. The broker said it was required to withhold taxes on my interest and dividend income in accordance with tax law and tax treaty rates, if applicable. The good news was the broker told me it would not withhold taxes on my capital gains. At tax time, the broker sent me a Form 1042-S, reporting my U.S. tax withholding on interest and dividend income. I also understand that I don't have to file a U.S. nonresident tax return (Form 1040NR), because the tax withholding took care of my responsibilities to pay U.S. taxes.

My proprietary trading firm sent me a Form K-1, reporting my share of trading gains in the firm, based on my sub-trading account performance (see information on proprietary trading). What shall I do with this K-1? Am I required to file a U.S. tax return and pay taxes on this income?

Others questions we receive indicate the firms withheld taxes on this income, and traders want to know what to do in this situation as well.

Quick Answer: Based on the information provided (and assuming the trader doesn't have a green card, meaning he isn't a legal U.S. resident and doesn't meet the "substantial presence test"), the IRS will consider the trader a nonresident for U.S. tax purposes.

Good News: Because the trader did not spend more than 183 days in the United States in 2003, his capital gains income is not taxable in the United States.

Good News: The IRS exempts the income generated by the foreign trader's direct-access business income from the effectively connected income (ECI) rules for operating a business in the United States.

Other types of businesses operated in the United States are deemed to have ECI income, and they must pay U.S. taxes on that ECI income. We believe the IRS exempted traders because it would be hard to determine where the business was operated from. Many international taxpayers trade remotely from abroad, and it would have been unfair to tax them on ECI income in the United States. One note of caution: If you come to the

United States to trade, you may trigger residency. If this occurs, you will have to pay taxes on your trading income based on the residency rules rather than the ECI rules for nonresidents.

Bad News: The IRS does not exempt a foreign trader's K-1 income resulting from proprietary trading business activity from the effectively connected income rules for operating a business in the United States. In this case, you are required to prepare a U.S. income tax return for nonresidents, Form 1040NR. You should report this K-1 income and pay the appropriate U.S. taxes on this income.

Don't be alarmed by paying U.S. taxes. Be aware that your home country most likely allows you to claim a foreign tax credit for the U.S. taxes you pay on this ECI K-1 income. If your home country has a higher tax rate than in the United States, then you may get a dollar-for-dollar tax (foreign tax) credit.

Another Note of Caution: Answers to international tax questions for traders, investors and others are complex, and the answers depend on each taxpayer's individual facts and circumstances. Many countries have income tax treaties with the United States, and taxpayers may find relief provisions in those treaties. Each treaty varies considerably. Our international tax attorneys at GreenTraderLaw.com can help.

Summary

International taxpayers who are deemed non-residents (no U.S. green card and do not meet the substantial presence test) are subject to U.S. taxes in the following situations:

- If the nonresident has a U.S.-based brokerage account as a trader (in the business) or investor, their U.S. broker will withhold taxes on interest and dividends only (using lower tax treaty rates if applicable). No withholding will be made on capital gains. The international taxpayer does not need a U.S. tax identification number, and they are not required to file a U.S. nonresident tax return, Form 1040NR.

- If the nonresident has a U.S.-based brokerage account as a trader (in the business) or investor, and they spend more than 183 days in the United States, they owe U.S. taxes on their net U.S. source capital gains. Many tax treaties contain provisions that reduce or eliminate taxation on capital gains.
- If the nonresident has a U.S.-based brokerage account and qualifies as a trader (in the business), they are exempt from the effectively connected income (ECI) rules for international taxpayers conducting business activities in the United States.
- If the nonresident is a member of a U.S.-based pass-through taxable entity (such as a Limited Liability Company [LLC] taxed as a partnership, a general partnership, a limited partnership, or S-corporation), in the business of trading securities or commodities, then that person has effectively connected income (ECI). That person must file a nonresident tax return, Form 1040NR, to report their ECI income and pay U.S. taxes on that income.
- An international proprietary trader who is an LLC member in a U.S.-based LLC proprietary trading firm (taxed as a partnership) has ECI income (K-1) and must file a Form 1040NR and pay tax on that ECI K-1 income. (See ideas for foreign tax credits mentioned previously.)
- An investor in a U.S.-based hedge fund limited partnership (or other pass-through entities like a LLC) with trader tax status also has this ECI problem, which is why foreign investors chose to invest in "offshore" hedge funds instead.

SOME TAX LAW DETAILS WITH OBSERVATIONS

General Tax Rules for Nonresident Aliens

Foreign aliens who have a green card (U.S. permanent resident card) are considered "legal" U.S. residents, and they are taxed like any other U.S. citizen or resident on their worldwide income. Foreign aliens, without a green card, may also be considered U.S. residents if they meet the "substantial presence test" in the United States.

Useful information can be obtained at the IRS website by searching for such topics as Topic 851: Resident and Nonresident aliens; international taxpayers; and green cards.

Tax Rules for Nonresident Investors

If a nonresident alien opens a U.S. brokerage account and buys and sells U.S.-based securities as an investor or a trader, and that person does not spend 183 days or more in the United States in a given tax year, that nonresident alien is not subject to U.S. taxes on his or her U.S. brokerage account capital gains.

If the nonresident does spend more than 183 days in the United States, they owe U.S. taxes on their net U.S. source capital gains. See an excerpt from "International Taxpayer—The Taxation of Capital Gains of Nonresident Alien Students, Scholars, and Employees of Foreign Governments," published on the IRS website.

In general, all nonresident alien investors are subject to U.S. tax withholding by their U.S.-based brokerage firms on their interest and dividend income, and certain master limited partnerships (e.g.. oil and gas deals) from U.S. securities. Search the IRS website for Form 1042-S.

Tax Rules for Nonresident Traders

Generally, when a foreign person engages in a trade or business in the United States, all income from sources within the United States other than certain investment income, is considered to be effectively connected income (ECI).

This categorization applies whether or not any connection can be made between the income and the trade or business being carried on in the United States during the tax year.

Generally, you must be engaged in a trade or business during the tax year to be able to treat income received in that year as ECI. You usually are considered to be engaged in a U.S. trade or business when you perform personal services in the United States. Whether you are engaged in a trade or business in the United States depends on the nature of your activities. Deductions are allowed against ECI, and it is taxed at the graduated rates or lesser rate under a tax treaty. The discussions that follow will help you determine whether you are engaged in a trade or business in the United States.

Certain kinds of fixed, determinable, annual, or periodical (FDAP) income are treated as ECI income because:

- Certain Internal Revenue Code sections require the income to be treated as ECI.
- Certain Internal Revenue Code sections allow elections to treat the income as ECI.
- Certain kinds of investment income are treated as ECI if they pass either of the two following tests:

    - *The Asset-Use Test.* The income must be associated with U.S. assets used in, or held for use in, the conduct of a U.S. trade or business.
    - *Business Activities Test.* The activities of that trade or business conducted in the United States are a material factor in the realization of the income.

In limited circumstances, some kinds of foreign source income may be treated as effectively connected with a trade or business in the United States. Refer to Publication 519, U.S. Tax Guide for Aliens.

The following categories of income are usually considered to be connected with a trade or business in the United States.

- You are considered to be engaged in a trade or business in the United States if you are temporarily present in the United States as a nonimmigrant on an F, J, M, or Q visa. The taxable part of any U.S. source scholarship or fellowship grant received by a non-immigrant in F, J, M, or Q status is treated as effectively connected with a trade or business in the United States.

- If you are a member of a partnership that at any time during the tax year is engaged in a trade or business in the United States, you are considered to be engaged in a trade or business in the United States.
- If your only U.S. business activity is trading in stocks, securities, or commodities (including hedging transactions) through a U.S. resident broker or other agent, you are not engaged in a trade or business in the United States.
- You usually are engaged in a U.S. trade or business when you perform personal services in the United States.
- If you own and operate a business in the United States selling services, products, or merchandise, you are, with certain exceptions, engaged in a trade or business in the United States. For example, profit from the sale in the United States of inventory property purchased either in this country or in a foreign country is effectively connected trade or business income.
- Gains and losses from the sale or exchange of U.S. real property interests (whether or not they are capital assets) are taxed as if you are engaged in a trade or business in the United States. You must treat the gain or loss as connected with that trade or business.
- Income from the rental of real property may be treated as ECI if the taxpayer elects to do so.

Note: Certain kinds of income that are normally treated as ECI or FDAP may not be treated as ECI or FDAP for withholding tax purposes.

Applicable Tax Rate

Income you receive during the tax year that is effectively connected with your trade or business in the United States is, after allowable deductions, taxed at the rates that apply to U.S. citizens and residents.

Tax Year

Generally, you can receive effectively connected income only if you are a nonresident alien engaged in a trade or business in the United States during the tax year. However, income you receive from the sale or exchange of property, the performance of services, or any other transaction in another tax year is treated as effectively connected in that year if it would have been effectively connected in the year the transaction took place or you performed the services.

Observations

If you are a member of a partnership that at any time during the tax year is engaged in a trade or business in the United States, you are considered to be engaged in a trade or business in the United States.

This law requires a nonresident member of a proprietary trading firm, organized as a limited liability company (LLC) in the U.S. (taxed as a partnership), to pay U.S. taxes on this effectively connected income on a Form 1040NR nonresident tax return.

If your only U.S. business activity is trading in stocks, securities, or commodities (including hedging transactions) through a U.S. resident broker or other agent, you are not engaged in a trade or business in the United States.

This rule saves direct-access traders from paying taxes in the United States. Other types of businesses operated in the United States are deemed to have ECI income, and they must pay U.S. taxes on that ECI income. We believe the IRS exempted traders because it would be difficult to determine where the business was operated from. Many international taxpayers trade remotely from abroad, and it would have been unfair to tax them on ECI income in the United States. One note of caution: If you come to the United States to trade, you may trigger residency. Then, you will have to pay taxes on your trading income based on the residency rules rather then the ECI rules for nonresidents.

Notice that this investment income is exempt from effectively connected income. See the following rules on investment capital gains.

These ECI rules only deal with business income and they recognize "U.S. business activity is trading in stocks, securities, or commodities (including hedging transactions) through a U.S. resident broker or other agent," as being exempt from ECI.

INTERNATIONAL TAXPAYER: FIXED, DETERMINABLE, ANNUAL, PERIODICAL

Fixed, determinable, annual, or periodical (FDAP) income is all income except the following:

- Gains derived from the sale of real or personal property (including market discount and option premiums but not including original issue discount)
- Items of income excluded from gross income without regard to the U.S. or foreign status of the owner of the income, such as tax-exempt municipal bond interest and qualified scholarship income

Income is fixed when it is paid in amounts known ahead of time. Income is determinable whenever a basis is established for figuring the amount to be paid. Income can be periodic if it is paid from time to time. It does not have to be paid annually or at regular intervals. Income can be determinable or periodic even if the length of time during which the payments are made is increased or decreased.

Tax Treatment of FDAP Income That Is Not Effectively Connected Income

Tax at a 30 percent (or lower treaty) rate applies to FDAP income or gains from U.S. sources, but only if they are not effectively connected with your

U.S. trade or business. The 30 percent (or lower treaty) rate applies to the gross amount of U.S.-source fixed or determinable annual or periodic gains, profits, or income. Deductions are not allowed against FDAP income.

The following items are examples of FDAP income:

- Compensation for personal services
- Dividends
- Interest
- Original issue discount
- Pensions and annuities
- Alimony
- Real property income, such as rents, other than gains from the sale of real property
- Royalties
- Scholarships and fellowship grants
- Other grants, prizes, and awards
- A sales commission paid or credited monthly
- A commission paid for a single transaction
- The distributable net income of an estate or trust that is FDAP income and that must be distributed currently, or has been paid or credited during the tax year, to a nonresident alien beneficiary
- A distribution from a partnership that is FDAP income, or such an amount that, although not actually distributed, is includible in the gross income of a foreign partner
- Taxes, mortgage interest, or insurance premiums paid to or for the account of, a nonresident alien landlord by a tenant under the terms of a lease
- Prizes awarded to nonresident alien artists for pictures exhibited in the United States
- Purses paid to nonresident alien boxers for prize fights in the United States
- Prizes awarded to nonresident alien professional golfers in golfing tournament in the United States

Notice capital gains income does not fit into any of the preceding FDAP definitions. Rather, special rules for capital gains apply. Further note that those special rules apply to investment activities with additional complications arising for trading business activities.

Social Security Benefits

A nonresident alien must include 85 percent of any U.S. social security benefit (and the social security equivalent part of a tier 1 railroad retirement benefit) in U.S.-source fixed or determinable annual or periodic income. This income is exempt under some tax treaties. Refer to Table 1 in Publication 901, U.S. Tax Treaties, for a list of tax treaties that exempt U.S. social security benefits from U.S. tax.

Capital Gains

If you were present in the United States for 183 or more days during the tax year, and you are still a nonresident alien, your net gain from sales or exchanges of capital assets is taxed at a 30 percent (or lower treaty) rate. For purposes of the 30 percent (or lower treaty) rate, net gain is the excess of your capital gains from U.S. sources over your capital losses from U.S. sources. This rule applies even if any of the transactions occurred while you were not in the United States. The 183-day test here is not the same as the 183-day test used in the substantial presence test. See the "Taxation of Nonresident Alien Students, Scholars, and Employees of Foreign Governments" section for further information.

If you were in the United States for fewer than 183 days during the tax year, you will not be taxed on your capital gains except for the following types of gains:

- Gains that are effectively connected with a trade or business in the United States during your tax year

- Gains on the disposal of timber, coal, or domestic iron ore with a retained economic interest
- Gains on contingent payments received from the sale or exchange of patents, copyrights, and similar property after October 4, 1966
- Gains on certain transfers of all substantial rights to, or an undivided interest in, patents if the transfers were made before October 5, 1966
- Gains on the sale or exchange of original issue discount obligations

Many tax treaties contain provisions that reduce or eliminate taxation on capital gains.

Capital Gains from the Sale of Property

These rules apply only to those capital gains and losses from sources in the United States that are not effectively connected with a trade or business in the United States. They apply even if you are engaged in a trade or business in the United States. These rules do not apply to the sale or exchange of a U.S. real property interest or to the sale of any property that is effectively connected with a trade or business in the United States.

Reporting Gains and Losses

Traders must report gains and losses from the sales or exchanges of capital assets that are not connected with a trade or business in the United States on page 4 of Form 1040NR. Gains and losses from sales or exchanges of capital assets (including real property) that are connected with a trade or business in the United States are reported on a separate Schedule D (from Form 1040) and page 1 of Form 1040NR. Schedule D is attached to Form 1040NR.

Most nonresidents who are in the United States for more than 183 days meet the substantial presence test and they are taxed like U.S. residents, making this point moot.

Taxation of Nonresident Alien Students,
Scholars, and Employees of Foreign Governments

The following discussion assumes that the capital gains in question are not effectively connected with the conduct of a trade or business in the U.S.

Under the residency rules of IRC § 7701(b), most foreign students, foreign scholars, and alien employees of foreign governments and of international organizations in the United States are considered to be exempt individuals. That is, they are exempt for extended periods of time from counting days of presence in the United States for the purposes of determining their residency in the United States. Thus, most foreign students, foreign scholars, and the alien employees of foreign governments and of international organizations in the United States remain nonresident aliens in the United States for extended periods of time. Many of these nonresident aliens make personal investments in the United States, which generate income from capital gains.

IRC § 871(a)(2) imposes a flat tax of 30 percent on U.S.-source capital gains in the hands of nonresident alien individuals physically present in the United States for 183 days or more during the taxable year. The 183-day rule of IRC § 871(a)(2) bears no relation to the 183-day rule of the substantial presence test of IRC § 7701(b)(3) and the exceptions to the residency rules (e.g., exempt individual/days not counted) of that section. Thus, in some situations the 183-day rule of IRC § 871(a)(2) may apply to individuals who have not crossed the threshold of U.S. residence under IRC § 7701(b)(3). For example, a foreign diplomat, consular officer, or other nonresident alien employee of a foreign government, or nonresident alien employee of an international organization who is visiting the United States in A or G nonimmigrant status for a period longer than 183 days in a calendar year would be subject to the 30 percent tax imposed by IRC § 871(a)(2) on U.S.-source capital gains. The same rule applies to a foreign student or scholar visiting the United States in F, J, M, or Q nonimmigrant status whose presence in the United States exceeds 183 days in any calendar year.

Because IRC § 871(a)(2) applies only to U.S.-source gains, the sourcing rules of IRC § 865(g) must be considered when addressing the application of section 871(a)(2). If, under the rules of IRC § 865(g)(1), an alien is determined to be a nonresident of the United States, then the alien's U.S.-source capital gains would be treated as foreign-source and thus non-taxable. The key factor is whether the alien's "tax home" has shifted to the United States. Here, we must rely upon the tax home rules of IRC § 162(a)(2), IRC § 911(d)(3), Revenue Ruling 93-86, and Revenue Procedure 2000-9.

In general, under the tax home rules, a person who is away (or who intends to be away) from his or her tax home for longer than one year shifts tax homes to the new location upon arrival in that new location. Thus, under this rule, most foreign students and scholars and most alien employees of foreign governments and of international organizations shift tax homes to the United States on the day of their arrival in the United States unless the particular program or employment that brings them to the United States clearly terminates in less than one year and they have no intention to remain in the United States after the termination of such program or employment.

Conclusion

Nonresident alien students and scholars and alien employees of foreign governments and international organizations who, at the time of their arrival in the United States, intend to reside in the United States for longer than one year are subject to the 30 percent taxation on their U.S.-source capital gains during any tax year if during such tax year (usually calendar year) they are present in the United States for 183 days or more, unless a tax treaty provides for a lesser rate of taxation. This assumes that such capital gains are not effectively connected with the conduct of a U.S. trade or business. These capital gains would be reported on page 4 (not page 1) of Form 1040NR and would not be reported on a Schedule D because they are being taxed at a flat rate of 30 percent under IRC § 871(a) or at a reduced flat rate under a tax treaty.

PATTERN DAY TRADERS

The NASD passed new margin rules in September 2001, which require $25,000 of trading capital for pattern day traders (PDT). The SEC has a distinct definition of pattern day traders: anybody who makes four or more day trades in a five-day period in considered a PDT.

Being labeled a PDT does not mean the IRS will automatically grant you trader tax status. The details surrounding the PDT rules can be found at www.nasdr.com.

Our firm received this e-mail:

> I've learned from (my broker) that a new account will be created that will be considered a "Day Trading Account," and it has various requirements and restrictions. Explicitly, to be termed a day trader, you must make four intraday trades in a five-day period. Sometimes I do, sometimes I don't . . . sometimes I hold overnight . . . sometimes I hold a month or so. So, am I a day trader or not? My concern is that the IRS will pull up the new "Day Trading Account" ruling and say . . . if you didn't participate in this kind of account . . . you are not a day trader and therefore unable to claim MTM status . . . which I am heavily counting on for 2001 taxes. Am I going to be able to claim MTM status in 2001?

Here was our answer:

> The new NASD regulation margin requirements for "pattern day trader" are not coordinated with the IRS rules for trader tax status. The new margin rules do not set precedent for the IRS classification of who qualifies for trader tax status (i.e., rises to the level of being in the trading business). Therefore, this new rule does not affect nor change the current IRS requirements for who qualifies for trader tax status.

Example: An active trader has four brokerage accounts, but he is not classified as a PDT in any of the accounts. When you look at all four accounts together, the trader would be deemed a PDT and also qualify for trader tax status. It seems obvious to us that if you are classified as a PDT, the IRS would be more willing to accept on the face of things (without examining your trading records) that you might qualify for trader tax status.

Note of Caution: We have been contacted by many traders who complained about the new PDT rules. These traders don't have the necessary $25,000 of capital required to open a PDT account. Prior to the new PDT rules, smaller traders could operate a trading business with $5,000 of capital. Now, smaller traders have few choices if they want to be in the trading business. One option is to take one of the many proprietary trading jobs or LLC opportunities currently being advertised.

PROPRIETARY TRADERS

When you take a job or position with a proprietary trading firm and trade the firm's capital (instead of trading with your own money), you are considered to be proprietary trading. Proprietary firms handle tax matters in a variety of ways: employees get a W-2; a Form 1099-Misc is used for independent contractors; and Form K-1s for LLC members.

In Chapter 1, we discuss some tax information for proprietary traders. Learn move about proprietary trading agreements, legal, tax, and business matters in Chapter 9.

In some cases, the firm handles taxes for its traders in a way contrary to the best tax interests of the trader. Some proprietary traders can benefit from overriding the firm's tax handling, gain trader tax status, and report their true economic gains and losses as a "trader in securities and/or commodities." Consult with a trader tax expert and proceed with caution.

Proprietary traders receiving Form 1099-Misc for compensation generally owe self-employment (SE) taxes on this earned income (net of business expenses). However, in some cases a trader can argue they are truly like retail traders in securities responsible for their own trading gains and losses—and the compensation payments are disguised trading gains. With this override, they can avoid owing SE taxes—a significant savings. If a trader in this circumstance wants to contribute to a tax-deductible retirement plan, they may be happy to have "earned income" and not do this override.

Proprietary traders receiving Form K-1s for their share of trading gains, losses, and expense if any are exempt from SE tax plus they have opportunities to deduct nonreimbursed business expenses, including but not limited to home office expenses. However, if your proprietary trading firm has an expense reimbursement plan make sure to use or lose it before year-end.

Many traders are interested in job offers from proprietary trading firms. These offers often allow traders with minimal trading capital the opportunity to trade the firm's capital (in a subaccount). Traders are offered a certain percentage (usually between 60 percent and 95 percent) of their trading gains in the form of an LLC Form K-1, Form 1099-Misc (nonemployee compensation) or Form W-2 employee compensation. The only risk for these proprietary traders is any money they are asked to deposit with the firm.

These offers sound great, but many complex tax and business issues are involved. The good news is that we have figured out tax-advantaged solutions for multiple scenarios. These solutions include avoiding self-employment taxes in certain situations, deducting your trading losses as ordinary with mark-to-market accounting, and deducting all your trading business expenses (which are not reimbursed by the firm). If you are a proprietary trader, you should consult with a trader tax expert. Consider engaging our firm GreenTraderTax.com for a consultation and to prepare your tax returns.

Important Tax Matters for Proprietary Traders

Some proprietary traders are treated as independent contractors (who receive Form 1099-Misc), others are LLC members (who receive Form K-1s), and still others are employees (who receive a W-2). Proprietary traders need to understand their underlying agreements and utilize tax-wise strategies that match their facts and circumstances. Not all proprietary traders and firms are alike, and different tax planning and reporting strategies are warranted.

Proprietary trading firm agreements are complex, and the entire industry is in a state of flux. Our firm is following several new developments that may significantly affect proprietary traders. You should follow these developments in the book's free update area (see Introduction for details).

Independent Contractors Receiving Form 1099-Misc

In most cases, these independent contractor proprietary traders work for a firm and get paid by them to trade a subtrading account. For tax purposes at year-end, the firm reports their compensation on a Form 1099-Misc (line 7, nonemployee compensation). The proprietary trader is generally required to report this income on an individual tax return Schedule C (Business Profit and Loss, line 1, gross receipts). The trader should deduct his or her trading business expenses not reimbursed by the firm on Schedule C, and the net income is then subject to self-employment taxes on Schedule SE. Per the IRS website, the total self-employment tax rate for 2004 is 15.3 percent of your net earnings from self-employment. The tax is made up of two parts. The maximum amount of net earnings subject to the social security part, 12.4 percent, is $87,900 (for 2004). All net earnings of at least $400 are subject to the Medicare part, 2.9 percent.

In some cases, the underlying agreement with the firm can be interpreted to show that the proprietary trader qualifies as a "trader in securities"; in fact, these traders risk their own money (their deposits). Traders in securities are exempt from self-employment taxes, so these traders will have significant tax savings. If the trader lost money against a "deposit" account, in some cases the trader can also deduct losses on his or her tax returns.

LLC Members Receiving Form K-1

These traders usually become a limited liability company (LLC) member in a broker-dealer entity by contributing a certain "deposit" amount (usually about $25,000) to the firm. In most cases, the proprietary trader is assigned a subtrading account, and the trader is allocated a high percentage of the trading gains. If the trader loses money, the firm usually charges expenses and losses to their LLC member capital account and ultimately to the trader's deposit account.

The firm provides the trader with more leverage through the broker-dealer registration. The firm insists on strict trading controls to make sure the trader does not lose their firm money, because the firm is providing the leverage capital at its risk.

In almost all cases, LLCs are taxed as partnerships, and the firm files an annual Form 1065 partnership tax return. The firm gives each LLC member (a partner for tax purposes) a Form K-1 at year-end. Technically, some LLCs can choose to be taxed as C-corporations. However, this case is rare and not tax-beneficial.

Although the proprietary trader is an LLC member and partner in the partnership tax return, in most cases, the proprietary trader does not share in any of the overall gains and losses of the firm or other partners. This arrangement is contrary to what happens in most partnerships, where partners do share in firmwide gains and losses. Most proprietary trading firm LLCs are structured so that the Class A members (i.e., the owners) share in the gains and losses of the firm (including but not limited to their share of the proprietary trader's gains and commissions). The proprietary trader is usually a Class C or D member who only shares the sub-trading account gains and losses (the trading gains that he or she generates). Sharing agreements vary widely from firm to firm and among individual traders within each firm. Different classes of LLC equity are designed for these purposes.

The key point for tax purposes is that the allocation of gains and losses must follow "substantial economic effect." Therefore, the K-1 tax reporting must "follow the money."

It is odd that one LLC member may report a $1 million gain and another a loss, but the IRS should accept this tax reporting as proper because it does have substantial economic effect.

LLC members are like traders in securities trading for their own account, except they are trading for a firm's account with more leverage.

Traders for their own account have more tax flexibility and chances for tax savings strategies.

Most proprietary trading firms use mark-to-market accounting as a broker-dealer, so the proprietary traders do have the benefits of MTM on their individual tax return. However, most firms do not pass through losses to prop traders and instead the Class A owners take these tax loss benefits.

The proprietary trading firm passes through the trading gains to the proprietary trader as being exempt from self-employment (SE) taxes.

If you are a foreign trader LLC member of a U.S.-based proprietary trading firm LLC, you owe U.S. taxes on your K-1 income.

Here are some tax limitations and strategies for proprietary traders in LLC proprietary trading firms:

- Almost all proprietary trading firms allow individuals to join only as LLC members. This restriction is primarily for SEC compliance reasons, because the proprietary trader will be a registered individual member of the broker-dealer firm.
- Several key tax advantages accrue to traders who set up entities, principally the opportunity to set up and fund a tax-deductible retirement account and to deduct health insurance premiums. Proprietary traders in LLC proprietary trading firms are not able to take advantage of these benefits. Some firms are trying to set up plans to accommodate traders in this regard. Ask your firm about it.
- Most LLC firms do not reimburse traders for their trading business expenses outside of the firm, including but not limited to home office expenses, meals, travel, supplies, Internet services, and other trading expenses. Some firms have instituted plans to reimburse traders, but many traders don't know about it or don't take advantage of it. Caution, if your firm has a reimbursement plan, you must "use or loose" the plan benefits before year-end.
- LLC members report their "partnership" ordinary gains and losses on Schedule E, page 2. If you submitted expenses to the

firm for reimbursement, your Schedule E income will be lower. If you could not submit any expenses, you should deduct your expenses as a second line item on Schedule E. This strategy is important if you want to save a significant amount of taxes.

Employees Receiving W-2s

These jobs are the real jobs. Employees are rarely asked to put up any money, so they are truly risking a firms' money and none of their own money. There are a few firms that offer "hybrid" jobs, which also require a deposit.

True employment jobs without requiring a deposit are rare. Only the best firms offer them, and they only offer them to proven traders with good performance records. They are not "come-ons" designed to lure new traders.

Although they have a good job, when it comes to taxes, employees get reduced tax benefits versus the independent contractor using Schedule C and the LLC member using Schedule E.

Try to get the firm to reimburse you for your trading expenses outside the firm. Report your remaining "unreimbursed employee business expenses" on Form 2106. The problem is that Form 2106 expenses are miscellaneous deductions subject to a 2 percent AGI limitation and additional itemized deduction limitations and not deductible for alternative minimum tax (AMT).

Nonresident Proprietary Traders

Nonresident proprietary traders in U.S. proprietary trading firms are subject to U.S. income taxation and withholding solely on the earnings reported by the U.S. firm.

Most U.S. proprietary trading firms are organized as LLCs, and they file a U.S. partnership income tax return. Each LLC member, including nonresident aliens, are given a Form K-1 to report the member's share of gains, losses, income, and expense. In effect, your Form K-1 represents what you earned at the firm. You owe U.S. taxes based on the earnings, not cash distributions. So, even if the firm did not pay you all your earnings, you still owe taxes in the United States.

It is important to note a key difference in U.S. tax treatment. Traders outside the United States have tax benefits in trading direct access (or otherwise) versus being a member of a U.S. proprietary trading firm that files a partnership tax return. The direct-access trader does not owe U.S. taxes on their trading gains, whereas the proprietary trader member of a U.S. LLC does owe U.S. taxes.

Our international tax attorneys are familiar with almost all tax treaties with other countries, and we can help you plan how to best handle your global tax matters (in the United States and your home country).

Take a Close Look at the Firm's Agreements

- When you take a job or position with a proprietary trading firm (allowing you to trade the firm's capital), the first thing you should find out is whether you are required to risk any of your own money. The next thing to find out is how the firm will treat you for tax purposes, and if you will be entitled to trader tax benefits.
- Proprietary trading firms (PTFs) handle tax matters in a variety of ways.
- Some pay their proprietary traders a salary, which is reported on a W-2 for employees. Others pay their traders as independent contractors and report the nonemployee compensation on Form 1099-Misc.
- Finally, other proprietary trading firms are organized as limited liability companies (LLC) and issue their LLC member proprietary traders a Form K-1 (Partner's Share of Income, Credits, Deductions, etc.).

PTFs That Offer True Employment

Some PTFs offer true employment: They hire you to trade their firm's capital and you get paid a salary, which is reported on a W-2. These PTFs do not require you to risk any of your own money, nor do they request a deposit (as many other firms do).

The PTFs maintain a subtrading account for your trading activity, and your W-2 compensation is calculated as a percentage of your net trader profits (after the PTF charges you for various fees and expenses). Compensation percentages vary by firm, but 60 percent is probably average. These firms offer what we consider to be legitimate employer-employee relationships. The problem is that these PTFs only hire experienced and successful traders. You can't blame them, because they are taking all the risk of losses. Some firms may not pay their traders bonus compensation until the trader makes new high net profits, that is, they make back their trading losses.

Some PTFs require you to deposit money for what they consider a job. However, when you look at the fine print, you realize it's not really a job. Some PTFs hire traders only on the condition that the trader deposits some of their own money into the PTF. This deposit will be used to cover the trader's losses and expenses, and some firms require as little as $5,000. When you read the fine print of these employment agreements, you realize that the employee is 100 percent responsible for their own PTF subtrading account losses, trading expenses, and education, but only up to the amount of their deposit.

The employee is also entitled to receive (in the form of W-2 employee compensation) about 60 percent of his or her PTF subtrading account net gains, after all trading expenses have been deducted.

The agreement provides that the PTF may charge all trading losses and expenses against the trader's deposit, and that the trader must add more money to keep the deposit amount at the original amount per the agreement (e.g., $5,000). Many of these types of PTF agreements also require the proprietary trader to pass certain training sessions, which the PTF also charges the trader for in advance.

When you read the fine print of these agreements, you see that in almost all cases—good, bad, and ugly—the PTF ends up keeping the trader's deposit.

Example of a Small, Inexperienced Trader

Joe Proprietary Trader wants to enter the trading business. Joe will trade actively, and he will be classified as a pattern day trader. Joe does not have $25,000 to open a direct-access trading account, and he sees an ad to join a PTF. He has an interview with the firm and is convinced the firm is willing to train him and sponsor him for his securities registration (Series 7 or otherwise).

Joe thinks that the firm's request for a $5,000 deposit plus $1,000 more for training is reasonable; in any event, that is all he can afford. He figures it is his only chance to enter the trading business, and in a worst-case scenario he will lose $6,000 (or a little more) and walk away with a Series 7 license. So far, Joe is correct.

We caution Joe to read the fine print. We have, and we notice that the PTF has so many strings attached that Joe might end up with large trading losses he is responsible for.

Tax Problems: Joe may end up paying a significant amount of money for the deposit, and he won't be able to deduct those losses as ordinary losses on his tax return as someone with trader tax status could. However, on exit from the firm, he can deduct the lost deposit as an ordinary loss— a business bad debt on Schedule C.

The Bottom Line: If you make money, all is okay, because both the firm and you make money. If you lose money, you lose your deposit and perhaps more. Plus, you subject yourself (in our opinion) to tough conditions, including high leverage (it takes money to lose money), pressure by the firm to close out your positions whenever they want (profitable or not), and trading in proximity to other inexperienced traders (some are not the pros you think they are). Remember the old saying: "If it looks too good to be true, it probably is." For some traders, PTFs offer an excellent solution. Find what's best for you.

PTF Limited Liability Companies

Many PTFs are organized as limited liability companies (LLCs). Some of these firms previously hired traders and provided their tax information on a Form 1099-Misc, but the SEC forced them to change their business model to become LLCs.

The SEC also required that all proprietary trader members of these LLCs be registered with the SEC (Series 7 or other).

These PTF LLCs usually require LLC members to contribute a minimum of $25,000 as a deposit or to the LLC member capital.

When you read the fine print of the LLC operating agreement, you see similar provisions to deposit accounts as mentioned earlier. The LLC member proprietary trader must maintain his or her deposit account at $25,000. All the losses and expenses incurred by the trader are charged against his or her capital account. All distributions (advances or compensation, whatever you want to call them) are also charged against the trader's capital account. Deposit accounts are used to cover losses in capital accounts.

The proprietary traders are usually a different type of LLC member from the member managers. They are the real owners who manage the company and share in a portion of the LLC proprietary traders gains, in addition to earning brokerage commissions.

Tax Matters

LLC proprietary traders receive a Form K-1 with special allocations, meaning they receive their exact net trading gain or loss share after all their expenses are charged. Form K-1 does not reflect any companywide gains or losses, only the specific gains and losses of the trader. Taxwise, these allocations are correct because they have substantial economic effect, meaning the taxable income and loss follow the money.

Many of these LLC operating agreements do not allow the LLC member proprietary traders to submit their home office or other trading expenses for reimbursement. If reimbursed, the LLC would charge the trader on the Form K-1. That practice would be fine, because it would reduce the trader's net income for tax purposes. The problem is that many of these LLCs do not reimburse their proprietary traders, and the proprietary traders do not know how they can deduct these expenses. Earlier, we showed you how.

CHAPTER SUMMARY

Trader tax status is always beneficial to investor tax status and should be declared by every trader. However, the qualifications to trader tax status mean that a trader should be absolutely certain he or she has reached the level of business trader before proceeding. Because of increased IRS scrutiny of trader tax returns, you should consult with a trader tax expert if you are at all unsure about your status.

CHAPTER 2

Mark-to-Market Accounting

The second part of trader tax status is the opportunity for qualified traders to elect mark-to-market (MTM) accounting (Internal Revenue Code § 475). This code section has the effect of converting capital gains and losses into ordinary gains and losses. Short-term capital gains are taxed the same as ordinary gains, but ordinary losses are far superior to capital losses. By default, traders and investors use the cash method of accounting, which means trading gains and losses are treated as capital gains and losses subject to the wash sale loss-deferral rules, and capital loss limitations.

Mark-to-market refers to the procedure you follow at year-end, when you mark all your open positions to market prices. In effect, you are calculating a sale of all open positions (long and short) at year-end using the year-end market prices. On the first day of the following year, you input the buy-back of those positions at the same market prices. In effect, you end up reporting on your tax return all realized and unrealized gains and losses. MTM converts unrealized positions to realized positions for tax purposes.

MTM is similar to the accrual method of accounting in the sense that the economic reality—not just the cash settlement, as would be done using the cash method of accounting—is reported on your tax returns. MTM only applies to trading gains and losses; it does not apply to a trader's business expenses, as would the accrual method of accounting. A trader may elect MTM for trading gains and losses and use the accrual or cash method of accounting for business expenses.

By default, all traders and investors use the cash method of accounting for trading gains and losses, and their trading expenses. A trader in securities and/or commodities who qualifies as "being in the business of trading" may elect to use MTM for trading gains and losses.

MTM trading gains and losses differ from the amount of gains and losses you would have using the cash method. The difference is the year-end MTM unrealized trading gains and losses that are calculated as realized.

MTM trading gains and losses are considered ordinary gains and losses, and they are reported on Form 4797 (Sale of Business Property). *Ordinary* is the key word; it means that trading losses may be deducted in full against any type of tax return income (ordinary, passive, investment, capital). Ordinary business losses (MTM trading losses) comprise part of one's net operating losses (NOLs), which are net business losses for the tax year. NOLs may be carried back up to two years for immediate tax refunds (on Form 1045 or Form 1040X). Or, you can elect to forgo an NOL carry back and carry forward the NOL twenty years. NOLs not used up in prior years are automatically carried forward.

Ordinary MTM trading gains are taxed at ordinary tax rates, which are the taxpayer's marginal tax rates. Short-term capital gains, using the cash method, are also taxed at ordinary tax rates, which eliminates any difference between MTM and the cash method as it applies to short-term gains on securities. MTM would not apply to a trader's segregated investment positions (i.e., a joint investment account held with a spouse), so one does not give up the opportunity to benefit from long-term capital gains tax rates, which are significantly lower than ordinary tax rates (e.g., 15 percent instead of 35 percent).

If you want to elect mark-to-market (MTM) accounting treatment for your current tax year (and future years), you need to attach an election to your prior year tax return or extension and file it by the due date of your prior year tax return (April 15 for individuals and March 15 for calendar-year corporations). The election process is important. If you make any mistakes or file it late, you will lose out on these trader tax benefits.

When you change your accounting method from cash to MTM for the current tax year, you need to also later file a Form 3115 (Change of Accounting Method) with the filing of your current year's tax return. Do not panic—the Form 3115 is not filed with your MTM election by April 15. This change of accounting is automatic, meaning you do not require consent from the IRS (as some other changes of accounting method require). Two steps are necessary in electing MTM; first electing it on time, and later filing the Form 3115. Make sure to do both properly or you will jeopardize your MTM election and usage. That error can cost you up to 40 percent (assumed tax rates) of your trading losses when it comes to claiming a refund. For example, elect MTM on April 15, 2004 for tax year 2004. Next, file a Form 3115 with your 2004 federal tax return in 2005, by the 2004 tax return due date including extensions. Many traders make a serious error by filing a Form 3115 in lieu of the election statement on April 15, 2004—a one-step process. The IRS most likely will return that filing and that trader won't have MTM.

You also will need to calculate and report a Section 481(a) adjustment on the Form 3115 and on your tax return Form 4797. A Section 481 adjustment is intended to report the accounting effect of changing your accounting method. If you elect MTM for the current tax year, you need to start your accounting on January 1 with all open positions valued at market prices on January 1. When you ended the prior tax year, you were using the cash method of accounting, which means all open positions were valued at cost. Hence, the section 481 adjustment is the difference in those open positions at cost versus the January 1 market values (prior year-end prices).

Your section 481 adjustment is your unrealized gain or loss on securities held in your trading business as of the end of the prior tax year. Remember, cash method traders only report their realized gains and losses in the prior tax year.

If your section 481 adjustment is positive, you are required to prorate the adjustment on your income tax return over four years. If it is less than

$25,000, you may use the "de minimis rule" and report the entire amount in the year of change.

Negative section 481 adjustments are 100 percent deductible in the year of change. Rev. Proc. 2002-9 and Rev. Proc. 2002-19 provide that, in the case of changes in method of accounting that result in a negative (i.e., taxpayer-favorable) IRC § 481(a) adjustment, the entire amount of the adjustment will be taken into account in the year of change. This rule change applies to 2001 and later years.

For example, a 2004 section 481 adjustment on January 1, 2004, in the amount of $40,000 is reported as $10,000 (one-quarter) on your 2004 tax return (Form 4797, Sale of Business Property), and the remaining three-quarters is divided evenly over the following three tax years (providing you remain in the trading business). If you exit the trading business, you must accelerate the entire remaining income adjustment to that tax year. If you have a deferred income adjustment, plan for this taxable income in later years.

MTM ELECTION STATEMENT TO USE

The IRS has not yet provided taxpayers with a form to use for the MTM election, as they indicated in the MTM tax laws. In lieu of a tax form, you may attach the following election statement to your prior year federal tax return or extension (Form 4868), which states:

> Pursuant to IRC 475(f), the Taxpayer hereby elects to adopt the mark-to-market method of accounting for the tax year ended December 31, 2005 year, and subsequent tax years. The election applies to the following trade or business: Trader in Securities as a sole proprietor.

Be careful to change this statement to commodities, or securities and commodities as appropriate.

Note: we don't recommend IRC § 475 for commodities, for the following reasons.

Some nuances are involved in electing MTM. If you have a large capital loss carryover, you cannot apply it against future MTM trading gains (capital losses can only be offset against capital gains). Many traders face this predicament: they want MTM "loss insurance," but they also want to use up their carryover capital losses.

Caution: Please note that when a partner contributes an asset to a partnership where the asset has a "built-in" capital loss in the hands of the partner (i.e., the cost basis of the asset is more than the fair market value at the date of the contribution to the partnership), the loss from the sale of the asset is still treated as a capital loss by the partnership if the asset is sold within five years of the date it was contributed to the partnership. This treatment is true even if the partnership has trader status and has properly elected MTM. IRC § 724(c) specifically prevents the conversion of built-in capital losses on security transactions to ordinary losses by contributions from a cash basis trader/investor to a trading entity that has properly elected MTM. This section applies also to an LLC, including a single-member LLC. However, it does not apply to S-corporations. Our firm, GreenTraderTax, has found a few exceptions to this rule so see our updates area.

A Missed Mark-to-Market Election for the Current Tax Year

If you missed the mark-to-market election deadline for the current year (by April 15), you can still benefit from the first part of trader tax status, reporting your trading business expenses on a Schedule C. You might also file an extension with a Private Letter Ruling or form an entity which may elect MTM within seventy-five days of inception.

Extensions for MTM Elections

If you miss the MTM election by April 15, and you act by October 15, you may be able to receive an extension of time to file your current year MTM election. Reg § 301.9100-1 "Extensions of time to make elections" provides relief for late elections. Note the maximum extension period is six months. One big catch, you need to file a Private Letter Ruling.

Private Letter Rulings

In order to file an extension for an MTM election, you must file a Private Letter Ruling (PLR). The PLR procedure is painstaking and expensive, and for traders seeking relief to use MTM, the chance of success is extremely small. To date, the IRS website has published only four PLRs for traders seeking to use MTM, and all have been denied.

It is useful to read the IRS rulings for the four cases. In each case, the IRS discussed Reg § 301.9100-1 "Extensions of time to make elections." The trader did not qualify for Reg § 301.9100-1 relief.

> www.irs.gov/pub/irs-wd/0209052.pdf
> www.irs.gov/pub/irs-wd/0209053.pdf
> www.irs.gov/pub/irs-wd/0209054.pdf
> www.irs.gov/pub/irs-wd/0304006.pdf

Net Operating Losses

Business taxpayers are allowed a special huge tax benefit: net operating loss (NOL) tax laws. These laws provide the opportunity to carry back and/or forward business losses. Make a fortune in one year and pay your taxes, then lose a fortune in the following years and carry back your NOLs to get huge refunds of taxes paid in the prior (profitable) years. MTM is an important component of NOLs

Securities Trading

Securities business traders should elect mark-to-market accounting for several reasons. In the event they lose money trading in any given year, which is highly likely because of the ups and downs of the trading business, they are protected with MTM tax loss insurance. Electing MTM allows them to get immediate tax refunds on their unlimited ordinary trading losses. Non-MTM traders using the default cash method of accounting are stuck with capital loss carryovers that may never result in a tax refund (unless they generate capital gains in future years).

Profitable securities business traders do not need tax loss insurance, and they want to know what MTM has to offer them. The answer is that with MTM, traders are exempt from the onerous wash sale loss-deferral rules (and straddles and constructive receipt rules) that apply to non-MTM traders and all investors. For example, a non-MTM trader might be profitable for the year, but may also have hundreds of wash sale loss transactions during (and especially toward the end) of the tax year. These wash sale losses are deferred to the following tax year, thereby increasing the non-MTM trader's tax bill significantly.

Profitable securities business traders with MTM owe as much in taxes as a non-MTM trader with the same amount of trading gains assuming no unrealized gains or losses at year-end. Each takes his or her ordinary income tax rate (graduated rates, depending on the level of income) and multiplies it by the amount of trading gains. Cash method short-term capital gains are subject to ordinary income tax rates.

Both MTM and non-MTM traders are able to receive long-term capital gains rate tax relief by segregating investment positions from their trading positions (i.e., keeping them in different accounts is suggested but not necessary). The tax code has historically always had a material difference in ordinary (and short-term capital gains) tax rates versus long-term capital gains tax rates. The 2003 Tax Act widened the difference to 35 percent (ordinary) versus 15 percent (long-term). Both rates may vary and in relation to each other, but the difference is usually a material savings. MTM traders get the benefits of both worlds.

In summary, MTM is the preferred method for securities business traders for four reasons:

1. You don't pay more taxes if you have trading business gains.
2. You benefit greatly if you have losses.

3. You are exempt from the wash sale (straddle and constructive receipt) rules.
4. You still benefit from lower long-term capital gains rates on your segregated investment positions.

Wash Sales

Securities traders and investors are subject to the wash-sale loss-deferral rules. Securities traders using mark-to-market accounting, (§ 475(f)), are exempt from wash sales. Wash sales are a major headache for active traders, because they are difficult to calculate and increase a trader's tax bill. Wash sale losses are not realized in the current tax year, but instead deferred to the next tax year. If you exceed the $3,000 capital loss limitation, wash sales can be desirable. When electing MTM in the following year, wash sales are part of your Section 481 adjustment ordinary loss or part of your realized ordinary loss, which is better than an excess unutilized capital loss.

Commodities and Futures Trading

Commodities and futures are taxed differently from securities. You need to learn about IRC § 1256 contracts, Form 6781, special carrybacks, and how they relate to IRC § 475(f), the new mark-to-market rules.

MTM (IRC § 475) is not a preferred method for profitable commodities and futures business traders for one reason: With the default method, commodities and futures trading gains are 60 percent long-term and 40 percent short-term; MTM (IRC § 475) commodities and futures trading gains are all short term. The current maximum blended tax rate on commodities and futures is 23 percent versus 35 percent on securities, a significant 12 percent difference.

Electing MTM IRC § 475 under these new rules converts your commodities and futures trading capital gains and losses (60/40 treatment) to ordinary gain or loss treatment, a 12 percent tax rate increase.

So, commodity traders face a trade-off. The default method (IRC § 1256—another type of MTM) is better if you have gains.

Section 1256 also has a loss carryback feature; you can carry back commodities and futures trading losses three tax years, but only against commodities and futures trading gains in those years. This loss carryback feature is not as useful as MTM IRC § 475 losses, which are full net operating losses (NOLs) that may offset any type of income in the prior two tax years.

In summary, commodities and futures business traders usually skip electing MTM IRC § 475 because they would increase their taxes on gains and only marginally improve their ability to carry back losses. This result is a stark contrast to securities business traders who get tax loss insurance for no cost (same tax on gains).

Here is one idea: If you incur large commodity trading losses before the election deadline for the current tax year (April 15), elect MTM IRC § 475 so you can deduct your commodity trading losses as ordinary losses. That decision will offset any type of income in the current tax year, and also excess losses can generate refunds in the prior two tax years (regardless whether you have commodities or futures trading gains in prior years).

If you trade both securities and commodities/futures, you may elect MTM IRC § 475 for securities only and not also for commodities and futures—a wise move for many business traders.

If your trading in securities and commodities/futures are unrelated activities (e.g., you trade stocks and also currency and interest futures—rather then securities indexes), the IRS may deem you have separate and unrelated businesses and require you to qualify for trader tax status in each business—meaning you must trade each enough to rise to business treatment.

TABLE OF COMPARISON:
TRADERS VERSUS INVESTORS

Table 2.1 points out the numerous benefits for taxpayers using trader tax status and MTM (or even just trader tax status).

Analysis

1. Higher tax rates on short-term (ST) capital gains

2. Lower tax rates on long-term (LT) capital gains

Short-term capital gains (for securities held less than one year) are taxed at a taxpayer's maximum ordinary income tax rates, which vary depending on a taxpayer's income level (graduated tax rates). Long-term capital gains (for securities held longer than one year) are taxed at long-term capital gains rates, which are significantly lower than ordinary income tax rates. For tax year 2004, the maximum long-term capital gains rate is 15 percent; the maximum ordinary income tax rate is 35 percent. This difference represents a huge tax savings, which both investors and traders may benefit from.

Traders qualify for lower long-term capital gains if they segregate their investment positions from their trading positions. This separation can be easily done by holding your investments in an online investment account and conducting your trading in your direct-access brokerage account. Traders really have nothing to lose by gaining trader status; it is extremely rare that a trader would hold a trading position for more than one year. Usually, if that is the case, the position is a loser, or it's a segregated investment position.

As is the norm, Congress makes traders "pay for" tax benefits by offsetting the benefits with limitations and restrictions. Congress makes investors pay for the tax benefit of long-term capital gains rate reduction with the following offsetting restrictions and limitations.

Table 2.1 Comparison of Business Trader vs. Investor

Trader with MTM vs. Without for Securities (not Commodities)	Investors	Business Traders Using Cash Basis Accounting	Business Traders Using Mark-to-Market Accounting
1. Higher tax rates on short-term (ST) capital gains	Yes	Yes	Yes
2. Lower tax rates on long-term (LT) capital gains	Yes	Yes	Yes
3. Limitations on capital losses	Yes Individuals limited to $3,000 net capital loss per year.	Yes Individuals limited to $3,000 net capital loss per year.	No Capital losses are converted to unlimited ordinary losses.
4. Wash sale loss-deferral rules apply	Yes	Yes	No
5. Limitations on investment expenses	Yes	No limitations on business expenses	No limitations on business expenses
6. Limitations on investment interest	Yes	No limitations on business expenses	No limitations on business expenses
7. Qualified traders may use Schedule C for business expenses	No	Yes	Yes
8. Qualified traders may elect mark-to-market accounting	No	Yes	Yes, using MTM
9. Report year-end unrealized gains and losses on trading positions, not investment positions	No	No	Yes
10. Allowed home office and education expenses	No	Yes	Yes
11. Allowed full depreciation on computers and office equipment	Yes (w/limitations)	Yes	Yes
12. Exempt from self-employment taxes	Yes	Yes	Yes
13. Allowed net operating loss carryback refund claims	No	Yes, but only on business expenses	Yes, on business expenses and trading losses

3. Limitations on capital losses

Net capital losses (all capital gains and losses summarized) are limited to a net deduction of $3,000 per year on an individual's tax return; a C-corporation entity tax return cannot deduct any net capital losses. Individual capital losses in excess of the allowable capital loss limitation are carried over to the following tax years, where they may only offset the following year's capital gains. Capital losses may not be carried back to prior tax years.

Traders should watch out for capital loss limitations! If you trade for a living, you are probably risking tens (or hundreds) of thousands of dollars, and it is conceivable that you can end any given year with a trading loss much greater than $3,000, the capital loss limitation amount.

Traders can overcome this limitation. For this reason alone, it is imperative that traders (those that qualify for trader tax status) elect mark-to-market accounting. With MTM, traders' capital losses are converted to ordinary losses, thereby avoiding the capital loss limitation. MTM ordinary trading losses may be used to offset all other types of income on a trader's tax return (spouse's salary, etc.). Traders that incur large trading losses usually have negative taxable income and a net operating loss.

4. Wash sale loss-deferral rules apply

Under the wash sale loss-deferral rules for investors (and traders without MTM), if you sell a stock for a loss and buy it back within thirty days before or after the sale date, the loss cannot be claimed for tax purposes. This rule is designed to prevent taxpayers from selling stock to claim the loss while buying it back within a short period of time to retain ownership. Although a wash sale loss cannot be claimed, the disallowed amount is added to the cost of the new stock. Thus, it can be claimed when it is finally disposed of in a manner other than via wash sale.

Traders Watch Out! Wash sale rules are another compelling reason why investor tax status doesn't make sense for day traders and why Congress changed the tax laws for traders. By nature, day traders trade every day and often focus their trading plan on a few different securities. As a result, it is inevitable that day traders will have multiple occasions of wash sale loss deferrals, which can be extremely complicated to account for. Congress realized that it makes no sense to punish a trader with wash sale violations if that trader has little prospect or desire to hold positions for twelve months or longer to benefit from lower long-term capital gains tax rates.

Traders can overcome this limitation. Qualified traders may elect MTM accounting treatment, thereby becoming exempt from the wash sale loss-deferral rules on their trading accounts. These traders are still subject to wash sale loss rules on their segregated investment accounts.

5. Limitations on investment expenses

Investors are limited in the types of investment expenses they may deduct on their tax returns. Investment expenses are reported as itemized deductions, subject to further limitations from the 2 percent floor for miscellaneous itemized deductions (i.e., these deductions must be more than 2 percent of your adjusted gross income) and the itemized deduction phase out for higher-income taxpayers.

Your itemized deductions will be reduced by the lesser of 3 percent of the excess of adjusted gross income (AGI) above the threshold amount; or 80 percent of the itemized deductions subject to the reduction rules. Investment expenses are also not deductible when computing alternative minimum tax (AMT), a nasty tax that is creeping up on many more taxpayers each year.

Traders Watch Out! By default, direct-access traders are serious traders in the business of trading. Direct-access traders are self-empowered and they use plenty of computers, software, tools, and services to operate their trading business.

Traders can overcome this limitation. Qualified traders are entitled to deduct all their business expenses on Schedule C (Profit or Loss From Business) as ordinary losses.

6. Limitations on investment interest

Investors may deduct investment interest expenses (e.g., margin interest) only to the extent of their net investment income. Any excess investment interest expenses are carried over to the following tax year to be applied in the same manner.

Investment income includes nonqualified dividends and interest earned on your investments, but not income from passive activities (e.g., tax shelter-type investments). Net short-term capital gains from the sale of your holdings are included in investment income. However, net capital gain, defined as the excess of net long-term capital gain over net short-term capital loss, and dividends that qualify for capital gains rates are excluded unless you elect to include some or all of them. Making this election will cost you the lower long-term capital gains rates.

Investment interest expenses are reported as itemized deductions. However, investment interest expenses are *not* subject to the itemized deduction phase-out rules for higher income taxpayers (your itemized deductions will be reduced by the lesser of 3 percent of the excess of AGI above the threshold amount or 80 percent of the itemized deductions subject to the reduction rules).

Traders Watch Out! Many traders use leverage on accounts that have quite a significant balance, which results in many thousands of dollars of margin interest expense. Traders usually do not have much investment income. Compared with investors, they have less chance to deduct their investment interest expenses.

Traders can overcome this limitation. Qualified traders report their margin interest expenses as a business expense instead of as an itemized deduction. Business expenses are not subject to limits.

7. Qualified traders may use Schedule C for business expenses

Qualified traders report their business expenses on Schedule C (Profit or Loss From Business). These expenses include but are not limited to margin interest expenses; depreciation on computers and equipment; amortization on software; Internet service; chat room services; training, supplies, postage, and couriers; phone; online and print research; travel; entertainment; gifts; business accessories; and home office expenses.

8. Qualified traders may elect mark-to-market accounting

Mark-to-market (MTM) accounting treatment for traders is the crux of the trader tax laws. A trader using MTM accounting will implicitly close out all open trading positions (open long positions and short sales) using the market value on the last trading day of the year. These MTM traders report both realized and unrealized trading gains and losses as ordinary gains and losses rather than capital gains and losses, which are limited.

The reason traders should use MTM is because their losses are treated as ordinary rather than capital. MTM traders pay the same ordinary income tax rates on securities trading gains as traders and investors using the cash method.

Traders in securities are similar to traders in commodities—both buy and sell frequently to make money on quick changes in market price. A different type of MTM is the required method of accounting for trading in commodities (per the Tax Act of 1986). IRC 1256 MTM has capital loss treatment unlike IRC 475(f) MTM, which has ordinary loss treatment. Congress required commodity brokers to report commodity trading gains and losses to traders using the MTM method because they wanted to close loopholes in the tax law being abused by commodity traders (e.g., straddles, loss deferrals, etc.). Congress considers MTM the proper accounting method for traders because it is based on the economic reality. Congress also realized that day trading involves thousands of transactions and that it would be difficult for the IRS to audit a trader's tax return using the cash basis, but much easier to audit the tax return of a trader using MTM.

9. Report year-end unrealized gains and
losses on trading positions, not investment positions

The reason traders should use MTM IRC 475(f)is because their losses are treated as ordinary rather than capital. Their potential for unrealized gains or losses on trading positions is not material, because active traders normally close out trading positions by the end of each day. Swing traders normally close out trading positions before year-end.

All MTM traders may still segregate investment positions. Traders may not use MTM on investment positions, so traders who have large unrealized gains on long-term investment positions do not report these unrealized gains on their tax returns until the year these investments are actually sold.

10. Allowed home office and education expenses

Most business traders convert one or more rooms in their home to an office and use it exclusively for their trading business. With the new, more liberal home office deduction rules, most traders can receive a tax benefit of more than $5,000 per year just on this one deduction. Investors are not allowed to deduct home office expenses, even if they use a room exclusively for investing activities.

Investors may not deduct education expenses, but traders in business may. Pretrading business education expenses may be included in IRC § 195, Start-Up Expenses, if they are for investigating and inquiring about a trading business. (More information on education expenses is provided later in the book.)

11. Allowed full depreciation on computers and office equipment

Most business traders use computers and other office equipment to operate their trading business. Traders may fully depreciate the cost of their computers and equipment, whereas investors are subject to the listed property rules using straight-line depreciation. These rules say that any computers and office equipment used for investment activities can only be depreciated if they are predominately used (i.e., used more than 50 percent of the time) for investing activities. Many investors also use their computers for personal use (entertainment, general news, taxes, etc.). The IRS frowns on these deductions for investors, but welcomes them for traders. Business traders may also use IRC § 179, the 100 percent depreciation rules, providing they have trading gains —otherwise this depreciation deduction is carried forward. Business traders may also use accelerated and bonus first year depreciation methods.

12. Exempt from self-employment taxes

Traders in securities and commodities using the cash or MTM methods of accounting are exempt from self-employment (SE) taxation. A trader qualifies as "being in the business of trading," which normally requires that SE taxes apply. However, Congress passed a special exemption for traders from the SE tax in the 1998 Tax Act. One exception, a commodities dealer or trader registered on a commodities exchange does owe SE taxes (IRC § 1402 (i)).

13. Allowed net operating loss carryback refund claims

Net operating losses (NOL) are usually comprised of a trader's business expenses and ordinary trading losses from using MTM accounting.

Traders may file amended tax returns or a preferred Form 1045 (quickie refund claim) carrying back their NOLs to their two prior tax return years. The NOL offsets taxable income in those prior tax years and reduces the tax liability accordingly. The decrease in tax liability then becomes an immediate refund claim.

Rather than carrying back a NOL, a taxpayer may elect to forgo the NOL carryback and instead carry it forward (to be applied against all and any ordinary, capital, or other type of income in the following tax year for up to twenty years).

Even traders not using MTM may have a NOL caused by their trading business expenses.

NOLs

Business taxpayers are allowed a special huge tax benefit through net operating loss (NOL) tax laws. These laws provide the opportunity to carry back and/or forward business losses. Make a fortune in one year and pay your taxes, then lose a fortune in the following years and carry back your NOLs to get huge refunds of taxes paid in the prior (profitable) years. If this sounds too good to be true, it isn't.

In 2001, Congress passed temporary relief extending the carryback period from two to five years for 2001 and 2002 NOLs. This news was fantastic for traders, because most traders made a fortune in 1997, 1998, and 1999 and then lost a fortune in 2000, 2001, and 2002. For example, a trader can carry back a 2001 NOL to 1996 through 2000, instead of just carrying it back to 1999 and 2000 (which was the previous law). This tax law change has great significance for traders, because many already carried back 2000 losses to 1998 and 1999 and already used up the gains for those years. In summary, this tax law change put hundreds of thousands of dollars in the pockets of many traders. Unfortunately, Congress failed in its attempt to extend the five-year NOL carryback period beyond 2002, so only two-year NOL carrybacks apply afterwards.

Our firm has many trader clients and we have prepared hundreds of net operating loss tax returns over the past few years. Our clients received their refunds, even in those cases where the IRS asked some questions. In a few cases, the refunds are delayed. NOL refund claim tax returns are complex and require exact execution. Otherwise, they can lead to questions from the IRS.

The IRS discusses NOLs on its website at www.irs.gov/publications/p536/index.html. IRS Publication 536 provides information on how to claim an NOL deduction.

The following excerpts come from Robert A. Green's article in the September 2002 issue of *Active Trader* magazine.

Net Operating Losses (NOLs)

A trader who qualifies as being in the business of trading (trader tax status) has ordinary losses from trading business expenses. If that trader elected MTM on time, they also have ordinary loss treatment on trading losses. If that trader has negative taxable income, because their trading losses and expenses exceed their other income, then that trader most likely has a Net Operating Loss (NOL).

Taxpayers may carry back 2001 and 2002 NOLs two or five tax years, or they may elect to forgo a carryback to instead carry their NOL forward to future tax years (twenty years).

The 2002 Tax Act provides temporary relief: the normal two-year carryback period is changed to two or five years back for 2001 and 2002 NOLs only, and Alternative Minimum Tax rules are relaxed in connection with NOLs. These new rules are boon for traders, since many traders have significant taxable income in years prior to 2000; allowing a better opportunity to utilize NOLs for tax savings.

An NOL carryback has the consequence of amending a tax return for prior tax years. The NOL is a new tax deduction for that amended tax year and the NOL deduction may be applied against taxable income of any kind in that year, whether or not the trader qualified as a trader in that prior tax year.

NOL tax returns may be filed on Form 1045 (Application for Tentative Refund) within one year of filing your current year tax return that generates the NOL. Alternatively, you may file your NOL return on a Form 1040X (Amended US Individual Income Tax Return) within three years of filing your current year's tax return. Form 1045s are filed faster than Form 1040X, so you get your refunds faster. Form 1040X returns are more scrutinized. Both returns for trader NOLs are very complex and you should engage a proven trader tax CPA firm for help. One error on these returns often results in IRS questions, or an exam or delayed refunds.

The article also gave an example of how a trader could save significant money with NOLs by using an actual return prepared by our firm.

Joe Trader has a job as a full-time consultant for a high-tech company. Joe also qualifies as a part-time securities trader for 2001. Joe elected mark-to-market (MTM) accounting on time, by attaching an election for IRC § 475(f) to his 2000 federal tax extension, filed by April 15, 2001.We reported Joe's 2001 trading business expenses on Schedule C (Profit or

Loss From Business). The net Schedule C loss of ($3,428) is reported on Form 1040 page 1, line 12. This loss is not limited in any way.

We reported Joe's MTM securities trading losses on Form 4797 (Sale of Business Property), part II Ordinary Gains and Losses. The Form 4797 loss of ($1,613,068) is reported on Form 1040 page 1, line 14. This loss is not limited in any way.

Joe elected MTM for 2001, and he had trading positions open at the end of 2000. We calculated Joe's IRC § 481(a) adjustment as negative ($22,050). On Joe's Form 4797 (Federal Statement), we report the entire IRC § 481(a) adjustment loss of $22,050.

Joe's Form on 1040 page 2 shows a negative taxable income of ($1,518,050) on line 37 before exemptions. Joe's trading losses and business expenses fully offset all of Joe's other income, of any kind.

On Form 1045 and the Election statement, Joe elected to forgo the five-year carryback (from the 2002 Tax Act changes), and we carried his 2001 NOL back two years to 1999 and 2000 (because he did not utilize the NOL fully in 1999).

Joe received a 2001 tax refund on Form 1040 page 2 in the amount of $9,457. Had Joe not elected MTM, he would have owed $6,614, an increase in tax versus using MTM in the amount of $16,071. With the cash method, Joe would have a capital loss limitation of $3,000, so his large trading losses would not offset his other income.

With MTM, Joe had a significant 2001 NOL, and he received tax refunds on his Form 1045 as follows: $186,506 for 1999; and $385,034 for 2000.

Joe also received interest from the IRS on his tax refunds, because these changes in tax liabilities are for prior tax years. Joe's total refund checks come close to $600,000.

Joe already received his tax refund checks, and he used them to replenish his otherwise depleted trading accounts. Joe is thrilled he elected MTM on time.

Notes About Form 1045: The 2002 Tax Act adds a five-year NOL carryback choice to the existing two-year carryback law. This temporary change only applies to NOLs generated in 2001 and 2002; the rule reverts to only the two-year carryback period starting again in 2003. The IRS planned a revised Form 1045 for late summer 2002 release to reflect the new five-year carryback choice.

A complex area for NOL returns is the alternative minimum tax (AMT). The 2002 Tax Act temporarily changed the AMT NOL from 90 percent to 100 percent for 2001 and 2002 NOL returns only. This good news for traders means with 100-percent AMT NOL, the nasty AMT tax won't reduce a trader's NOL refund claim. AMT is a second set of tax calculations that differs from regular tax calculations; the ones you focus on most. AMT has nasty surprises for many taxpayers, not allowing certain deductions for AMT taxable income and requiring other adjustments, all of which can increase your tax liability.

NOL carryback tax returns are complex in cases where a taxpayer had a different filing status in the NOL carryback years.

The Bottom Line: Taxpayers in the securities trading business should use trader tax status (Schedule C) and mark-to-market accounting (Form 4797). With this trader tax status, profitable traders maximize their tax savings (using ordinary business deductions), and losing traders have ordinary losses that often times generate a net operating loss (NOL).

NOL refund claims are great news for traders. NOL refunds are often the last resort for replenishing a trader's working capital. However, NOL tax returns are complex and often scrutinized by the IRS. One small error or omission can cause an IRS exam or significantly delay your NOL refunds. It is highly recommended that you consult with a proven trader tax professional experienced with NOL returns.

CHAPTER SUMMARY

MTM is a powerful weapon in delivering maximum tax benefits to traders. It helps allow traders to claim NOL deductions, which can be huge. Remember, though, a taxpayer is not eligible to elect MTM unless he first qualifies for trader tax status, and MTM must be elected on time, by April 15 of the current tax year. Failure to do so can cost traders thousands of dollars in lost refunds.

CHAPTER 3

Entities for Traders

Business traders are, by default, considered sole proprietors. However, many traders choose to incorporate their trading business. A good reason for forming a trader entity is it allows you to establish a retirement plan or other tax-deductible and tax-deferred employee benefit plans. These options are not available for sole proprietor traders (who otherwise receive all trader tax status and MTM accounting benefits). Another good reason is that a trader entity can deliver business tax breaks to your spouse or investors. If you miss the April 15, MTM election, you can form an entity to elect MTM for the balance of the tax year.

Entities are also useful for part-time traders who just barely qualify for trader tax status and want to use a separate entity tax return to reduce their chance of IRS questions or to combine trading activity with other traders or investors (prop traders, family members, and more). However, forming a separate legal entity to conduct your trading activity without rising to the level of trading as a business will not automatically entitle you to trader tax status. You still may have an investment entity and must use investment tax rules, which allow few breaks.

When it comes to entities for traders, the correct and best way happens to be the simple and easy way. We usually advocate a pass-through entity in your home state. Pass-through entities mean that your entity does not pay a tax; instead, gains, losses, or expenses on the entity are passed through to your individual tax return to be taxed there. Pass-through entities file their own tax return and allocate income, gain, loss, and expense to partners on a Form K-1.

In many cases, the best approach is a single-member LLC (SMLLC). With this entity, you do not file a partnership tax return. Instead, you report all the entity-level income, gain, loss, and expense on your individual return directly. This approach is by far the simplest, and it is the same as being a sole proprietor, except that with the LLC you may have a retirement plan.

SINGLE-MEMBER LLCS

A single-member LLC is a pass-through entity. However, because it includes only one member (you), a partnership tax return may not be filed (as would be the case with two or more partners). This news is good because you don't have to spend extra time and money filing a separate tax return for the entity.

SMLLCs can be formed quickly, providing you with mark-to-market accounting and the opportunity to create earned income, which is required for retirement plan contributions and health insurance premium tax deductions (from adjusted gross income). An unincorporated trader does not have earned income, and therefore cannot receive any of these tax benefits. There is one exception for a commodities, futures, or options dealer registered on an exchange—those traders do have earned income (IRC § 1402(i)).

The ability to deduct health insurance premiums is quite helpful. Self-employed taxpayers with earned income can deduct 100 percent of their health insurance premiums. This deduction is a dollar-for-dollar deduction from adjusted gross income (AGI), just as an ordinary business expense would be. If you don't qualify for an AGI deduction then you may deduct health insurance premiums as "medical expenses"—part of itemized deductions on Schedule A—but only in excess of 7.5 percent of AGI. Few taxpayers get a benefit here, so an AGI deduction is preferred.

If you missed the mark-to-market accounting election, you can still achieve MTM status for the balance of the trading year, but not for the year to date. With a new entity, you can elect MTM status internally (no IRS filing is required) within seventy-five days of inception. This election will provide you with "tax loss insurance" for the balance of the calendar year.

A single-member LLC tax return is basically the same as a sole proprietor (unincorporated) trader's tax return. In both cases, all trading expenses are reported on Schedule C (Profit or Loss From Business), MTM trading gains and losses are reported on Form 4797 (Sale of Business Property—Part II Ordinary Gain or Loss), and interest and dividend income are reported on Schedule B (Interest and Dividends).

The differences with the single-member LLC are that the LLC tax identification number (EIN)—as opposed to the sole proprietor's social security number—is reported on the Schedule C, and the LLC is entitled to pay the owner a fee to create earned income. The key tax difference (and source of tax benefits) is that a single-member LLC may have a second Schedule C, filed by the administrator of the LLC trading business. The second Schedule C reports a fee from the LLC trading business, which is the filer of the first Schedule C. This reporting creates a wash and results in no overall difference in income—the first Schedule C deducts an amount equal to what the second Schedule C reports as income. The tax benefit comes from the second Schedule C being earned income, which unlocks retirement plan and health premium deductions, saving income taxes in excess of self-employment taxes.

The one thing to be cautious about is that when a partner contributes an asset to a partnership where the asset has a built-in capital loss in the hands of the partner (i.e., the cost basis of the asset is more than the fair market value at the date of the contribution to the partnership), the loss from sale of the asset is still treated as a capital loss by the partnership if the asset is sold within five years of the date it was contributed to the partnership. This treatment applies even if the partnership has trader status and has properly elected MTM. Internal Revenue Code § 724(c) specifically prevents the conversion of built-in capital losses on security transactions to ordinary losses by contributions from a cash basis trader/

investor to a trading entity that has properly elected MTM. This restriction applies also to an LLC, including a single-member LLC. However, it does not apply to S-corporations.

INVESTOR VERSUS SOLE PROPRIETOR
VERSUS SINGLE-MEMBER LLC

The following example shows how a business trader gets tax breaks beyond that of an investor, and how a trader who forms a single-member LLC gets even more tax breaks.

Joe Trader is single, twenty-six years old, and a resident of California. He trades securities (no commodities) every day and all day from his one-bedroom office (in his two-bedroom apartment).

Joe assumed he would qualify for trader tax status, so he elected mark-to-market accounting (MTM) by April 15, 2002.

Joe has the typical business expenses for margin interest ($15,752), depreciation on equipment ($6,413), amortization on software ($646), supplies, travel, meals and entertainment, postage, telephone, tax and accounting services, chat rooms, Internet service providers, online information services, publications and books, and seminars.

Joe has a trading account at a direct-access brokerage and in 2002 his realized trading gains on securities was $248,558. He did not keep any open positions at year-end. Because Joe has MTM, he reports his trading gains on Form 4797, Part II Ordinary Gain or Loss. His trading account had interest income of $795 and dividend income of $99.

If Joe had fewer than 400 round-trip trades for the year and he held positions open for sixty days on average and he did not meet the other tests for sole proprietor status, he might consider filing as an investor.

On the other hand, if Joe had more than 1,000 round-trip trades and kept the positions open for minutes to a few days and if he easily meets the other tests, then he should file as a sole proprietor.

If Joe filed as an investor, his Schedule A itemized deductions (from restricted investment expenses) would be $21,789. If he were able to file as a sole proprietor, he would have net (unrestricted) deductions of $48,600, comprised Schedule C ordinary deductions of $43,900, and the standard deduction of $4,700. The sole proprietor version unlocks more of the exemption amount. The net effect is lower taxable income of $27,831 on the sole proprietor return. The tax savings as a sole proprietor versus an investor is $12,415 (44.6 percent of the additional deduction savings).

Had Joe formed a single-member LLC in 2002, he could have saved an additional $7,345, providing he executed the primary beneficial trader tax strategy for forming an entity; which is forming and funding a retirement plan.

Forming a SMLLC in Joe's home state of California costs about $215 (with an online incorporator) and is simple and quick to do. The only entity-level tax is a fixed state tax of $800 and a nominal fee depending on the level of income. In many states, either no stealth taxes (hidden entity-level taxes) are assessed on a SMLLC or there is an annual fee or charge of up to a few hundred dollars. These taxes are deductible.

A SMLLC has the same tax treatment as a sole proprietor in the following ways: all trading business expenses are reported on a Schedule C; all trading gains are reported on a Form 4797; and all interest and dividend income is reported on Schedule B.

A SMLLC has different tax treatment from a sole proprietor in the following beneficial ways, providing the retirement plan strategy is executed.

Joe's SMLLC pays a fee to himself for administration, reported on a second Schedule C. Joe pays the minimum fee necessary ($152,320 for 2002) to drive the maximum Mini 401(k) retirement plan contribution of $40,000 (the 2002 limit, which rises in future years—$41,000 for 2004).

The second Schedule C with the $152,320 of net income is subject to self-employment (SE) taxes. Adjusted gross income deductions in the amount of $49,719 are taken. These are not available on the sole proprietor return. These additional deductions lower the federal and state income taxes, which offset the SE taxes created in this scenario (but do not apply on the investor and sole proprietor returns, because traders are not subject to SE taxes).

Joe could have saved $7,345 more in taxes with this SMLLC and replaced "bad" income taxes with "good" SE taxes (SE taxes provide retirement benefits, but income taxes provide no benefits). Joe cashed in on this incentive from the IRS to fund a retirement account, which is wise financial planning. Joe can actively trade his Mini 401(k) plan assets and grow this account tax-free until he retires. Joe can also borrow money from his Mini 401(k) plan. Mini 401(k) plans and other retirement plans will be explained in greater detail in Chapter 4.

Another good idea for a trading entity is the husband-wife partnership.

HUSBAND-WIFE PARTNERSHIP

One benefit for married traders is that marriage can unlock some incredible tax savings strategies in connection with your trading business.

It is not necessary for your spouse to also be a trader in your business or otherwise active. However, a few requirements must be met:

- You must qualify for trader tax status.
- You must have some or all of the following husband-wife trading business factors:
    (a) Your spouse is listed on your trading statements.
    (b) Part of your trading capital belongs to your spouse.
    (c) Your spouse participates in your trading business,
        as a trader, manager, or administrator.

If your spouse is passive in your trading partnership, he or she will be subject to investment interest expense rules, which are not a big deal.

Many traders list their spouse's name on their trading business brokerage accounts for various reasons: joint tenancy, in case one spouse dies, the money belongs to both spouses, or both spouses are in the trading business. If your spouse is part of your trading business (a co-trader, manager, or otherwise), the IRS does not allow a joint sole proprietor Schedule C (Profit of Loss From Business) filing. Instead, it requires you to report the trading business activity on a general partnership tax return (Form 1065).

Don't be alarmed by this IRS tax rule clearly stated in the Schedule C instructions. It can be beneficial in many instances. The IRS does not require a formal partnership agreement or any filing whatsoever, except the partnership tax return. It is a "general partnership" for legal purposes and not a limited or other type of partnership. Other types of partnerships may require formal agreements or state filings. Most states follow the federal rules and don't have minimum taxes for general partnerships. Check with your home state or their website.

In the case of a husband and wife trading partnership, the entire partnership activity ends up on the "married filing joint" (or separate) individual tax return. The only difference is that instead of having a Schedule C for the trading business expenses and a Form 4797 for mark-to-market trading gains and losses, the entire net amount (trading gains minus losses minus expenses) is reported on your individual tax return Schedule E, page 2, Part II (Income or Loss from Partnerships and S-Corporations), Non-Passive Income and Loss section. In both cases, you get tax-beneficial ordinary loss treatment.

New taxpayer trading entities (never filed a tax return before) may elect mark-to-market accounting by filing an internal resolution within seventy-five days of inception. Existing taxpayers must file external MTM elections. If a spouse joins your trading business, you implicitly formed a partnership on the date he or she joined your business, and you have seventy-five days from that partnership inception date to elect MTM internally.

This option can be beneficial to traders who missed the April 15 MTM election deadline. Their spouse can join their trading business and they can then elect MTM for this partnership after the April 15 date (assuming you start your partnership during the year). Be careful with this tax strategy. If your spouse was part of your trading business from January 1, you had to elect MTM by March 15.

In the case your spouse joins mid-year, split your trading business activity between Schedule C for the prepartnership period and the partnership return afterwards. Use the cash method of accounting for the Schedule C period and the MTM method for the partnership return.

Your Spouse Listed as a Joint Tenant Only

If your spouse is not part of your trading business, and you merely listed him or her on your trading brokerage statements (and Form 1099s) for joint tenancy reasons, that approach should not affect your sole proprietor trading business reporting on Schedule C.

Watch out, though, for complications. Assume you lose your spouse's share of the trading account assets and your spouse is not part of your trading business. If you are using mark-to-market accounting, you may not use ordinary loss treatment for your spouse's lost money. First of all, you don't have basis; secondly, your spouse may not use MTM accounting. Rather, your spouse should take a capital loss for his or her share of the loss.

Names on the Trading Accounts

If your spouse is not in your trading business, be careful not to list his or her name as the only name on your trading brokerage accounts. The IRS may prevent you from using trader tax status and MTM because the money belongs to your spouse. One solution involves using a note payable to show that you borrowed the money from your spouse and it's your money to gain or lose trading. If any of the tax returns are prepared incorrectly and don't have the correct footnotes, you are putting the tax benefits in jeopardy.

As is the case with SMLLCs, a husband-wife partnership has built-in capital losses.

Example of a Husband-Wife Trading Partnership Solution

Joe and Nancy were happily married in 2000. Joe was a stock broker and Nancy a banker.

In June of 2001 Joe wanted to pursue his dreams of being an entrepreneur, and he left his job to start a trading business.

Joe opened a direct-access trading account in 2001 and funded the account with some of his and Nancy's capital. They agreed that Nancy would help Joe manage the trading business, but that Nancy would not interfere with Joe's day-to-day trading decisions. Nancy agreed to help with bookkeeping, strategy, risk assessment, and general business and finance issues.

Nancy insisted that her name be listed on the trading brokerage accounts, as a joint tenant, because some of the money was hers and if anything happened to Joe, she could immediately have access to these funds. Unfortunately, their prior accountant did not inform them about MTM accounting or husband-wife partnerships.

On their 2001 individual income tax returns, their prior accountant treated Joe as a sole proprietor and reported trading business expenses, including margin interest expenses, on Schedule C (Profit or Loss From Business) for full ordinary loss treatment. These Schedule C losses offset Nancy's W-2 wage income and generated a tax refund.

The bad news was that Joe and Nancy did not know about MTM; even if they did, it was too late to elect MTM in June 2001, when Joe started the trading business. Joe's 2001 trading losses were $53,000, but their prior accountant limited them to a $3,000 capital loss limitation. Had Joe elected MTM by April 15, 2001 (with good planning), they could have deducted the entire $53,000 as an ordinary loss and received additional tax refunds of $20,000.

Their prior accountant put them into a tax predicament, because they had a capital loss carryover of $50,000 for 2002. He then compounded the error by skipping the MTM election for 2002. He made this decision because Joe had gains year-to-date in 2002, and the accountant figured by not electing MTM, he could offset 2002 capital gains with 2001 carryover capital losses. Had Joe elected MTM for 2002 (by April 15, 2002) and had gains for 2002, those gains would be ordinary gains and he could not deduct his capital loss carryover. As a result, they would increase his 2002 tax liabilities.

As it turned out, though, Joe ended up losing $43,000 more in trading for 2002, and the decision to not elect MTM was the wrong one. When Joe and Nancy visit their prior accountant for preparing their 2002 tax returns, he tells them the bad news. He tells them, "Tough luck. You can only deduct the $3,000 capital loss limitation, and you'll have to carry over a capital loss of $90,000 to 2003" ($50,000 from 2001 and $40,000 from 2002).

Joe and Nancy need to lose this accountant and seek better advice from a proven trader tax expert.

The Potential Fix for 2001

Joe and Nancy may have a de facto general partnership for 2001 from the inception date of their trading business. As new taxpayers (a new general partnership), Joe and Nancy could have verbally elected MTM accounting internally within seventy-five days of inception of their trading business. An IRS Form SS-4 can later be filed to get a tax identification number for their trading general partnership. They can file a late (but acceptable) general partnership tax return (Form 1065) for calendar year 2001, using MTM accounting. Late penalties are only $500.

Additionally, federal and state amended individual tax returns for 2001 are filed, reporting the partnership return Form K-1 ordinary losses (from trading losses and expenses) on Schedule E. The result of these new tax return filings are refunds of approximately $20,000 or more, depending on the marginal tax rates. Rather than having nondeductible capital losses, Joe and Nancy have full ordinary loss treatment on the $53,000 worth of trading losses for 2001.

The Fix for 2002

Partnership and individual tax returns for 2002 are filed using MTM. The result is approximately $16,000 or more of additional tax refunds from a full ordinary loss on the $43,000 trading loss. It is preferred if the 2002 partnership tax extensions are filed by April 15, 2003, but late partnership tax returns can still be filed, with a small penalty. The penalty is $50 for each month or part of a month (for a maximum of five months) after the due date of the return (April 15, 2003), multiplied by the total number of partners in the partnership.

Tax Planning for 2003

Joe and Nancy turn it around and as of mid-year 2003 are on target to make about $200,000 trading in 2003. Having the general partnership in place will afford them the opportunity to benefit from having a separate legal entity.

Joe plans to open a Mini 401(k) retirement plan and contribute and deduct up to $40,000 to that plan. This retirement plan deduction will save Joe and Nancy several thousand dollars in taxes and provide Joe with tax-deferred retirement assets. Paying into social security and Medicare will also benefit Joe come retirement. If Joe was a sole proprietor, he could not establish a retirement plan.

Joe and Nancy get immediate tax refunds for all of their trading losses and are not stuck with 2003 capital loss carryovers of $90,000.

Note: Assuming Joe generates large trading gains in 2003, he could utilize $90,000 of capital loss carryovers from 2002 (assuming no fix herewith). It should be noted that many traders don't turn it around like Joe and wind up with large capital loss carryovers they have little chance of ever recovering. Certainly, getting immediate refunds on ordinary trading losses with MTM is much better then hoping to generate capital gains in the future.

The Bottom Line: Take advantage of all the benefits of marriage, which include some tax benefits for traders. If you have a clear opportunity to file amended tax returns for immediate refunds, consider that strategy. Note that the IRS frowns on paying large tax refunds on amended tax returns, so you should carefully weigh all factors beforehand.

Here is an excerpt from the IRS website as well as an observation:

> If spouses carry on a business together and share in the profits and
> losses, they may be partners in a partnership whether or not they have a

formal partnership agreement. Spouses should report income or loss from the business on Form 1065, U.S. Partnership Return of Income. They should not report the income on a Form 1040 Schedule C, Profit or Loss From Business in the name of one spouse as a sole proprietor.

If each spouse is a partner in a partnership, each spouse should carry his or her share of the partnership income or loss from Form 1065, Schedule K-1, Partner's Share of Income, Credits, Deductions, etc., to their joint or separate Form(s) 1040. Each spouse should include his or her respective share of self-employment income on a separate Form 1040 Schedule SE, Self-Employment Tax. Self-employment income belongs to the person who is the member of the partnership and cannot be treated as self-employment income by the nonmember spouse, even in community property states. This generally does not increase the total tax on the return, but it does give each spouse credit for social security earnings on which retirement benefits are based. However, this may not be true if either spouse exceeds the social security tax limitation. Refer to Publication 553, Highlights of 2001 Tax Changes, for further information about self-employment taxes.

Observation: The preceding explanation hints at what the IRS is after with de facto partnership treatment. The government's goal is collecting more self-employment taxes to improve funding of social security and Medicare. Allocating net income between a husband and wife versus just one of the spouses creates two rather than one self-employment tax bases. Trading gains are not subject to self-employment taxes.

NASDAQ Data Feed Fees

One potential drawback to forming an entity is that NASDAQ charges higher data fees to professionals, and an entity might increase your chances of being deemed a professional. NASDAQ offers significantly lower fees to nonprofessionals, but qualifying for these lower fees is a challenge for some traders.

In general, if you trade for your own individual account, are not registered as a security professional, and use the NASDAQ market information for your own personal use, you qualify for the lower nonprofessional rates. By default, everyone is a professional unless you can document that you meet the facts and circumstance NASDAQ tests to qualify for nonprofessional status.

The first test is whether you are a registered security professional. If you are exempt from registration but still a security professional such as an exempt investment advisor, you fail this first test.

If you pass the first test, the second test is whether you are a natural person or your trading account is opened in the name of an entity. Only individual trading accounts pass this test. There may be some new exceptions here.

Finally, the last test is whether you are using the NASDAQ market information for your own personal use or for the benefit of others. If you are managing money for investors or friends (family members are exempt here), or operating a website or financial newsletter, you are using this market information for third parties and not just for your personal use. In that case, you fail the third and final test.

The spirit of the rules is clear. You can be a hyperactive trader and qualify for business tax treatment with the IRS, and still qualify for the lower nonprofessional NASDAQ rates, if you are not a security professional, trade as an individual, and do not share your market information for the benefit of others. Most traders fall into this window of nonqualification.

Triggering Higher Rates

Forming an entity for additional tax savings is wise, but it is important to figure out beforehand whether you will be forced into the higher professional data feed rates and how much that additional cost will be. Keep in mind that many brokers cover the cost for nonprofessional data feed fees, so the entire amount of the professional fees may be additional costs to your trading business. If you are using a lower tier of NASDAQ services, this additional cost may be small versus the tax savings you will generate with a business entity tax strategy.

A few ways are possible to form an entity and still qualify for the nonprofessional rates. The first one is the previously mentioned husband-wife general partnership. This type of partnership means the brokerage accounts can be left in the individual names of the husband and wife. In that case, when your broker executes the NASDAQ data feed agreement, the agreement is in the name of a natural person. To avoid further confusion, it is best to sign that agreement with the name of one spouse only, to prevent the case of possibly owing two sets of fees.

Another possibility is that your broker may be able to help. Some brokers may allow you to open an entity account and still not charge you for the professional rates. Perhaps they will eat the additional cost themselves or finesse the NASDAQ subscription agreement to claim you still are a nonprofessional.

Caution: It is important for you to understand what position your broker is taking on your behalf and to fully understand the questions and forms your broker asks you to answer and fill out. NASDAQ will hold you responsible for your claimed non-professional status. Your broker will rely on your representations on the subject. NASDAQ will only hold your broker partially responsible if your broker purposely attempts to skirt any responsibilities in this regard. For example, if your broker knows you don't qualify for nonprofessional status and tells you to just sign the forms without explaining them, then you can seek some indemnity from your broker, but again you are at risk and the responsible party.

SMLLCs and S-Corporations and Nonprofessional Status

A husband-wife general partnership can navigate around the NASDAQ rules and keep nonprofessional status. However, other trader business entities such as SMLLCs, LLCs, and S-corporations will be considered professionals by default.

Our firm has been working with NASDAQ to clarify their definition for nonprofessional rates. Our goal is to change the current definition so that traders, who trade solely for their own accounts, but use an entity (i.e., for retirement plans and health insurance deductions) may still qualify for nonprofessional rates. As of the time of this writing, all entities without exception should pay the professional rates. You should visit the free update area at www.greencompany.com/Book/index.shtml for any changes.

Again, speak to your broker. Perhaps the broker can take a position that you own 100 percent of your SMLLC and as a sole proprietor you qualified as a nonprofessional. In spirit, you should otherwise still qualify except for the SMLLC technicality. Perhaps, they can find a way for the NASDAQ agreement to be executed in your individual name. This option may or may not pass muster with the NASDAQ. In theory, it seems fair and not abusive to the spirit of the rules.

Trader Tax Status and the "Trading Rule" for Business Tax Breaks in Entities

Active traders/managers in hedge funds, family trading entities, and other types of trading companies can use trader tax status and the trading rule to deliver business tax breaks, including mark-to-market accounting, to their investors.

Investors in businesses are normally subject to the passive activity loss rules, but the trading rule tax loophole exempts investors from passive activity rules in a trading company. The net result is your investors get full business expense treatment for all expenses in your entity, including but not limited to all trading expenses (supplies, services, chat rooms, seminars, travel, meals and entertainment, professional fees), your management fees (payments to you as manager), depreciation on computers and equipment, and more. The one exception is investment interest expense, which is discussed next.

This option provides a huge edge. Your competitors in investment company hedge funds pass through deductions from portfolio income on their K-1s, and their investors are stuck with limited investment expenses. The bottom line is that your investors can have a higher after-tax return, which is a huge benefit in marketing.

The second key tax benefit is your ability to use mark-to-market accounting on the entity level. With MTM, if you lose money while trading, you can pass through those losses as ordinary losses to your investors, rather than loading them up with even more unusable capital losses, which your competition did during recent bear markets.

Sure, you plan to have gains, but your investors will really value this tax loss insurance when evaluating your private placement memorandum against your investment company competition.

Don't worry if you have gains, MTM still comes in handy.

Unique Trading Hedge Funds

Thousands of new hedge funds have sprung up the past few years, but the majority of their trading programs are not short-term trading. Only short-term trading programs have a shot at qualifying for trader tax status. Non-short-term trading funds are investment funds and they are stuck with the less tax-beneficial investment company rules.

Difference Between Business and Investment Treatment

First, all income and losses are broken down between business and investment treatment. Business treatment is only for situations when you are involved in a trade or business. The IRS considers this effort serious and allows you to deduct every type of expense and loss in connection with pursuing business income.

Investment treatment applies when a taxpayer pursues growth in assets and is not doing this activity on a daily or full-time basis. All taxpayers focus their main efforts on making a living from a job or a business, and they try to grow their assets with investments.

The IRS has special tax rules for investment activities including, but not limited to, lower long-term capital gains tax rates, capital loss limitations, wash sale and straddle loss deferral rules, investment interest expense limitations, and investment expense limitations. Basically, the IRS gives taxpayers a break on long-term capital gains and then really makes you pay for that one special break with severe limitations on losses and expenses.

The problem for investors is that it takes money to make money. You need special tools and skills, and it costs money to acquire them. The IRS restricts investor's abilities to deduct those expenses. The markets are dangerous, and a puny $3,000 capital loss limitation is ridiculous. Congress has not increased that amount for decades.

Obviously, business treatment is far superior to investment treatment. A key point to remember is that trading companies with business status can also segregate investments to generate long-term capital gains. So, they can have the best of both worlds.

Passive Activity Loss Rules

If you are an investor in a company with business treatment, unless you are active in management on a daily basis (and the rules are complex), you are subject to the third type of tax treatment: the onerous passive activity treatment. However, the trading rule tax loophole exempts portfolio investors from these passive activity loss rules.

The passive activity loss rules are meant to prevent investors in businesses from getting business tax breaks. The passive activity rules are supposed to suspend those losses into the future. In some cases, this treatment is even worse than getting investment treatment on the losses. The trading rule exception basically gives investors in trading businesses a special break. Rather than force them into investment treatment, it allows business treatment for all income, losses, and expenses, except one item: investment interest expenses.

Origination of This Special Loophole

The IRS created the passive activity loss rules to combat the proliferation of real estate and other tax shelters in the 1980s. Promoters would set up business partnerships in real estate, movies, and other activities, use nonrecourse debt to shield the investors from risk, and then pass through huge business losses to the investors. These were tax losses but not true economic losses.

The passive activity loss rules were successful in killing off these tax shelters. What good were all those business losses if you could not deduct them on your tax return? The losses were suspended until the investor had sufficient passive activity income to offset only true economic losses.

Promoters never take new tax laws lying down. They scurried to create reverse tax shelters that could generate passive activity income. Their first idea was business partnerships engaged in trading to generate portfolio income, which they figured would be easy enough. A proven trader can generate income without much risk, but the IRS fought back with the trading rule, which says that trading partnerships are not subject to passive activity rules.

The end result is that the IRS won their war on those types of tax shelters. The IRS may realize the trading rule gives a tax shelter of sorts to investors in trading companies, but we believe they think it's just for expenses. MTM only came into existence for traders and trading businesses in 1997, and the IRS may not yet realize that investors will be able to get huge MTM trading loss benefits on their tax returns and large refunds with net operating losses. At least these are true economic losses.

The IRS "State of the Law"

The following excerpt from an IRS Field Service Advice document, which is not technically tax law, represents the IRS view of the "state of tax law." The IRS summarized the issues and conclusions as follows:

ISSUES

1. Whether a partner in a "trader" partnership may claim as a trade or business expense the operating expenses of the partnership.
2. Whether a partner in a "trader" partnership should treat his ordinary income or losses from the partnership as arising from a passive activity for purposes of section 469 (the passive activity regulations).

3. Whether section 163(d) (limitation on investment interest) limits the deduction of any interest expense flowing through to a noncorporate partner from a "trader" partnership.

CONCLUSION

1. A partner in a "trader" partnership may claim as a trade or business expense the section 162 (trade or business expenses) expenses of the partnership.
2. A partner must treat his ordinary income or losses from a "trader" partnership as not arising from a passive activity.
3. For noncorporate partners, section 163(d) will limit the deduction of interest expense that is not attributable to the partnership's trading activity. In addition, for those noncorporate partners who do not materially participate in the trading activity, section 163(d) also will limit the deduction of interest expense that is attributable to the partnership's trading activity.

Observation: The passive investor receives complete business tax breaks on ordinary business expenses except for investment interest expenses. The structure helps the investor get maximum possible benefit from those investment interest expenses.

The Best Hedge Fund Tax Strategy

Before you proceed, think about what tax strategy is best for you as the trader/manager of your trading company, and what is best for your investors. In one area your interests are the same as your investors: you both want trader tax status for ordinary loss treatment.

Fee or Profit Allocation

In the case of trading companies, though, your interests may be different from your investors in some areas. A trader/manager in a hedge fund is entitled to an incentive compensation payment (usually 20 percent) for their efforts in managing money for the investors. In the case of investment companies, the structure can either provide for a fee, which is classified as a deduction from portfolio income (a restricted itemized deduction), or it can be structured as profit allocation, which is a share of capital gains. Note that a recent IRS audit manual is claiming profit allocations are disguised fees. Many lawyers are contesting this.

Most investment companies use profit allocations to prevent the investors from being stuck with nondeductible itemized deductions. Deductions from portfolio income are investment expenses reported on Schedule A as miscellaneous deductions. They are only deductible in excess of 2 percent of adjusted gross income. Investment expenses are an alternative minimum tax (AMT) preference item (not deductible for AMT). Many taxpayers are hit with the dreaded AMT increasingly more each coming year.

For an investment company example, rather than report on your investors' K-1s a $50,000 capital gain and a $10,000 investment expense (the incentive fee), it is beneficial to use a profit allocation and report on the K-1 a capital gain of $40,000 and no deductions from portfolio income. You will have to report the other expenses as deductions from portfolio income, unless you are a trading company. In that case, you pass through business expenses without limitation for your investors.

In a trading company, the trader may want to use a fee structure in lieu of a profit allocation. The investors may prefer an ordinary business loss for fees and a higher capital gain (that $50,000) to offset their unutilized excess capital losses.

Consider the earned income issue for the trader/manager. Fees are considered earned income, whereas a share of capital gains (the profit allocation) are not earned income. This appears to be one reason why the recent IRS audit manual is arguing for fee treatment.

It may work out well for both the manager and the investors to use fees. If the manager wants to limit the earned income and related self-employment taxes due on earned income, an S-corporation can be used for the manager (as the managing member vehicle in the hedge fund LLC).

S-corporations are not subject to self-employment taxes, whereas LLC income is. The S-corporation can pay a smaller salary to the manager to drive the retirement plan strategies, and satisfy the IRS on reasonable compensation rules. This strategy saves a considerable amount of self-employment or payroll taxes.

Commodities traders may prefer the profit allocation over the fee in all cases, because the trader/manager also wants to benefit from the lower taxes on commodities capital gains (a 60/40 split in which 60 percent of gains are taxed at lower long-term capital gains tax rates).

Investment Interest Expenses

The one exception to the trading rule tax loophole is that investment interest expenses are not considered business interest expenses for all passive investors. All the other expenses are business expenses rather than investment expenses.

Passive investors may deduct investment interest expenses only if they have investment income and pass other tests. Investment interest deductions are also an AMT tax preference item.

A hedge fund with capital gains rather than MTM ordinary gains may help investors increase their investment interest deduction, because investors may choose to include capital gains in their investment income formula for this deduction.

Investment Interest Expense Rules

The following excerpt comes from the IRS:

> The amount you can deduct as investment interest expense may be limited in two different ways. First, you may not deduct the interest on money you borrow to buy or carry shares in a mutual fund that distributes only exempt-interest dividends.

Second, your deduction for investment interest expense is limited to the amount of your net investment income.

Net Investment Income This is figured by subtracting your investment expenses other than interest from your investment income. For this purpose, do not include any income or expenses taken into account to figure gain or loss from passive or business activities.

Investment Income Investment income generally includes gross income derived from property held for investment (such as interest, non-qualified dividends, annuities, and royalties). It generally does not include net capital gain derived from disposing of investment property qualified dividends, nor does it include capital gain distributions from mutual fund shares. However, you can choose to include part or all of your net capital gain and qualified dividends in investment income.

Investment Expenses Investment expenses include all income-producing expenses relating to the investment property, other than interest expenses, that are allowable deductions after subtracting 2 percent of adjusted gross income. In figuring the amount over the 2 percent limit, miscellaneous expenses that are not investment expenses are disallowed before any investment expenses are disallowed.

Scams and Alerts Regarding Multiple Entities Schemes

The idea of avoiding taxes on income sounds appealing to many traders, but look before you leap because the IRS considers tax avoidance against the law. Many tax avoidance schemes using multiple entities are marketed to traders, and traders need to stay clear of these schemes and the firms that promote them.

Popular books on the market feature complex strategies for estate and family planning, and fringe benefits. In our opinion, most of these strategies don't work as designed for traders, and they cost thousands of dollars to set up. Finding a good CPA to file these annual returns will be a challenge, because most competent CPAs will balk.

Caution: Some of these books suggest that traders use family limited partnerships as an integral part of their trading businesses. This idea is always bad as far as we are concerned. Trouble may lie ahead for you if you follow this advice.

Avoid those authors who would advise parking your trading business in a flawed corporate structure and promote complex entity strategies that utilize a C-corporation for the management company. We totally disagree with these strategies and find them expensive and a waste of a trader's money. We believe that this tactic sells traders an unnecessary bill of goods just so the firm can make lots of money setting up the entities and filing extra tax returns every year (at additional profit for them, not you).

CHAPTER SUMMARY

A business trader is, by default, a sole proprietor. Although this status is good enough to unlock numerous tax breaks, forming an entity can in some cases be the preferred route for traders. An entity allows a trader to have earned income, which can be used to fund retirement plans and for other benefits. A simple entity is the best, and a husband-wife partnership (if you're married) or a single-member LLC are preferred. Watch out, though, because some entity scams floating around will only wind up getting you in trouble with the IRS.

CHAPTER 4

Retirement Plans

Even traders will retire someday, and it's never too early to consider a retirement plan. Every consistently profitable trader should have a retirement plan. Recent tax law changes increased the deductible contributions dramatically.

Remember, you need to first form an entity to pay yourself an administration fee so that you have earned income, which is the basis for a tax-deductible retirement plan contribution. Part-time traders may have other sources of earned income or be covered in their employers' retirement plans, so they may not need an entity.

The two most basic retirement plans are the traditional individual retirement account (IRA) and the Roth IRA. A traditional IRA is tax-deferred (i.e., you will not be taxed on income in your account until you eventually tap into those funds). Annual contributions are tax-deductible.

Roth IRAs are the opposite: Annual contributions are not tax-deductible, but you also are not taxed when you withdraw funds. This option can result in significant tax savings if the IRA has gained substantially over the years. It's especially attractive to traders.

MINI 401(K) PLANS

For traders, though, a Mini 401(k) plan (also known as solo or individual 401(k) plan) is the plan of choice. You get both an elective deferral from a traditional 401(k) plan plus a maximum defined contribution profit-sharing plan, all in one. Many other advantages include consolidation of all retirement plans into one and plan loans. The main tax benefit for traders is that you can save self-employment taxes by paying yourself a lower fee from your entity in reaching the plan contribution limits versus just having a defined contribution plan like a SEP IRA, or profit sharing plan.

Here is an example of how a Mini 401(k) can save you $4,929, based on a 2003 tax return. Assume the trader has adjusted gross income (AGI) deductions in the amount of $17,499, comprised of the following:

- $14,132 tax-deductible contribution to your Mini 401(k) plan; the maximum 401(k) elective deferral amount of $12,000 for 2003, and $13,000 for 2004. In addition, you are entitled to a profit-sharing contribution of 20 percent of your net fee income (after deducting 50 percent of your self-employment tax).
- $2,130 of deductible health insurance premiums. For 2003, you may deduct 100 percent of your health insurance premiums (up to your earned income).
- $1,237, or one-half your SE taxes of $2,473 due on your $17,500 fee income. Notice the AGI deduction is 100 percent of the fee amount.

You save $7,402 in income tax, assuming a combined federal and state marginal income tax rate of 42.3 percent. You owe SE taxes of $2,473 ($17,500 fee income multiplied by 92.35 percent multiplied by 15.3 percent SE tax rate).

Plus, you replaced bad income taxes with good SE taxes. Paying SE taxes increases your retirement benefits (social security and Medicare insurance); income taxes never benefit you in the future.

Your cost of forming the entity (needed for a trader retirement plan) is around $750 (varies by state). In future years, you don't have this one-time cost.

If you have a successful year and can afford to contribute more to your retirement plan, we recommend you contribute the maximum allowed—$41,000 (2004 maximum) to a Mini 401(k) plan or other type of defined contribution plan.

In that case, you can expect even greater net savings, and you'll be able to grow more money in a tax-deferred account.

The major tax reason why the Mini 401(k) profit-sharing plan is the most attractive retirement plan for traders is that you can contribute the maximum $41,000 on a lower fee income. With other profit-sharing retirement plans, you must use the maximum fee compensation allowed of $205,000 to reach the $41,000 contribution limit. With the Mini 401(k) plan, you save a few thousand dollars of SE taxes—you pay SE taxes on under $150,000 instead of $205,000.

Be Flexible

The cardinal rule for retirement planning tax strategies for small business owners is to figure out:

- How much they can contribute on a before-tax basis to a retirement plan
- How much salary or fees are required to make that contribution
- How much income taxes will be saved with that retirement plan tax-deductible contribution versus the extra cost of paying payroll taxes due on the compensation amount

Not One Size Fits All

Several different types of retirement plans are eligible for the tax advantages of a qualified plan. The owner gets a tax deduction from income for contributions and the plan has a tax-free buildup of plan investments providing deferral of income until periodic distribution of the funds at retirement age.

The type of plan you choose will depend on your individual needs and circumstances, like your age and how much cash you have available to contribute.

Of the two basic types of plans, one family of plans defines the annual contribution to the plan. The second type of plan defines the retirement benefits to be provided.

A *defined benefit plan* provides for a fixed benefit at retirement based generally upon years of service and compensation. Adoption of a defined benefit plan is a nondiscretionary commitment to fund the plan. These plans will often provide the greatest current deduction from income, and the greatest retirement benefit, where the owners of the business are older and nearing retirement.

Defined benefit plans are more complex and costly than *defined contribution plans*, because they require the use of an independent actuary to set your annual contribution and the plan documents must be tailor-made by an experienced retirement attorney. Defined contribution plans are available from many brokerage firms or banks and little customization is required. Profit-sharing plans are defined contribution plans and can provide you with the flexibility of determining the amount of contributions to be made for a particular year.

TRADING YOUR RETIREMENT PLAN

The bear market clawed away at many traders' working capital. Traders seek new sources of capital to ride the bull (markets) again. Some traders are interested in joining proprietary trading firms to gain access to a firm's trading capital, with a subtrading account using greater leverage. Most proprietary trading firms require a brokerage license and minimum capital of $25,000 or more.

Other traders are interested in forming their own hedge fund to raise capital from investors (friends, family, and others) and to make money off other people's money. This plan is a good opportunity for successful traders, but losing traders may have trouble executing this business plan.

A last resort for many traders is closer to home—their own retirement plan assets. But before you start day trading your retirement assets, you should learn about many restrictions that apply. Various government agencies regulate retirement account investments. For the benefit of tax-free deferral or permanent savings, the government insists on investment protection, prudence, diversification, liquidity, and no self-dealing.

Navigating around these rules to actively trade your retirement accounts is limited. In all cases, try to follow the spirit of the law; prudence is a virtue, and you want to retire one day on these assets. Throwing caution to the wind and losing all your retirement assets in risky day trading is not a wise undertaking.

It's Not a Perfect World!

In a perfect world, a business trader has sufficient capital to fund his or her trading business. If a reasonable-to-aggressive return on trading capital is 25 to 50 percent, a trader needs capital of $200,000-plus to generate income of $100,000. This amount is what many traders need to cover their living and business expenses. Certainly, the past few years have not been a perfect world for traders and many have suffered losses to their trading capital. Can you make a good living on trading capital of $25,000 or less?

For many traders their last resort for trading capital is their retirement plan assets. It's not easy finding ways to take money out of your retirement plans to put in your trading accounts. If you take money out of your retirement plan before retirement age, it's an early withdrawal subject to regular income tax (at ordinary tax rates up to 35 percent), plus a nasty excise tax penalty of 10 percent (with few exceptions). Many traders tap into their retirement plans figuring they have no income or losses and can take the distribution into income. They are later surprised and upset about the 10 percent penalty.

Most qualified retirement plans allow for loans, and you can use the loan proceeds to fund your taxable trading accounts. IRAs are not qualified plans, and they do not allow loans.

Leave the Money in Your Plan and Benefit from Tax-Deferred Trading

You don't have to pay taxes and excise tax penalties on early withdrawals to have access to trading your retirement plan assets. Some limited ways allow you to leave the money in your retirement plans and trade it there for continued tax-deferral on the existing money and all the trading gains you generate.

Short-term trading on securities is taxed at ordinary tax rates anyway, so when you retire and take distributions, you will pay those same ordinary tax rates (tax laws can change the rates at retirement).

Find a financial calculator on the Internet and see the power of tax-free compounded returns; you will be impressed. However, many pitfalls, restrictions, and possible violations await, so read on.

Brokers Take a Pound of Flesh

Barron's reviews and rates online and direct-access brokerage firms each year, and they design charts showing off who has the lowest commissions. They are all low these days, which is a huge benefit for traders. The problem is that when it comes to retirement plan accounts, brokerage firms cover the gamut in terms of commissions (most are high), number of allowed trades, and other terms and conditions. Some of their terms are based on ERISA and IRS rules, and others are simply their own policies.

WHAT IS ERISA?

ERISA stands for the Employee Retirement Income Security Act of 1974 and is administered by the U.S. Department of Labor. ERISA was passed in order to better protect employees' retirement plan assets. Far too many companies were abusing their company retirement plans for the benefit of management and shareholders and not employees.

Before ERISA, companies could purchase only their own stock in their retirement plans. Bankrupt companies ended up taking jobs and retirement plan assets. A Department of Labor (DOL) ruling for ERISA on plan diversification prevents a company from investing all retirement plan assets into its own stock, or any one stock.

Under ERISA, company administrators are charged with a fiduciary duty to diversify investments and manage the risk of losses. Traders are familiar with this type of risk management, but this rule presents a problem for many traders. Is active trading in an ERISA-covered retirement plan a violation of the plan diversification rules?

No clear DOL or ERISA guidance or case law indicates how to apply the plan diversification rule to active trading. Each case should be evaluated on individual facts and circumstances in consultation with a CPA or tax attorney specializing in ERISA and tax regulations.

Before you start worrying about ERISA rules, though, find out whether your retirement plans are even subject to ERISA regulations. If you have an IRA or individual-level plan, you are exempt from ERISA rules. SEP IRAs and Mini 401 (k) plans set up on the individual level (with no employees) are not covered by ERISA. SEP IRAs and Mini 401 (k) plans set up on the company level are ERISA-covered plans. This distinction makes sense because retirement plans that include third-party employees are ERISA-covered to protect those employees. On the other hand, plans for individuals without employees have significantly less government oversight and protection.

RESTRICTIONS ON IRA INVESTMENTS

IRA investment guidelines limit what investments can be made and disallow self-dealing or prohibited transactions. Some investments that are allowed generate unrelated business income (UBI), which leads to the payment of taxes (UBIT) on that income, even though the investment is made in a tax-deferred IRA account.

IRAs may not invest in life insurance and collectibles (art works, antiques, and most precious metals). Foreign investments should be limited to ADRs and domestic mutual funds. Real estate investments are allowed, providing your trustee is a qualified provider, and he or she allows it and can navigate around complex rules.

When it comes to brokerage accounts, IRAs are cash accounts and may not use margin to buy stocks (or other forms of debt-leverage for purchasing stocks). An IRA that invests in a hedge fund or other investment company that uses leverage is breaking the rule on the use of leverage. The consequence is the generation of UBI from the income in the hedge fund and taxes on that income.

Taxes on Day Trading of Your IRA

Many traders are interested in actively trading their IRA accounts, even though they can't use margin to buy stocks. Some traders will enter and exit trades on a daily basis, similar to how they operate their day trading business in taxable accounts. This activity raises an important question of great concern to many traders: Will the IRS consider day or swing trading in an IRA account a camouflaged profit-producing activity that is subject to UBIT? Many traders may not mind paying taxes on their day trading gains in their IRA account, because they would have to pay similar taxes anyway in a taxable account. Their goal may be to tap additional sources of trading capital, and they don't mind losing the tax-deferral benefits. If a trader stops trading, then the future profit growth is tax-deferred in the IRA account.

Prohibited Transactions and Self-Dealing

The IRS does not allow self-dealing or prohibited transactions between your retirement plan assets and yourself. For example, if you actively trade your retirement plan assets (ERISA or not), you may not pay yourself a management or administration fee. Such activity is deemed self-dealing and subject to prohibited transaction tax penalties. The initial tax on a prohibited transaction is 15 percent, which is not your only problem. You also have an early withdrawal subject to ordinary taxation plus a 10 percent excise tax penalty (Form 5329).

Other self-dealing and prohibited transactions need to be avoided:

- Your retirement plan may not be a partner in your trading entity.
- You can't sell securities from your taxable accounts to your retirement accounts.
- You and your family members may not invest their retirement plan assets into your own hedge fund.

Based on a more aggressive interpretation of the law, some CPAs and attorneys may not categorize an owner's IRA investment in their own hedge fund as a self-dealing prohibited transaction, providing the following facts and circumstances apply:

- The managing member does not earn any revenue from his or her own IRA (i.e., fees at zero).
- The IRA capital may not be material enough to help the managing member launch the hedge fund (showing others that the fund has other investors of certain magnitude).
- The IRA does not help pay the fund expenses in a material manner.

Taking this more aggressive approach may give you the answer you want to hear, but recognize that you may turn your tax-deferred or tax-exempt IRA into a taxable account. This approach is not suggested.

Solo Traders with ERISA Plans

Traders may raise the following question: I don't have any employees, so why should this ERISA plan diversification rule apply to me? If you have an ERISA plan, the rule applies to you even if you don't have any employees. If you trade an ERISA plan that only includes yourself (no employees) you may think, "What's the risk if no employees can sue me for ERISA violations?" You should also consider that if you get divorced and it's contested, your spouse's attorney can allege ERISA violations. A spouse may be entitled to half or another portion of your ERISA retirement plan assets and deserve the protection of ERISA.

Consider the following example of trading in an ERISA plan: A business trader actively trades 10 stocks on a daily basis and does not keep any positions overnight. This trader hedges positions and monitors risk closely, using stops and other available methods. This trader is diversified and, notwithstanding the perceived risk of day trading, is consistently profitable. The spirit of the plan diversification rule calls for risk management, liquidity, and diversification. It does not specifically state that active trading is prohibited. It can be argued that this trader is not buying and holding one or a few stocks with great market risk. In fact, the trader is diversified and trading with lots of risk management.

What can be argued is that the pursuit of day trading is risky. A profitable trader can argue that consistent profitability proves that day trading is not high risk for that trader.

Of course this trader may not need to tap into retirement plan assets. On the other hand, a consistent losing trader may need to tap these retirement plan assets and, as such, may have a problem with this argument. This more aggressive approach is based on theory and has not been tested under the law; so proceed with caution and at your own risk. Consult with an expert to better assess this risk.

Consider the reverse example: A consistent losing trader actively trades stocks in an ERISA plan in a risky manner without the use of stop losses or hedging. An argument can be made that this trader violated ERISA rules by not diversifying out of risky swing and day trading activities.

Trader Tax Status Benefits and Trading Your Retirement Accounts

Now that you solved how to actively trade your retirement plan accounts without ERISA or tax trouble, keep in mind that you are still lacking trader tax status unless you actively trade a taxable account as well. If you just trade retirement plan accounts and no taxable accounts, all your expenses are matched to your retirement plan income, which is tax-deferred, making your expenses also tax-deferred. It will be difficult (but possible) to keep appropriate records so that when you retire and take taxable distributions, you can reduce that income by the deferred expenses. An administrator will not allow you to record those tax-deferred expenses in the retirement account.

To protect against deferral of your expenses, achieve trader tax status on at least a small taxable trading account. Within reason, you can allocate all your business expenses to the taxable account and not be stuck with any expense deferral. You will then get the best of both worlds.

The Bottom Line: If you want to actively trade your retirement plan accounts, first determine which EIRSA and IRS rules may apply to your trading plan.

It's a mine field with gray areas, and you need to protect yourself against ordinary taxation on unrelated business income or early withdrawals, plus the 10 percent excise tax penalties on early withdrawals, plus the 15 percent tax penalties on prohibited transactions on self-dealing.

Ask yourself whether these extra costs, uncertainties, and headaches are worth putting your retirement accounts at great risk. For some the answer may be Yes, so do your homework and try to stay clear of these extra costs and gray areas.

FRINGE BENEFIT PLANS

As an owner/employee of your trading business, you have limited opportunities for fringe benefit plans. By employing your spouse and classifying yourself as a spouse of a nonowner/employee, you can unlock valuable fringe benefit plan tax savings.

Fringe benefits, commonly known as perks, include retirement plans; health, life, and disability insurance; education, dependent care, and adoption assistance; meals, lodging, and parking; and many other types of plans.

The Details

If you are interested in opportunities to convert more of your nondeductible family expenses into deductible business expenses, you should learn about fringe benefit plans. Most small businesses, including trading businesses, overlook fringe benefit plans; many larger companies rely on fringe benefit plans to attract and retain employees.

These plans are somewhat complex and some require written accountable plans with annual reporting. So, you will need the help of a competent CPA or attorney specializing in employee benefits. It's wise to get a quote on costs and a projection of tax benefits to see whether it's worthwhile for you.

If you can convert $15,000 of family expenses into business expenses and save taxes at 40 percent marginal tax rates, you generate tax savings of $6,000. If your professional fees and other costs are $1,500, your return is 4:1. Plus, your costs are deductible business expenses, and tax credits are also available for forming retirement plans.

Easy Basic Plans

Most business traders want to cover the basic employee benefits, which include compensation, retirement plans, and health insurance coverage. These plans are relatively easy to set up for owner/traders.

Retirement plans are available "off the shelf" from most financial institutions, and require no additional expenses. No additional expenses are part of obtaining a health insurance plan; the only costs are the monthly premiums.

Sole proprietor (unincorporated) business traders may not set up retirement plans or deduct health insurance premiums (both are AGI deductions) because trading gains are not earned income, except for commodities dealers registered on an exchange.

Business traders need to form a separate legal entity to pay themselves a fee or salary on which they can then base tax-deductible retirement and health insurance plans.

Other Fringe Benefit Plans

Fringe benefit plans are designed for larger companies with lots of rank-and-file employees. Discrimination rules are intended to prevent highly compensated employees (owner types) from monopolizing the majority of the plan benefits. If owners and management want these benefits, they must also cover all employees.

The problem for owner/traders is that their entities of choice are pass-through entities and many fringe benefit plans are not allowed for these types of owner/employees. Self-employed individuals (and pass-through entity owner/employees) who want to benefit from fringe benefit plans can do so if their spouses work for the business. By covering employees and spouses, they become entitled to benefits by virtue of being the spouse of an employee.

The Power of Fringe Benefit Plans

An effective way for small businesses to maximize tax savings is to find ways to convert fixed personal expenses into allowable business expenses. For example, many traders convert some of their home expenses into deductible home office expenses. At-home traders also take business depreciation on furniture, fixtures, and equipment.

Fringe benefit plans provide additional opportunities to convert more family expenses into business deductions. The employee (your spouse) is reimbursed by your trading business for his or her nonbusiness-related education, dependent care, at-home meals, and more. These types of expenses would not otherwise qualify for business expense treatment, because they are not "ordinary and necessary" for a business.

Your company deducts the reimbursed amounts as a business expense and your employee excludes the reimbursement from income. In other words, the reimbursement is not included in their gross wages reported on a W-2 or gross compensation on a Form 1099-Misc. In many cases, the fringe benefit is also not included in wages calculating payroll taxes (FICA and Medicare).

For more information on all types of fringe benefits and what is excludable for income versus payroll tax, see IRS Publication 15-B, Employer's Tax Guide to Fringe Benefits, at www.irs.gov.

Don't Feel Bad for the IRS

Fringe benefit plans are win-win for the employer and employee; only the IRS loses. However, don't feel bad for the IRS because most fringe benefits plans are geared for C-corporations, which are subject to double-taxation (paying taxes first on the corporate level up to 35 percent, and then a second time on the shareholder level—qualifying dividends and long-term capital gains are taxed up to 15 percent).

But, you don't need a C-corporation for fringe benefits, so choose a much better type of entity for trading businesses. With a pass-through entity, a business trader avoids double taxation and gets immediate tax refunds on trading losses. All items of income or loss are passing through to the individual tax level, and taxes are not paid on the entity level.

Public companies and other larger companies don't have a choice of entities; they can only be a C-corporation. It is simply not possible (and not allowed) to pass items of income and expense to what could be thousands of individual shareholders. Smaller businesses are allowed to use pass-through entity taxation, and almost all prefer it.

Health insurance deductions were raised to 100 percent in 2003, putting them on par with C-corporations.

No further advantages accrue to a C-corporation. Business traders can use a pass-through entity coupled with the spouse of a nonowner/ employee strategy to unlock every conceivable tax benefit.

Choose the Best Pass-Through Entity

A sole proprietorship (unincorporated business) is good for all fringe benefit plans, except a retirement plan for the owner/employee. Because it is the biggest benefit, you should consider a separate entity instead. Limited liability companies (LLC) are good for many traders. An LLC files a partnership tax return, unless you elect to be taxed as a C-corporation (not recommended per the previous discussion).

If you are the single member, then it's a disregarded entity (no partner, so no partnership return) and you file a Schedule C, similar to a sole proprietorship (except you can have a retirement plan).

Most LLCs don't pay franchise taxes in their home state and have nominal annual report costs (less than a few hundred dollars). You can have special allocations with LLCs.

Single traders who have other jobs and are a close call for trader tax status may prefer an S-corporation over a single-member LLC; filing a separate tax return can deflect IRS questions. S-corporations may not use special allocations like LLCs and partnerships. Instead, S-corporations must allocate income and loss based on pro rata ownership of capital. This is not attractive to many traders.

Note: The IRS can argue that a sole proprietor who hires a spouse is really a husband-wife general partnership. This would make the spouse an owner and not entitled to many fringe benefits.

Statutory or Nonstatutory

Fringe benefit plans include statutory and nonstatutory plans. Statutory employee benefits (those benefits that are carved out by separate sections of the Internal Revenue Code).

Included are qualified retirement plans, group term life insurance, medical coverage, educational assistance, certain meals and lodging, dependent care assistance, and adoption assistance.

Nonstatutory fringe benefits (IRC § 132) include no-additional-cost services; qualified employee discounts; working condition fringes; de minimis fringes; certain transportation benefits; reimbursement of moving expenses; retirement, financial, and tax planning services; club dues; Christmas gifts; and interest-free loans.

Health Insurance Premiums

Health insurance premiums are rising dramatically and represent a significant cost for families. The new trend is for employers to cut back on these fringe benefits by passing on more of the premium to the employee, often times with a flexible spending account or wage withholding.

Business traders with entities can deduct health insurance premiums. These rules only apply for any calendar month in which a trader isn't eligible to participate in any subsidized health plan maintained by any employer of his or her spouse. No AGI deduction is allowed to the extent that the deduction exceeds the trader's fee earned from their trading business, with respect to which the plan providing the medical care coverage was established.

These rules also apply to partners in partnerships and more-than-2-percent shareholders of S-corporations where the partnership or corporation pays for health insurance coverage for its partners or shareholders.

If any of your health insurance premiums are not deductible from AGI, you can add those amounts to your itemized deductions for medical expenses, which are deductible if they are in excess of 7.5 percent of AGI.

Medical Reimbursement Plans

Families have lots of medical expenses not covered by insurance: co-pays, dental, vision, and noncovered procedures. Consider setting up an uninsured medical plan to pay noncovered medical costs (IRC § 105(b)).

Owner/employees are not covered, so set up the plan to cover nonowner/employees and their spouses (you the owner/trader). All medical benefits are excludable from income and payroll taxes.

Health Savings Accounts and
Health Reimbursement Arrangements

Recent tax law changes have created attractive new options for dealing with health insurance and medical expense reimbursement. Before these changes, one had fewer options: to buy health insurance or not (self-insurance), and how big a deductible to take, which affected the amount of your annual health insurance premiums.

With the creation of health savings accounts (HSAs), taxpayers received many new advantages: tax-deductible contributions to HSAs similar to deducting health insurance premiums from AGI (adjusted gross income); more control and flexibility over paying medical expenses; and most important, a better chance to save money and not overpay your insurance company for benefits you never get. With HSAs, you, not the insurance companies, own the unused premiums.

Here is how HSAs work. First you need to have a high-deductible health insurance plan as your base plan, so you are not fully self-insuring, rather it's a combination.

This high-deductible plan allows you to obtain much lower insurance premium rates (whether you are in a group plan or not). In lieu of higher premiums, you pay the difference (give or take) to your own HSA account.

It's sort of like a hybrid health insurance and self-insurance plan, sanctioned by the IRS with tax-deferral benefits. The IRS patterns this concept off the IRA, where you provide for your own retirement funds with tax advantages.

After paying your high-deductible premiums (which are much lower than before), you next fund your own HSA account. Like an IRA, an HSA account is in your own name and the money in the account belongs to you, not an insurance company. So any money left over after paying eligible medical expenses belongs to you—and that's how you better your chances at winning the insurance game! Instead of giving all your money to the insurance company in premiums, you divide up the money and pay some to the insurance company and the rest to yourself in the HSA account.

If you have a serious medical problem and the bills are outrageously large, no problem; the insurance company pays those bills—over the $1,000 (single) or $2,000 (family) deductible amounts—which are the minimum deductibles. You can have higher deductibles as you see fit. Some insurance plans pay medical expenses without application of your deductible, saving you more of your HSA funds.

Like an IRA, you get a tax deduction for your contributions to your HSA, but this is not really an advantage over AGI deductions for health insurance premiums. Traders have the same problem of needing earned income for either deduction. Also like an IRA, an HSA has the tax advantage of tax-free buildup of assets.

The worst tax scenario for taxpayers is going out of pocket on medical expenses without any insurance or HSA plan and then not being able to get any tax deduction for those expenses due to itemized deduction limitations.

Medical expenses are only deductible if they are in excess of 7.5 percent of AGI, and they are not deductible at all for alternative minimum taxes (AMT).

Like any retirement funds, HSAs are especially attractive for traders because traders more than other types of taxpayers can really take advantage of the tax-free buildup from trading their HSA assets.

Note: Many HSAs only pay interest income and don't allow trading. This should change over time.

You also can use the HSA assets to pay your eligible medical expenses that are not paid by the insurance company—those expenses you do not submit above your deductible amount and/or copays.

The GTT Alliance for Traders, an advocacy alliance of traders seeking tax reform and help for traders on health and other types of insurance, mortgages, and much more, provides the following information on their insurance Website:

> Congress has passed a new tax favored insurance plan that replaces Medical Savings Accounts. The new plan is now referred to as a Health Savings Accounts (HSAs). All Americans under the age of 65, regardless of their employment status, now qualify for an HSA.
>
> An HSA is a medical savings account without the restrictions or limitations the old legislation created. The new legislation allows people who buy medical policies with deductibles of at least $1,000 for a single person or $2,000 for a family to establish a tax-free "health savings

account" and potentially reduce their health insurance premiums by as much as 50 percent.

They, or their employers, can fund these accounts with an amount equal to the deductible and the money can be used to pay health care expenses. If the money is not needed, the money can be invested. All money going in the HSA are pretax dollars and withdrawals for health care, including dental services, are tax-free. All existing MSAs will be converted to HSAs during the 2004 year.

Another new option created from recent legislation is a health reimbursement arrangement (HRA). The GTT Alliance for Traders health site lists the following benefits for employees and employers:

- HRAs are the newest way for employers to give their employees freedom of choice in health care planning while controlling their own costs.
- HRAs are similar to Flexible Spending Accounts (FSAs) except that employees do not lose money at the end of the year. Unused dollars may be rolled over into the next year!
- HRAs are similar to Medical Savings Accounts (MSAs) except that HRAs are funded by employers, HRAs are available to employers of all sizes, and HRAs are flexible in design.
- HRAs permit the employee to accumulate money for future health care needs such as retirement health care expenses
- HRAs allow employers to redefine employer-employee health care financing and responsibility.
- HRAs allow employers to offer a high deductible plan and allocate the savings to the HRA for future employee-directed health care.

For more details on HSAs and HRAs, visit the GTT Alliance for Traders Website at GTT (GreenTraderTax) at http://www.greencompany .com/ Traders/ Advocacy.shtml.

Life Insurance Plans

Nonowner/employees can exclude the first $50,000 of group term life insurance coverage (IRC § 79). Excess coverage is taxable to the employee. Your trading business can deduct the life insurance premiums, and your spouse (the nonowner/employee) only reports taxable income on the excess coverage. Compare the actual premium cost to the IRS table rates (the phantom income) to see whether it's beneficial for excess coverage in this plan.

You can also have a "carve-out" plan—a replacement individual plan or cash in lieu of the policy.

Dependent Care Assistance Plans

Many traders with families spend money on dependent care assistance and can benefit from this type of fringe benefit plan. Employees can exclude up to $5,000 of employer-paid dependent care costs (not to exceed earned income, as covered in IRC § 129). The plan must be written. These excluded amounts cannot be part of a child care tax credit. You should consult with your accountant to see which is preferable for your situation. If you opt for a child care credit instead, note both spouses need earned income. Using a pass-through entity, a trader can pay a fee (earned income) to both spouses.

Benefits of Flexible Spending Accounts for Traders

Big companies use flexible spending accounts (FSAs) with salary reduction to shift the cost of fringe benefit plans onto employees. It's good for employees because it lowers their taxable salary amount; the excluded amounts are pretax. With some FSA plans, the excluded benefits are also exempt from payroll taxes (such as is the case with dependent care assistance FSA plans).

Be careful of the "use it or lose it" features in FSAs. If you don't use the FSA amount deposited or withheld, you may lose it for good.

Business traders don't need FSAs because they are not concerned with shifting the burden to other family members.

Educational Assistance Plans and Education Deductions

Employees can exclude up to $5,250 of employer-paid educational assistance (IRC § 127). It applies to just about any kind of course or program including graduate-level courses, even if it isn't job or business related.

Excess amounts can still qualify for the exclusion under the working condition fringe benefit rules. For example, if you take computer training for $10,000 it can all be excluded (because it's job-related). Excludable amounts are not subject to payroll taxes.

Traders face challenges in deducting education expenses as normal business expenses. Business-related educational expenses paid after a trading business is commenced are deductible. However, education expenses paid before business commencement may be nondeductible, or start-up expenses IRC § 195 (amortized over sixty months on a straight-line basis.)

For a tax deduction, your education expenses must help you maintain or improve your employment or business skills, or be required for you to keep your job (or your business), your salary level, or your current status. The education cannot, however, enable you to meet the minimum qualifications for your job, or qualify you for a new trade or business.

A stock broker is already in the trading field, so pretrading business education can be deductible. An attorney studying the trading business before starting to trade may be denied the deduction. Protect your deduction by paying education bills after you commence actual trading. Many types of educational credits are also available for all family members.

Adoption Assistance

Employees can exclude adoption assistance up to $10,000 if their AGI is below set limits (IRC § 137). The exclusion applies to income and payroll taxes.

Meals and Lodging Plans

These expenses can be fully excluded providing you meet the following conditions:

- The meals must be provided on the employer's premises. Many traders don't go out to lunch; they are glued to their screens throughout the day, just like other traders working for large firms.
- Lodging must be furnished on the employer's premises and the employee must accept it as a condition of employment. This lodging exclusion is too aggressive to consider for at-home traders. The home office rules are intended to cover these expenses.

Shift of Income to Children

If your children are of working age and truly capable of helping you in your trading business, consider paying them wages or fees and including them in your employee and fringe benefit plans. This approach also shifts some of your income from higher marginal tax rates to a child's lower marginal tax rates. Consider Roth IRAs for your working children. You can trade their Roth IRA, and all the income builds tax-free on a permanent basis.

The Bottom Line: Fringe benefit plans are somewhat complex and cost some money to implement, but they can be well worth the effort and cost. Consult with a trader tax expert who also is experienced in benefits law. They can determine whether any or all of these plans are right for you and your family.

SELF-EMPLOYMENT TAXES

Unlike all other types of sole proprietorship or unincorporated businesses, securities and commodities traders, with trader tax status, are exempt from self-employment taxation (SE taxes). The exception is that options, commodities, and futures dealers or traders who are registered on commodities exchanges owe SE taxes. Saving SE taxes are great, but you may want to create earned income with an entity to have tax-deductible retirement and fringe benefit plans, in which case you will owe SE tax on that earned income (but you can limit the amount).

Here are the details: Per IRS Publication 550, "Gains and losses from selling securities as part of a trading business are not subject to self-employment tax." This is true whether the MTM election is made or not.

Internal Revenue Code Section 1402, the code section on self-employment taxes, has "special rules for options and commodities dealers."

- The general rule of Section 1402 states that gains and losses from trading in securities and commodities are not subject to self-employment taxation.
- This special rule, 1402(i), states, "in determining the net earnings from self-employment of any options dealer or commodities dealer, there shall not be excluded any gain or loss (in the normal course of the taxpayer's activity of dealing in or trading section 1256 contracts) from section 1256 contracts or property related to such contracts. The term 'commodities dealer' means a person who is actively engaged in trading section 1256 contracts and is registered with a domestic board of trade which is designated as a contract market by the Commodities Futures Trading Commission."

Proprietary traders who receive a Form 1099-Misc for nonemployee compensation are also subject to SE tax.

CHAPTER SUMMARY

Retirement plans are a great idea for traders, but they cannot be formed without earned income. Forming an entity provides earned income and can help traders enjoy fringe benefit plans, most notably a retirement fund. One of the best retirement plans around is the Mini 401(k). It offers tax savings not available in plans such as the IRA. You can also trade your retirement plan, although you must observe certain restrictions.

CHAPTER 5

Commodities, Securities, and Currencies

COMMODITIES AND FUTURES TRADING

Commodities and futures are taxed differently from securities. You need to learn about IRC Section 1256 contracts, Form 6781 and special carrybacks, and how they relate to IRC Section 475(f), the new mark-to-market rules.

MTM (IRC § 475) is not a preferred method for profitable commodities and futures business traders for one reason: With the default accounting method, commodities and futures trading gains are 60 percent long term (i.e., lower rates) and 40 percent short term; MTM (IRC § 475) commodities and futures trading gains are all short term. So, commodity traders experience a trade-off. The default method (IRC § 1256—another type of MTM) is better if you have gains.

Section 1256 also has a loss carryback feature; you can carry back commodities and futures trading losses three tax years, but only against commodities and futures trading gains in those years. This loss carryback feature is not as useful as MTM IRC § 475 losses, which are full net operating losses (NOLs) and may offset any type of income in the prior two tax years.

In summary, commodities and futures business traders usually skip electing MTM IRC § 475 because they would increase their taxes on gains and only marginally improve their ability to carry back losses. This result is a stark contrast to securities business traders who get tax loss insurance with MTM IRC § 475 for no cost (same tax on gains).

Here is one idea: If you incur large commodity trading losses before the MTM election deadline for the current tax year, elect MTM IRC § 475 so you can deduct your commodity trading losses as ordinary losses. That deduction will offset any type of income in the current tax year, and excess losses can generate refunds in the prior two tax years (regardless of whether you have commodities or futures trading gains in prior years).

If you trade both securities and commodities/futures, you may elect MTM IRC § 475 for "securities only" and not also for commodities and futures—a wise move for many business traders. If your trading in securities and commodities/futures are unrelated activities (e.g., you trade stocks and also currency and interest futures rather than securities indexes), the IRS may deem you have separate and unrelated businesses and require you to qualify for trader tax status in each business, meaning you must trade each enough to rise to business treatment.

Distinguishing Between a Security and a Commodity

The universe of trading instruments is growing every day, providing traders with many new opportunities for profits. Taxwise, the IRS forces all these instruments into two main tax categories: securities or commodities. Figuring out how to treat all the new products is a challenge.

For securities, business traders report capital gains and losses on Schedule D (default cash method) or ordinary gains and losses on Form 4797 Part II (if mark-to-market accounting is elected). Securities traders rarely hold positions for more than twelve months, so the bulk of their trading gains are short-term capital gains subject to the ordinary income tax rates.

Tax Rates on Commodities Versus Securities

Commodities are section 1256 contracts taxed 60 percent at long-term capital gains tax rates and 40 percent at short-term capital gains tax rates (i.e., ordinary income tax rates).

$$60\% \times 15\% \text{ (maximum long-term capital gains tax rate)} = 9\%$$
$$40\% \times 35\% \text{ (maximum short-term capital gains tax rate, or}$$
$$\text{ordinary rate)} = 14\%.$$
$$\text{Net maximum 60/40 blended tax rate} = 23 \text{ percent}$$

Securities are usually all short-term for traders, because they hold positions for less than twelve months (maximum short-term capital gains tax rate [ordinary rate] of 35 percent).

It is important to note the net maximum tax rates are significantly better for commodities traders versus securities traders (23 percent versus 35 percent, respectively).

Regulated Futures Contracts

Regulated futures contracts (RFC) are traded on commodities exchanges and, as the regulated label suggests, are regulated by the exchange and the Commodity Futures Trading Commission (CFTC). Exchange-traded commodities, including currency RFCs are covered under IRC section 1256 contracts. Business traders and all investors report RFC section 1256 contracts as capital gains and losses on Form 6781 (Gains and Losses from Section 1256 Contracts and Straddles). This approach allows them to split the gains and losses 60/40 on Schedule D: 60 percent long-term, 40 percent short-term.

A 60/40 split gives commodities traders and investors an advantage over securities traders. For this reason, most profitable commodities business traders don't elect MTM IRC § 475. With § 475, commodities traders can have full tax loss insurance, (ordinary loss treatment), but they are reluctant to give up their beneficial tax rates on gains (the 60/40 split).

Section 1256 Contracts

Section 1256 contracts include regulated futures contracts, foreign currency contracts, nonequity options, dealer equity options, and dealer securities futures contracts. For a partnership that's a qualified fund, section 1256 contracts include bank forward contracts, foreign currency futures contracts, and similar instruments prescribed by IRS regulations.

Commodities are IRC section 1256 contracts. Section 1256 contracts are marked to market at the end of each tax year, so all traders and investors report realized and unrealized gains and losses. No election is necessary here. Do not confuse section 1256 mark-to-market accounting with IRC § 475(f):

- What is and is not a section 1256 contract? See the area titled Definitions in IRC Section 1256 law. Great confusion among trader taxpayers surrounds what is a §1256 contract and what is not.
- Section 1256 was introduced into law by the Economic Recovery Tax Act of 1981. Section 1256 contains special rules for reporting gains and losses from "section 1256 contracts."
- Section 1256(b) defines the term *section 1256 contract* (e.g., commodities) as including any regulated futures contract, any foreign currency contract, any nonequity option, any deal equity option, and any dealer securities futures contract. The Commodities Futures Modernization Act (CFMA) of 2000 established that broad-based indexes are also considered commodities.
- Section 1256(g)(1) provides that the term *regulated futures contract* means a contract (1) with respect to which the amount required to be deposited and the amount which may be withdrawn depends on a system of marking to market, and (2) which is traded on or subject to the rules of a qualified board or exchange.

A futures contract is not defined in section 1256. The CFTC defines a futures contract as "an agreement to purchase or sell a commodity for delivery in the future: (1) at a price that is determined at initiation of the contract; (2) which obligates each party to the contract to fulfill the contract at the specified price; (3) which is used to assume or shift price risk;

and (4) which may be satisfied by delivery or offset." Only a futures contract that has actually been traded on a CFTC-designated contract market
or subject to its rules is a regulated futures contract for purposes of §
1256(g)(1).

A regulated futures contract can be traded by either a taxpayer as a
principal or by a third party acting on the taxpayer's behalf as an agent.
Futures contracts that have been traded by two private parties over the
counter (OTC) are not traded on a contract market and are not regulated
futures contracts for purposes of § 1256(g)(1). See Revenue Ruling 87-43,
1987-1 C.B. 252.

A futures contract that does not meet these terms may be a nonregulated futures contract. The difference between forward contracts and
futures contracts is that the parties to a forward contact generally intend to
make and take delivery.

Parties to a futures contract are speculators who intend to close out
their positions by offset before delivery.

Section 1256(g)(7) provides that the term *qualified board or exchange*
means (1) a national securities exchange that is registered with the Securities and Exchange Commission, (2) a domestic board of trade designated
as a contract market by the Commodity Futures Trading Commission, or
(3) any other exchange, board of trade, or other market the Secretary
determines has rules adequate to carry out the purposes of this section.
Even though the Secretary of the Treasury has not taken up its congres-
sional mandate to create legislative certainty in this area, it can be argued
that the CFTC, by default, has filled the interstitial legislative gap.

Three-Year Carryback of Losses from Section 1256 Contracts

In the Form 6781 instructions, see the directive for Box D (Net Section
1256 Contracts Loss Election). When preparing Form 6781, all individual
taxpayers may mark Box D, thereby electing to carry back a net section
1256 contract loss three tax years.

You then file an amended return for the carryback year and you may apply the section 1256 carryback loss on your Form 6781 for that prior tax year.

Note: If you don't have Form 6781 gains in that prior carryback year, you won't get any benefit from this carryback. So check this aspect before you make this election. Unlike IRC § 475(f)(2), you can make this section 1256 carryback election when you prepare your tax return.

Why 60/40 Treatment Is Viable for Some Foreign Futures

Since the enactment of section 1256 in 1981, a number of contract markets throughout the world have implemented adequate rules and could be determined to be a qualified board or exchange within the meaning of section 1256(g)(7). The Treasury Department's recognition of the appropriate extension of 60/40 tax treatment to foreign exchanges, boards of trade, and other markets pursuant to section 1256(g)(7)(C) is long overdue and is not likely to be forthcoming anytime soon.

Although a formal designation as such by the Treasury would expressly make futures contracts traded on these foreign exchanges eligible for treatment as a section 1256 contract (e.g., eligible for 60/40 capital gain or loss treatment), the lack of such designation does not necessarily preclude 60/40 tax treatment.

OPERATIVE ANALYSIS

For purposes of determining the tax consequences of a transaction, it is necessary to ascertain the legal relationships that exist between the parties to the transaction. In the typical exchange clearing process for a futures or option contract, an exchange clearinghouse is interposed between the original parties to the transaction, namely, the clearing members who represent the purchaser and seller under the contract.

Because a series of steps are involved in the typical exchange clearing process, the step transaction doctrine provides that these steps are not analyzed separately but are viewed as component parts of a single transaction.

In the typical exchange clearing process, the legal relationship between the investor and the broker remains unchanged notwithstanding the fact that an exchange clearinghouse is interposed between the original parties to the transaction. Relying on this type of analysis, in Revenue Ruling 85-72, 1985-1 CB 286, the IRS determined that International Futures Exchange (Bermuda) Ltd. was a qualified board or exchange.

The Tax Court, in Johnson v. CIR, T.C. Memo (1993-178), stating that the purpose of section 1256 is to provide the system of taxation based on marking to market of regulated futures contracts, held the taxpayers' trading in futures contracts and in futures transactions on the London Metal Exchange were conducted subject to the rules of a board of trade or commodity exchange within the meaning of § 1256(g)(7).

However, in Revenue Ruling 87-43, 1987-1 CB 252, the IRS ruled that Singapore International Monetary Exchange Limited (SIMEX) was a foreign board of trade that was not a qualified board or exchange. In that ruling, the Chicago Mercantile Exchange (CME) and the SIMEX established the Mutual Offset System (System) to provide a process by which customers could establish new positions or offset existing positions on one exchange, during hours in which that exchange is closed for trading, by the execution of a contract on the other exchange.

COMMODITY FUTURES
TRADING COMMISSION ON FOREIGN FUTURES

The same type of legal analysis can be extended to decisions of the CFTC with respect to foreign contract markets. Part 30 of the CFTC's regulations establishes the regulatory structure governing the offer and sale of foreign futures and options contracts to U.S. persons by persons acting as futures commission merchants, introducing brokers, commodity pool operators, and commodity trading advisors.

Section 30.10 of these regulations allows the CFTC to, among other things, exempt a foreign firm acting in the capacity of a futures commission merchant from compliance with certain CFTC rules and regulations. To receive such relief under Rule 30.10, the firm's home-country regulator must demonstrate that it provides a comparable system of regulation and must enter into an information sharing agreement with the CFTC.

Once a firm receives confirmation of Rule 30.10 relief, it may engage in the offer or sale of foreign futures and options contracts to U.S. persons without registering with the CFTC on the terms specified in the Rule 30.10 Order.

A reasonable basis in fact and law allows the conclusion that futures traded on foreign contract markets with a Rule 30.10 exemption are entitled to classification as section 1256 contracts (e.g., commodities) with the result that 60/40 tax treatment is appropriate. All that is needed is a determination by the Treasury Secretary.

In the absence of a forward determination by the Secretary, it may be possible to develop an appropriate and reasonable tax return position in support of 60/40 tax treatment for futures contracts traded on the foregoing foreign contract markets.

The CFTC has effectively determined that the foregoing contract markets are exchanges, boards of trade, and other markets qualified within the meaning of § 1256(g)(7) as such boards and exchanges have rules adequate to support the purpose of section 1256. In addition, it can be posited because of the extensive review conducted by the CFTC's Division of Market Oversight, futures traded through the following foreign entities receiving No Action Letters from the CFTC are eligible for section 1256 60/40 tax treatment, pursuant to the preceding analysis.

- MEFF AIAF SENAF Holding de Mercados Financieros S.A. (MEFF), Madrid and Barcelona, Spain
- Bourse de Montreal, Inc., Montreal, Quebec, Canada
- London Metal Exchange Ltd., (LME) London, U.K.
- Eurex Zurich (Eurex CH), Zurich, Switzerland
- OM London Exchange Ltd., (OM), London, U.K.
- Hong Kong Futures Exchange Ltd. (HKFE), Hong Kong, China

- SGX-DT, Singapore
- International Petroleum Exchange of London Ltd., (IPE), London, U.K.
- Eurex Deutschland (Eurex), Frankfurt, Germany
- SFE Corporation Ltd., Sydney, Australia, and Auckland, New Zealand
- Euronext Paris, Paris, France
- London International Financial Futures and Options Exchange (LIFFE), London, U.K.

The IRS has not ruled on the argument that any foreign board or exchange that has received notification from the CFTC under Rule 30.10 is a qualified board or exchange under Section 1256(g).

The 1993 Johnson TC Memo case cited above holds that the London exchange was a board or exchange, under prior law dealing with the definition of a capital asset and holding periods, former Section 1222.

The court did not hold that the London exchange was a qualified board or exchange under Section 1256(g), as the case's facts arose before the enactment of Section 1256. Therefore, while Johnson is favorable, there is still a gap, which is made clear above.

Should an aggressive taxpayer conclude that a gap should be filled in by default? Our writing above certainly gives fair disclosure and leaves it up to the taxpayer. There is a reasonable basis for a return position. The IRS itself has acted recently to extend these interstitial gaps, in the area of "foreign currency contract" by arguing that the term includes not just interbank traded forwards but other OTC Forex contracts as well.

CURRENCIES AND FOREX TRADING

Special Tax Rules for Currency Trading

Currency traders transact in contracts on regulated commodities exchanges or in the nonregulated interbank market, which is a collection of banks giving third-party prices on foreign current contracts (FCC) and other forward contracts.

Currency traders are taxed similar to commodities traders, except that interbank currency traders must "elect out" of IRC § 988 (the ordinary gain or loss rules for special currency transactions) if they want the tax-beneficial 60/40 capital gains rate treatment of IRC § 1256.

Currency traders electing out of IRC § 988 are treated the same as other commodities traders in that their trading gains and losses are treated as section 1256 contracts. Business traders and all investors report section 1256 contracts as capital gains and losses on Form 6781 (Gains and Losses from Section 1256 Contracts and Straddles). This treatment allows them to split the gains and losses 60/40 on Schedule D: 60 percent long-term, 40 percent short-term.

IRC Section 988

The principal intention of IRC § 988 is taxation on foreign currency transactions in a taxpayer's normal course of transacting global business. For example, if a manufacturer purchases materials in a foreign country in a foreign currency, then the fluctuation in exchange rates gain or loss should be accounting for pursuant to IRC § 988.

IRC § 988 provides that these fluctuations in exchange rate gains and losses should be treated as ordinary income or loss and reported as interest income or interest expense. IRC § 988 considers exchange rate risk in the normal course of business to be like interest. Currency traders who trade regulated futures contracts (RFCs) are not affected by IRC § 988 because they are not trading in actual currencies. RFCs based on currencies are just like any other RFC on an organized exchange.

Additionally, because RFCs are marked to market at the close of each day (and year), in accordance with section 1256, the economic and taxable gain or loss is the same. IRC § 988 specifically mentions that RFCs and other mark-to-market instruments are exempt transactions:

(i) In general. Clause (iii) of subparagraph (B) shall not apply to any regulated futures contract or nonequity option which would be marked to market under section 1256 if held on the last day of the taxable year.

Section 988 Effects on Foreign Currency Contracts

A currency trader using the interbank market to transact in foreign currency contracts and other forward contracts is exposed to foreign exchange rate fluctuations, similar to a manufacturer as stated earlier. However, the currency trader looks upon currency positions as capital assets in the normal course of trading activity (business or investment). In other words, a currency trader may elect out of ordinary gain or loss treatment in IRC § 988, thereby using section 1256 contract treatment, which is 60/40 capital gains and losses.

Most currency traders will want to make this election for the tax-beneficial treatment of section 1256 (lower tax rates on gains).

IRC § 988(a)(1)(B) provides currency traders with an exception to the general ordinary gain or loss rule:

Special rule for forward contracts, etc. Except as provided in regulations, a taxpayer may elect to treat any foreign currency gain or loss attributable to a forward contract, a futures contract, or option described in subsection (c)(1)(B)(iii) which is a capital asset in the hands of the taxpayer and which is not a part of a straddle (within the meaning of section 1092(c), without regard to paragraph (4) thereof) as capital gain or loss (as the case may be) if the taxpayer makes such election and identifies such transaction before the close of the day on which such transaction is entered into (or such earlier time as the Secretary may prescribe).

(c)(1)(B)(iii) Entering into or acquiring any forward contract, futures contract, option, or similar financial instrument (with exception above for RFCs).

The Tax Differences on Stock Indexes,
Single-Stock Futures, and Other New Products

New financial products launched by securities and commodities exchanges the past few years include but are not limited to ETFs, E-minis, single-stock futures, new stock indexes, and options and futures on almost everything.

In particular, a rash of new stock indexes from various exchanges provide traders with new means to trade in securities markets. To date, most of these new indexes are, in fact, taxed like commodities, but some are taxed like securities. Coordinated legislation in 2000 from the IRS, Securities and Exchange Commission (SEC), and Commodity Futures Trading Commission (CFTC) set the new general rule.

- **Single-stock futures:** The IRS considers single-stock futures to be "securities futures contracts." Single-stock futures are taxed like their underlying securities (stock, options, and narrow-based indexes) and not like commodities (commodities, futures, Forex, and broad-based indexes). Plus, gains on single-stock futures are always short-term capital gains.
- **Stock indexes:** A narrow-based index is taxed like a security. Conversely, if the index is comprised of 10 or more securities, it is considered a broad-based index that resembles and is taxed like a commodity. E-minis are broad-based indexes taxed as commodities.
- **Securities:** These instruments include but are not limited to exchange-traded funds (ETFs) including QQQ, DIA, and SPDRs; stocks, stock options, mutual funds, and bonds; single-stock futures, otherwise known as "nondealer securities futures contracts"; and by default, any capital asset that is not otherwise defined as an IRC section 1256 contract (a commodity) or IRC § 988 (currencies, interbank foreign exchange, or Forex). For example, gold bullion sounds like a commodity or currency, but physical gold is neither included in IRC section 1256 or 988, and it's taxed like securities. Therefore, if you hold gold bullion bars

for more than twelve months, you are entitled to the lower long-term capital gains rate (currently up to 15 percent).

Tax Implications

If you are a business trader, understand ahead of time how incorporating some of these new products into your trading program may affect your trader tax status and MTM election. For example, if you elected MTM for your securities trading business only (and not for commodities) and you revise your business plan to trade E-Minis almost exclusively, you won't have ordinary loss protection on the E-Minis, because they are taxed as commodities.

Before the Internet revolutionized online trading in 1997, a trader's business and tax universe was in balance. The SEC and CFTC kept to their respective turfs for securities and commodities, and the IRS taxed all instruments as either securities or commodities. The lines of demarcation were clear for all. Most traders focused on securities or commodities trading and few actively traded both. Things changed dramatically with the passage of the Commodity Futures Modernization Act and the simultaneous creation of an entire assortment of new product hybrids.

Newly Created Products

The online trading revolution brought tremendous growth in the securities markets with the advent of hot IPOs. Trading in tech and NASDAQ stocks were all the rage in the late 1990s. By 2000, the stock market bubble burst and securities and commodities exchanges actively began to compete for customers by creating new products that mirrored products created by the other exchange.

Commodities exchanges felt they missed the stock market windfall, so they rushed to market new flavors of broad-based stock indexes. Commodity exchanges were successful, partially because of the tax advantages for commodities traders over securities traders.

These new hybrid products created with the CFMA raised the ire of the SEC. This new act solved many of the outstanding regulatory and tax treatment issues raised by these new products. The CFMA established a framework for joint regulation (by the SEC and the CFTC) of single-stock futures and narrow-based security indexes. IRS issues were also solved because the CFMA updated the IRS definition of "nonequity options" in IRC section 1256 contracts (commodities). Now, both the IRS and regulatory definitions of broad-based indexes are the same—10 or more stocks in an index. This definition is great news for traders because now almost all indexes are broad-based and taxed at the lower commodity tax rates.

Regulation-wise, broad-based security indexes, which are not considered security futures products, continue to trade under the sole jurisdiction of the CFTC. Security futures products (i.e., single-stock futures) are subject to the joint jurisdiction of the CFTC and the SEC. Methods for determining when an index is broad- or narrow-based (for tax and regulatory purposes) are discussed at www.cftc.gov/sfp/sfpbackground.htm. For indexes excluded from the definition of narrow-based security index, see www.cftc.gov/sfp/sfpcontractsapprovedprecfma.htm.

The main effect of the CFMA was to significantly expand the definition of a broad-based index, which is considered a commodity. Narrow-based indexes are considered securities. Under the CFMA, almost all futures and options on stock indexes, and smaller variations of indexes (commonly known as E-Minis), are considered broad-based indexes, and treated as commodities.

Single-Stock Futures Taxed as Securities

The IRS states,

> [A] gain or loss on the sale, exchange, or termination of a securities futures contract generally has the same character as gain or loss from transactions in the underlying security.
>
> For example, if the underlying asset would be a capital asset in the hands of the taxpayer, gain or loss from the sale of the contract is a

capital gain or loss. This rule does not apply to securities futures contracts that are not capital assets (they are inventory assets), nor does it apply to products identified as hedging transactions, or any income derived in connection with a contract that would otherwise not produce a capital gain. Except as provided in the regulations, capital gain or loss from the sale, exchange or termination of a securities futures contract to sell property is treated as short-term capital gain or loss.

A securities futures contract generally is defined as a contract of sale for future delivery of a single security or a narrow-based security index.

TAX HELP FROM CONGRESS

Congress should be applauded for acting in a smart manner in their passage of the CFMA. Traders are not investing in long-term securities, but instead looking to trade any feasible instrument for a quick swing in price for profit. For traders, it's a zero-sum game. Now with the CFMA, all those new indexes are treated as commodities and commodity tax law is better for traders. Commodities are marked to market at the end of each day (which is the way a trader thinks), and the tax rates are lower.

Congress needs to do more work and help more traders avoid the tax pitfalls of securities taxation. Traders can help themselves with an IRC § 475 mark-to-market election to avoid wash sales, straddle rules, and capital loss limitations.

CHAPTER SUMMARY

For tax purposes, securities and commodities are not alike. Commodities traders have a tax benefit over securities traders; they are taxed at a mixed 60/40 tax rate, regardless of how long they hold a position. Before you trade, it's important to know whether your trade will be taxed as a security or a commodity, because a new breed of hybrid products have characteristics of both. And, if you trade currencies, you must deal with entirely different tax implications.

CHAPTER 6

Accounting

COMPLEX ACCOUNTING FOR TRADING GAINS AND LOSSES

Most traders who qualify for trader tax status have more than 1,000 trades per year; some have hundreds of thousands. Figuring out your trade-by-trade accounting for securities can be a nightmare and cost a trader too much valuable time.

GTT TradeLog software programs from GreenTraderTax and Armen Computing completely automates your stock, options and futures trades, and tax accounting. Save days of time and professional fees by using our programs to import all your trades (prior and current years). Our program generates your Schedule Ds (cash method) and Form 4797 (mark-to-market method) tax reports. *Barron's* and *Active Trader* magazine have rated it among the best tax accounting solutions for traders. Learn more, take a tour, and get a free download at http://www.greencompany.com/Traders/Software.shtml.

Insufficient Help from Brokers

IRS Form 1099s sent by your broker at tax time do not include securities trading gains and losses; rather they only include proceeds. Some brokerage firms provide traders with reports of trading gains and losses; but most of these reports have unmatched trades or don't account for mark-to-market accounting or wash sales. Commodities and futures traders have it easy. Their Form 1099s do report "aggregate profit or loss."

Don't get lost trying to calculate each securities trade. Instead, use the inventory approach or performance record approach formulas with guidance to calculate an annual net gain or loss amount per brokerage account. The formulas and the annual gain or loss numbers generated are proven and acceptable to the IRS. You enter one line per brokerage account on your Schedule D or Form 4797. One drawback is these formulas cannot calculate wash sales, and you must determine them in another manner. If you use MTM IRC § 475, the formulas are 100 percent accurate.

Many traders use their own formulas or consumer finance software programs during the tax year, which is useful for knowing their profit and loss. Many of these traders have trouble generating accurate tax return numbers that reconcile to their Form 1099s, and they don't make correct adjustments for mark-to-market accounting, § 481(a) adjustments, or wash sales.

Inventory Approach

The formulas come in three different accounting scenarios:

1. Cash method of accounting
2. Mark-to-market method of accounting
3. Elect mark-to-market method of accounting

General Guidance for Inventory Approach

The inventory approach formulas use the same logic that is used in inventory accounting used by retailers and manufacturers. Revenue minus Cost of Goods Sold equals Gross Margin.

$$\text{Cost of Goods Sold} = \text{Opening Inventory}$$
$$+ \text{ Purchases} - \text{Ending Inventory.}$$

For the trading business, Revenue equates to Proceeds, and Opening and Ending Inventory equates to Opening and Closing Positions Held.

Cash Method of Accounting

Here's the formula for calculating your profit or loss for the tax year.

$$\text{Trading gain or loss} = R - CGSC$$

where

$$CGSC = OPC + P - EPC$$

where

R = Revenue or proceeds (from security sales)
P = Purchases (security purchases)
OPC = Opening positions held for tax period priced at original cost
EPC = Ending positions held for tax period priced at original cost

Mark-to-Market Method of Accounting

Here's the formula for calculating your profit or loss for the tax year:

$$\text{MTM trading gain or loss} = (R + EPM) - CGSM$$

where

$$CGSM \text{ (cost of goods sold)} = OPM + P$$

where

R = Revenue or proceeds (from security sales)
P = Purchases (security purchases)
OPM = Opening positions held for tax period priced at
market on January 1
EPM = Ending positions held for tax period priced at
market on December 31

Elect Mark-to-Market Method of Accounting

This method includes two components: (1) You start with the preceding mark-to-market method of accounting, and (2) then you add your § 481(a) adjustment. Here's the formula for calculating your § 481(a) adjustment.

$$\text{Section 481(a) adjustment} = OPM - OPC$$

where

OPM = Opening positions held for tax period
priced at market on January 1
OPC = Opening positions held for tax period
priced at original cost

You will need to perform the following steps to gather the necessary tax information to enter into the formulas.

- *Step 1.* Determine your opening inventory (your Opening Positions Held on January 1). You will find this information listed on your prior December 31 monthly brokerage statement. Opening Positions Held are listed at market prices as of December 31 (or last trade day of the prior tax year). If you are using the cash method of accounting (versus the mark-to-market accounting method), you will also need the original cost basis (or carryover cost basis with deferred wash sale losses) for the open positions. Note that monthly brokerage statements are based on settlement date, whereas tax returns and Form 1099s are based on trade date. Care needs to be taken to account for unsettled trades (trades clearing or settling in early January that were traded in the prior tax year).

- *Step 2.* Determine your total purchases of securities during the tax year. You can find purchases listed on most Form 1099 supplemental information. Some brokers report purchases in detail, but then don't total them up. You also may find purchases totaled each month on the monthly statements, but again take care about unsettled trades. Finding total purchases is usually the most difficult part of this exercise, if the broker doesn't total them up in the Form 1099 supplemental information.

- *Step 3.* Determine your total sales of securities during the tax year. Total sales of stocks, bonds, and mutual funds are reported on the first part of your Form 1099. You can usually find total sales of stock options in the supplemental information section of your Form 1099. If not, look in the monthly brokerage statements.

- *Step 4.* Determine your ending inventory (open positions at year-end). As with opening inventory, you can find these amounts on the monthly statement at the end of the tax year.

Performance Record Approach

Money managers use the performance record approach to report their trading activity to their investors. This approach works well for Forex traders too. Basically, you determine performance using the following formula: Ending net assets (ENA) minus additions (funds added to your accounts during the tax year) plus withdrawals (funds or expenses paid out of your accounts during the tax year) minus beginning net assets (BNA) equals total performance. Total performance minus portfolio income plus margin interest expense equals trading gains and losses.

$$\text{Trading gains and losses} = TP - PI + MIE$$

where

$$TP = ENA - A + W - BNA$$

where

TP = Total performance
ENA = Ending net assets
BNA = Beginning net asset
A = Additions
W = Withdrawals
PI = Portfolio income
MIE = Margin interest expense

Section 481(a) Adjustments

The performance approach has variations for cash or mark-to-market accounting methods. Most securities traders are better off using the inventory approach. The performance record approach is preferable when you have trouble determining total purchases or other information required for the inventory approach. It's always preferable for Forex traders.

The section 481(a) adjustment is required when you elect mark-to-market accounting. According to Rev. Proc. 99-17 (updated by Rev. Proc. 2002-19), mark-to-market accounting method for dealers in securities—election for traders and dealers, Section 6, Change in Method of Accounting; Clause.03 Section 481(a) Adjustment:

> If a taxpayer changes its method of accounting under section 6.01 of this revenue procedure, the taxpayer must take into account the net amount of the section 481(a) adjustment in the manner provided in section 5.04 of Rev. Proc. 98-60. Thus, the section 481(a) adjustment generally is taken into account ratably over four taxable years beginning with the year of change (modified by Rev. Proc. 2002-19 below). For purposes of section 481, a change in method of accounting made under this revenue procedure is a change in method of accounting initiated by the taxpayer.

According to the rules for Form 3115 (Change of Accounting Method), if the change results in a positive section 481 adjustment, the taxpayer must, beginning with the year of change, take the section 481 adjustment into account ratably over four taxable years in computing taxable income. However, the taxpayer may elect to take the entire positive section 481 adjustment in the year of change, providing the section 481 adjustment is under $25,000. Otherwise, the taxpayer is required to prorate this section 481 adjustment over four taxable years.

According to Rev. Proc. 2002-19, if the change results in a negative section 481 adjustment, the taxpayer must take the entire section 481(a) adjustment into account in the year of change.

Section 481(a) Adjustment Calculation

On January 1, the taxpayer started the year with Security Trading Positions.

Market value on January 1 of security trading positions	$903,221
Original cost basis of security trading positions	875,105
Section 481(a) adjustment	+$28,116

This amount is reported on Form 4797 Part II.

Deferral Required

The section 481 adjustment is over $25,000, so the taxpayer may not elect to report the entire amount in the current tax year; instead the taxpayer must prorate the adjustment over four years. The positive § 481(a) deferral is calculated as follows:

Sec. 481(a) adjustment of $28,116 ÷ 4 years × 3 years = $(21,087).

This deferral amount is also reported on Form 4797 Part II.

The taxpayer will report the balance of the positive deferral in the amount of $7,029 per year on his or her Form 4797 Part II for the following three tax years. In the event that the taxpayer exits his or her trading business, the taxpayer will accelerate the balance of his or her § 481(a) adjustment to the exit year. The § 481(a) adjustment is reported on Form 4797 Part II of your tax return and in the year of change it is also reported on Form 3115 covered later in this book.

INDIVIDUAL EXAMPLES

If you traded securities as a business during the year, you should learn how to file a proper income tax return, taking advantage of trader tax status and mark-to-market accounting tax laws. We provide examples of federal and state tax returns for many types of traders. This "Individual Examples" section is excerpted from the "2004 GTT Guide: 2003 Tax Return Examples for Securities Traders (Individual and Entities)" available at Green-TraderTax.com. Each complete federal and state tax return example in that guide is 50 to 100 pages, too big to include in this book. Some buyers of this book may feel the need to also purchase these companion guides, but others will be fine with the book alone. At the time of this writing, only 2003 tax forms were available. Trader types included:

Part-time traders: These traders have other full-time jobs or other business activities. They are the traders the IRS attacks in exams. Our example tax returns show part-time traders how to avoid raising red flags with the IRS, and they include footnotes to explain your status and prevent IRS questions and exams. We show you many clever tax-filing strategies, and you should not file a part-time trader tax return without these examples and this guide. We also show you examples of how the IRS may want to change your tax returns and how your return would look without trader tax status.

Money-losing traders: These traders lost money in their trading businesses in the current year and prior years. They are the traders the IRS attacks in exams. Our example tax returns show money-losing traders how to avoid raising red flags with the IRS, and they include footnotes to explain your status and prevent IRS questions and exams. We show you many clever tax-filing strategies to maximize your tax benefits and increase your carryovers to future years or carrybacks to prior years for immediate tax relief. You should not file a money-losing trader tax return without these examples and this guide. We also show you examples of how the IRS may want to change your tax returns and how your return would look without trader tax status.

Sole proprietor business traders: We have a few different example tax returns for profitable traders in a few different states. We show profitable traders how to maximize expense deductions, including home office, travel, meals, margin interest, and every conceivable trading business expense. We show you many clever tax-filing strategies to maximize your tax benefits.

For example, your trading business expenses are reported on Schedule C and your trading gains are reported on Schedule D (cash method) or Form 4797 (mark-to-market method). No gains or income is reported on Schedule C. If you file this way, you may invite IRS questions or an exam because of a large Schedule C business loss (for your expenses). Our many example tax returns show you how to transfer income from Schedule D or Form 4797 to Schedule C to do away with some or all of the loss.

This unlocks further tax benefits such as home office expenses and section 179 depreciation, which require Schedule C income. We also show you how to avoid self-employment taxes and to explain all these aspects to the IRS in customized footnotes. You should not file a profitable trader tax return without these examples and this guide.

Single-member LLC business traders: Both sole proprietor and single-member LLC (SMLLC) business traders can deduct all possible trading business expenses on Schedule C and elect mark-to-market (MTM) accounting for ordinary gain or loss treatment (tax loss insurance if you have losses). However, only a SMLLC trader can deduct health insurance premiums and contribute to a tax-deductible retirement plan.

Mark-to-market accounting traders: We cover examples of traders with or without MTM. A separate example also covers continuing MTM trader and those who first elected it for the current year (and have a Section 481 adjustment).

Part-year traders: We cover examples of traders who enter or exit their trading business during the tax year. We cover suspended MTM elections and whether a trader has to accelerate the remaining positive Section 481 adjustments (from electing MTM).

States: We will include examples for many states.

Form 3115 and more: The guide gives you everything you need at tax time including line-by-line guidance, Form 3115, footnotes, home office deductions, extensions, and more.

Tax reporting strategies and guidance: In our companion set of trader tax guides with complete example tax returns, at the end of each of the example tax returns (which are PDF files) and before the state return, are several pages titled "Supplemental Information." The first few supplemental information pages are marked "TAX RETURN FOOTNOTES," and just after them are "CLIENT NOTES— FOR INTERNAL USE ONLY." We include as much of this information as possible in this book.

Tax return footnotes: These notes are included with your tax return and help explain your complex tax status to the IRS. Some accountants advocate no footnotes, but we strongly believe that trader tax status is quite complex. To prevent IRS questions and exams, we have had great success with our clients using footnotes. The footnotes explain trader tax laws, your status, and the trader tax treatment used on the return.

Client notes—For internal use only: Do not file this section with your tax return. These notes are for internal use only. The notes are intended to explain to you how we prepared these example tax returns. We include guidance, notes, warnings, strategies, tips, and form references.

Following is an example of a tax return footnote which you can customize depending on what type of trader you are.

TAX RETURN FOOTNOTES

The example footnote that follows is for a part-time business trader in securities who elected mark-to-market accounting (MTM IRC § 475) for the tax year being filed.

The first paragraph explains the trader's part-time business status. This paragraph is added to answer any IRS questions about part-time status upfront with the intention of preventing IRS questions or an exam later on. If you are full time, you can delete this paragraph.

Note the paragraphs about electing mark-to-market (MTM) accounting IRC § 475(f) for 2003 and the related IRC § 481 (a) adjustment on the tax return and Form 3115 (Change of Accounting Method). If you did not elect MTM for the tax year being filed, you can omit those paragraphs.

The rest of the footnote is standard and is intended to explain business trader tax status and how you reported various items on your tax return.

Customized footnotes together with full federal and state tax return examples for every type of business trader are included in our companion *GTT Trader Tax Examples Guides*, published every tax season at www .greentradertax.com.

Example Tax Return Footnote

Note to Schedules C, Form 4797-Part II & Form 3115 in connection with taxpayer's business activity: "trader in securities."

Taxpayer operated a trading business, in accordance with the definition below during the entire year of 2003. From January through October of 2003, the taxpayer carried on two careers at the same time. The taxpayer's former job allowed him access to his trading business during trading hours using his computer and Internet connection at work. Taxpayer also operated his trading business before, during, and after work and on weekends. Taxpayer left his job as an attorney at the end of October to focus on his trading business full time. Considerable time spent every trading day, consistent and frequent number of trades, and trading proceeds all support taxpayer's raising to the level of conducting this activity as a business.

Summary

Taxpayer qualifies as a trader in securities for 2003 and he duly elected mark-to-market accounting IRC § 475(f) on time for tax year 2003. Taxpayer's trading business expenses are reported on Schedule C, and his trading gains and losses are reported on Form 4797, Part II—Ordinary Gain or Loss. Taxpayer is not subject to self-employment taxes on this trading activity. Taxpayer is also not subject to wash sale loss deferral rules on this trading activity.

Taxpayer's investment positions (if any) are not subject to the above trading business tax treatment and instead are subject to normal rules for investing activities, which is Schedule D capital gains or losses, wash sales, and Schedule A for related investment expenses.

Special Notes

If taxpayer has net business trading gains, sufficient trading gains are transferred from Schedule D or Form 4797 to Schedule C to cover taxpayer's related trading business expenses. This is done since Schedule C business expenses relate to taxpayer's trading gains and income is not otherwise reported on Schedule C. There is no change to the tax liability as a result of this transfer.

See additional tax return explanations that follow.

Taxpayer's business activities are described in IRS Publication 550, Chapter 4—Special Rules for Traders. We excerpt these rules below (and add some notes in parenthesis).

Special Rules for Traders in Securities

Special rules apply if you are a trader in securities in the business of buying and selling securities for your own account. To be engaged in business as a trader in securities, you must meet all the following conditions. (Taxpayer met all the following conditions for tax year 2003.)

- You must seek to profit from daily market movements in the prices of securities and not from dividends, interest, or capital appreciation.
- Your activity must be substantial.
- You must carry on the activity with continuity and regularity.

The following facts and circumstances should be considered in determining if your activity is a securities trading business.

- Typical holding periods for securities bought and sold. (Taxpayer had very short holding periods.)

- The frequency and dollar amount of your trades during the year. (Taxpayer traded frequently with lower dollar amounts—high turnover.)
- The extent to which you pursue the activity to produce income for a livelihood. (Taxpayer's intention is to earn a living from this trading business activity.)
- The amount of time you devote to the activity. (Taxpayer spends a good part of every day on this activity.)

Note: You may be a trader in some securities and have other securities you hold for investment. The special rules discussed here do not apply to the securities held for investment. You must keep detailed records to distinguish the securities. The securities held for investment must be identified as such in your records on the day you acquired them (for example, by holding them in a separate brokerage account). (If taxpayer has investment securities, they are clearly "segregated" from his or her trading securities in accordance with current IRS regulations.)

How to Report

Transactions from trading activities result in capital gains and losses and must be reported on Schedule D (Form 1040). Losses from these transactions are subject to the limit on capital losses explained earlier in this chapter.

Mark-to-Market Election Made

(Taxpayer elected mark-to-market accounting for securities only for 2003.)

If you made the mark-to-market election, you should report all gains and losses from trading as ordinary gains and losses in Part II of Form 4797, instead of as capital gains and losses on Schedule D. In that case, securities held at the end of the year in your business as a trader are marked-to-market by treating them as if they were sold (and reacquired) for fair market value on the last business day of the year. But do not mark to market any securities you held for investment. Report sales from those securities on Schedule D, not Form 4797.

Expenses

Interest expense and other investment expenses that an investor would deduct on Schedule A (Form 1040) are deducted by a trader on Schedule C (Form 1040), Profit or Loss From Business, if the expenses are from the trading business. Commissions and other costs of acquiring or disposing of securities are not deductible (on Schedule C) but must be used to figure gain or loss on Schedule D (if cash basis) or Form 4797 (if mark-to-market). The limit on investment interest expense, which applies to investors, does not apply to interest paid or incurred in a trading business. (Taxpayer duly reported his or her trading business expenses on Schedule C: Trader in securities.)

Self-Employment Tax

Gains and losses from selling securities as part of a trading business are not subject to self-employment tax. This is true whether the election is made or not.

How to Make the Mark-to-Market Election

To make the mark-to-market election for 2004, you must file a statement by April 15, 2004. This statement should be attached to either your 2003 individual income tax return or a request for an extension of time to file that return. (Taxpayer elected mark-to-market accounting for securities only for tax year 2003; by attaching that election to his 2002 tax return or extension filed by April 15, 2003. A copy of that election is included at the end of this footnote.) The statement must include the following information:

- That you are making an election under section 475(f) of the Internal Revenue Code.
- The first tax year for which the election is effective.
- The trade or business for which you are making the election.
- If you are not required to file a 2003 income tax return, you make the election by placing the above statement in your books and records no later than March 15, 2004. Attach a copy of the statement to your 2004 return.

After making the election to change to the mark-to-market method of accounting, you must change your method of accounting for securities under Revenue Procedure 2002-9 and 2002-19. Revenue Procedure 2002-9 requires you to file Form 3115, Application for Change in Accounting Method. Follow its instructions. Label the Form 3115 as filed under "Section 10A of the Appendix of Rev. Proc. 2002-9." (Taxpayer is filing his or her Form 3115 together with the Section 481 adjustment [if any applies] with this tax return. Taxpayer is filing a duplicate copy with the IRS national office as is also required.)

Once you make the election, it will apply to 2004 and all later tax years, unless you get permission from IRS to revoke it. The effect of making the election is described under mark-to-market election made, earlier.

For more information on this election, see Revenue Procedure 99-17, 1999-1 CB 503.

Section 481(a) Adjustment Tax Law for Traders

According to Rev. Proc. 99-17, 1999-7 IRB 1, IRC Sec(s)—
Mark-to-Market Accounting Method for Dealers in Securi-
ties—Election for Traders and Dealers. Section 6. Change in
Method of Accounting; Clause.03 Section 481(a) Adjustment:

If a taxpayer changes its method of accounting under section 6.01 of
this revenue procedure, the taxpayer must take into account the net
amount of the section 481(a) adjustment in the manner provided in
section 5.04 of Rev. Proc. 98-60. Thus, the section 481(a) adjustment
generally is taken into account ratably over four taxable years beginning with the year of change. For purposes of section 481, a change
in method of accounting made under this revenue procedure is a
change in method of accounting initiated by the taxpayer.

According to the rules for Form 3115, if the change results
in a positive section 481 adjustment, the taxpayer must, beginning with the year of change, take the section 481 adjustment
into account ratably over four taxable years in computing taxable income. However, the taxpayer may elect to take the entire
section 481 positive adjustment in the year of change, providing the Section 481 adjustment is under $25,000. Otherwise,
taxpayer is required to prorate this Section 481 adjustment over
four taxable years.

If the change results in a negative section 481 adjustment,
the taxpayer must take the entire section 481(a) adjustment
into account in the year of change (Rev Proc 2002-19).

Section 481(a) Adjustment—Calculation

On January 1, 2003, taxpayer started the year with "Trading
Positions."

Market value on January 1, 2003	$286,522
Original cost basis	170,979
Section 481 adjustment is the difference	+115,543

This amount is reported on Form 4797, Part II, and pro-rated over four years.

The Section 481 adjustment is greater than $25,000. As indicated above, taxpayer must prorate the greater than $25,000 positive adjustment over four tax years.

The total Sec 481(a) prorated deferral is calculated as follows:

Sec 481(a) adjustment of $115,543 ÷
by 4 years × 3 years = $ (86,658).

This amount is also reported on the Form 4797, Part II.

Taxpayer will report the deferred prorated income on his or her Form 4797 Part II in the amount of $28,886 per year for each of the following three tax years, 2004, 2005, and 2006. In the event that taxpayer exits the trading business before the final adjustment year, taxpayer shall be required to accelerate the remaining deferred income in that year of exit.

Copy of Taxpayer's Election for MTM Accounting

This election was attached to taxpayer's 2002 tax return or extension filed by April 15, 2003.

Pursuant to IRC 475(f), the taxpayer hereby elects to adopt the mark-to-market method of accounting for the tax year ended December 31, 2003, and subsequent tax years. The election applies to the following trade or business: Trader in Securities as a Sole Proprietor.

Example 1: Money-Losing, Full-Time Securities Business MTM Trader

Trader elected mark-to-market accounting for tax year with a negative section 481 adjustment. Home office for rental apartment.

> *Client facts:* This client is single and lives in California. He trades securities full-time and operates from his three-bedroom rental apartment. Even though he is full-time, he only had 1,000 round-trip trades, because he had a difficult year. He traded every day the market was open, except when he was sick or on vacation. His trading business is his only means of making a living. On average, his holding periods are less than a few days. On most days, he spends the entire day in his trading business, executing and researching trades, and doing management activities. The client's securities proceeds total over $27 million.

> *Trader tax status determination:* Based on the preceding facts, this trader has trader tax status for the entire year; therefore, his return was prepared as a sole proprietor (an unincorporated business). We reported all of the client's trading business expenses on Schedule C (Profit or Loss From Business) as shown in Figure 6.1. The client was trading full time, made a sufficient number of round-trip trades, had short holding periods, spent sufficient time in the business, and had large proceeds. Equally important, the client mentioned that his intention was to operate a trading business on a frequent, continuous, and regular basis, and his objective was to profit from quick swings in price, not long term price appreciation.

> *The mark-to-market accounting process:* The client elected mark-to-market (MTM) accounting (IRC 475) for the tax year by the due date of April 15 of the same tax year (i.e., April 15, 2003, for tax year 2003). See page 147 for a copy of the election that should be

Figure 6.1 Schedule C, Profit or Loss From Business

Schedule **C** (Form 1040) 2003 EX13 Fed-CA fulltime MTM, loss, 481 loss 111-11-1111 Page **2**

Part III   **Cost of Goods Sold** (see instructions)

33	Method(s) used to value closing inventory: **a** ☐ Cost **b** ☐ Lower of cost or market **c** ☐ Other (attach explanation)		
34	Was there any change in determining quantities, costs, or valuations between opening and closing inventory? If 'Yes,' attach explanation.		☐ Yes ☐ No
35	Inventory at beginning of year. If different from last year's closing inventory, attach explanation	35	
36	Purchases less cost of items withdrawn for personal use	36	
37	Cost of labor. Do not include any amounts paid to yourself	37	
38	Materials and supplies	38	
39	Other costs	39	
40	Add lines 35 through 39	40	
41	Inventory at end of year	41	
42	**Cost of goods sold.** Subtract line 41 from line 40. Enter the result here and on page 1, line 4	42	

Part IV   **Information on Your Vehicle.** Complete this part **only** if you are claiming car or truck expenses on line 9 and are not required to file Form 4562 for this business. See the instructions for line 13 to find out if you must file Form 4562.

43 When did you place your vehicle in service for business purposes? (month, day, year) ▶ _ _ _ _ _ _ _ _ _ _ _ .

44 Of the total number of miles you drove your vehicle during 2003, enter the number of miles you used your vehicle for:
  a Business _ _ _ _ _ _ _ _ _ _ _   **b** Commuting _ _ _ _ _ _ _ _ _ _ _   **c** Other _ _ _ _ _ _ _ _ _ _ _

45 Do you (or your spouse) have another vehicle available for personal use? ☐ Yes ☐ No

46 Was your vehicle available for personal use during off-duty hours? ☐ Yes ☐ No

47**a** Do you have evidence to support your deduction? ☐ Yes ☐ No

  b If 'Yes,' is the evidence written? ☐ Yes ☐ No

Part V   **Other Expenses.** List below business expenses not included on lines 8-26 or line 30.

Postage	195.
Trader tax and accounting	755.
Trading cable and internet service	652.
Trading chat room	1,350.
Trading newsletters and publications	1,145.
Trading online information services	2,988.
Trading seminars	3,225.
48 **Total other expenses.** Enter here and on page 1, line 27 48	10,310.

Schedule **C** (Form 1040) 2003

FDIZ0112L 10/14/03

Figure 6.1 Schedule C, Profit or Loss From Business, *continued*

attached to this tax return. This election completes the first part of the MTM process.

Filing of Form 3115: For the second step of completing the MTM election process, we attach a Form 3115 (Change of Accounting Method) including any required IRC § 481 adjustment to his 2003 tax return, shown in Figure 6.2. We also file a duplicate copy of Form 3115 only to the IRS National Office. This filing needs to be done by the due date of this tax return, including extensions. Many traders and accountants err by filing Form 3115 in lieu of the MTM election statement. They reduced two steps to one and wind up without MTM. Filing either the MTM election statement or Form 3115 late will invalidate MTM—so be careful to do both properly and on time.

Applying MTM: For the third and final step of completing the MTM election process, we make sure to mark all open trading positions at year-end to market prices. We also report MTM gains and losses on Form 4797 Part II, ordinary gain and loss (see Figure 6.3).

Warning: If any of the preceding steps is done incorrectly or late (after the extended due date), the IRS can challenge this client's right to use MTM. This challenge can have serious consequences. Without MTM, the IRS will require all capital gains and losses to be reported on Schedule D, and this client will lose all the ordinary loss benefits of Form 4797. Capital losses are limited to $3,000 per year, and the client will also be subject to wash sale loss and straddle loss deferral rules.

Section 481 adjustment: Because the client elected MTM for the tax year, the client had to calculate and report a section 481 adjustment. See the explanation of a section 481 adjustment and the related tax law in the Footnotes. Negative § 481 adjustments are taken 100 percent in the year of change.

Form **3115**
(Rev. December 2003)
Department of the Treasury
Internal Revenue Service

Application for Change in Accounting Method

OMB No. 1545-0152

Name of filer (name of parent corporation if a consolidated group) (see instructions)

EX13Fed-NY full-time MTM, loss. 481 loss

Identification number (see instructions)
111-11-1111

Principal business activity code number (see instructions)
523110

Number, street, and room or suite no. If a P.O. box, see the instructions.

Any Street

City or town, state, and ZIP code

New York, NY 10011

Tax year of change begins (MM/DD/YYYY) 01/01/2003

Tax year of change ends (MM/DD/YYYY) 12/31/2003

Name of contact person (see instructions)

Name of applicant(s) (if different than filer) and identification number(s) (see instructions)

Contact person's telephone number
( )

If the applicant is a member of a consolidated group, check this box . . . . ▶ ☐

If Form 2848, Power of Attorney and Declaration of Representative, is attached, check this box . . . . . . ▶ ☐

Check the box to indicate the applicant.

☒ Individual
☐ Corporation
☐ Controlled foreign corporation (Sec. 957)
☐ 10/50 corporation (Sec. 904(d)(2)(E))
☐ Qualified personal service corporation (Sec. 448(d)(2))
☐ Exempt organization. Enter Code section ▶

☐ Cooperative (Sec. 1381)
☐ Partnership
☐ S corporation
☐ Insurance co. (Sec. 816(a))
☐ Insurance co. (Sec. 831)
☐ Other (specify) ▶

Check the appropriate box to indicate the type of accounting method change being requested. (see instructions)

☐ Depreciation or Amortization
☒ Financial Products and/or Financial Activities of Financial Institutions
☐ Other (specify) ▶

Caution: *The applicant must provide the requested information to be eligible for approval of the requested accounting method change. The applicant may be required to provide information specific to the accounting method change such as an attached statement. The applicant must provide all information relevant to the requested accounting method change, even if not specifically requested by the Form 3115.*

Part I	**Information For Automatic Change Request**	Yes	No

1 Enter the requested designated accounting method change number from the **List of Automatic Accounting Method Changes** (see instructions). Enter only one method change number, except as provided for in the instructions. If the requested change is not included in that list, check "Other," and provide a description.

▶ (a) Change No. 64 (b) Other ☐ Description ▶

2 Is the accounting method being requested one for which the scope limitations of section 4.02 of Rev. Proc. 2002-9 (or its successor) **do not** apply? . . . . | X | |
If "Yes," go to Part II.

3 Is the tax year of change the final tax year of a trade or business for which the taxpayer would be required to take the entire amount of the section 481(a) adjustment into account in computing taxable income? . . . | | X |
If "Yes," the applicant is not eligible to make the change under automatic change request procedures.
Note: *Complete Part II below and then Part IV, and also Schedules A through E of this form (if applicable).*

Part II	**Information For All Requests**	Yes	No

4a Does the applicant (or any present or former consolidated group in which the applicant was a member during the applicable tax year(s)) have any Federal income tax return(s) under examination (see instructions)? . . . | | X |
If you answered "No," go to line 5.

b Is the method of accounting the applicant is requesting to change an issue (with respect to either the applicant or any present or former consolidated group in which the applicant was a member during the applicable tax year(s) either (i) under consideration or (ii) placed in suspense (see instructions)? . . . . |

Signature *(see instructions)*

Under penalties of perjury, I declare that I have examined this application, including accompanying schedules and statements, and to the best of my knowledge and belief, the application contains all the relevant facts relating to the application, and it is true, correct, and complete. Declaration of preparer (other than applicant) is based on all information of which preparer has any knowledge.

Filer

Preparer (other than filer/applicant)

Signature and date

Signature of individual preparing the application and date

EX13Fed-NY full-time MTM, loss. 481 loss

Name and title (print or type)

Name of individual preparing the application (print or type)

Name of firm preparing the application

For Privacy Act and Paperwork Reduction Act Notice, see the instructions.

Cat. No. 19280E

Form **3115** (Rev. 12-2003)

Figure 6.2

Form 3115 (Rev. 12-2003) | Page **2**

Part II Information For All Requests (continued)	Yes	No

4c Is the method of accounting the applicant is requesting to change an issue pending (with respect to either the applicant or any present or former consolidated group in which the applicant was a member during the applicable tax year(s)) for any tax year under examination (see instructions)? . . . .

d Is the request to change the method of accounting being filed under the procedures requiring that the operating division director consent to the filing of the request (see instructions)? . . . .
If "Yes," attach the consent statement from the director.

e Is the request to change the method of accounting being filed under the 90-day or 120-day window period? .
If "Yes," check the box for the applicable window period and attach the required statement (see instructions).
☐ 90 day   ☐ 120 day

f If you answered "Yes" to line 4a, enter the name and telephone number of the examining agent and the tax year(s) under examination.
Name ▶ _____ Telephone number ▶ _____ Tax year(s) ▶ _____

g Has a copy of this Form 3115 been provided to the examining agent identified on line 4f? . . . .

5a Does the applicant (or any present or former consolidated group in which the applicant was a member during the applicable tax year(s)) have any Federal income tax return(s) before Appeals and/or a Federal court? . | | X |
If "Yes," enter the name of the (check the box) ☐ Appeals officer and/or ☐ counsel for the government, and the tax year(s) before Appeals and/or a Federal court.
Name ▶ _____ Telephone number ▶ _____ Tax year(s) ▶ _____

b Has a copy of this Form 3115 been provided to the Appeals officer and/or counsel for the government identified on line 5a? . . . .   n/a

c Is the method of accounting the applicant is requesting to change an issue under consideration by Appeals and/or a Federal court (for either the applicant or any present or former consolidated group in which the applicant was a member for the tax year(s) the applicant was a member)?   X
If "Yes," attach an explanation.

6 If the applicant answered "Yes" to line 4a and/or 5a with respect to any present or former consolidated group, provide each parent corporation's **(a)** name, **(b)** identification number, **(c)** address, and **(d)** tax year(s) during which the applicant was a member that is under examination, before an Appeals office, and/or before a Federal court.

7 If the applicant is an entity (including a limited liability company) treated as a partnership or S corporation for Federal income tax purposes, is it requesting a change from a method of accounting that is an issue under consideration in an examination, before Appeals, or before a Federal court, with respect to a Federal income tax return of a partner, member, or shareholder of that entity? . . . .   n/a
If "Yes," the applicant is **not** eligible to make the change.

8 Is the applicant making a change to which audit protection does not apply (see instructions)?   X

9a Has the applicant, its predecessor, or a related party requested or made (under either an automatic change procedure or a procedure requiring advance consent) a change in accounting method within the past 5 years (including the year of the requested change)?   X

b If "Yes," attach a description of each change and the year of change for each separate trade or business and whether consent was obtained.

c If any application was withdrawn, not perfected, or denied, or if a Consent Agreement was sent to the taxpayer but was not signed and returned to the IRS, or if the change was not made or not made in the requested year of change, include an explanation.

10a Does the applicant, its predecessor, or a related party currently have pending any request (including any concurrently filed request) for a private letter ruling, change in accounting method, or technical advice? . . .   X

b If "Yes," for each request attach a statement providing the name(s) of the taxpayer, identification number(s), the type of request (private letter ruling, change in accounting method, or technical advice), and the specific issue(s) in the request(s).

11 Is the applicant requesting to change its **overall** method of accounting?   X
If "Yes," check the appropriate boxes below to indicate the applicant's present and proposed methods of accounting. Also, complete Schedule A on page 4 of the form.
Present method: ☐ Cash   ☐ Accrual   ☐ Hybrid (attach description)
Proposed method: ☐ Cash   ☐ Accrual   ☐ Hybrid (attach description)

12 If the applicant is **not** changing its overall method of accounting, attach a detailed and complete description for each of the following:

a The item(s) being changed. elected IRC 475(f) for trading securities
b The applicant's present method for the item(s) being changed. Cash
c The applicant's proposed method for the item(s) being changed. IRC Sec. 475(f)(1) mark to market
d The applicant's present overall method of accounting (cash, accrual, or hybrid). **

Form **3115** (Rev. 12-2003)

** Keep using cash for business expenses

Figure 6.2a

Form 3115 (Rev. 12-2003)   Page **3**

Part II	Information For All Requests (continued)	Yes	No

13 Attach a detailed and complete description of the applicant's trade(s) or business(es), and the principal business activity code for each. If the applicant has more than one trade or business as defined in Regulations section 1.446-1(d), describe: whether each trade or business is accounted for separately; the goods and services provided by each trade or business and any other types of activities engaged in that generate gross income; the overall method of accounting for each trade or business; and which trade or business is requesting to change its accounting method as part of this application or a separate application.

14 Will the proposed method of accounting be used for the applicant's books and records and financial statements? For insurance companies, see the instructions . . . .   **See Note ** Below**   X

    If "No," attach an explanation.

15a Has the applicant engaged, or will it engage, in a transaction to which section 381(a) applies (e.g., a reorganization, merger, or liquidation) during the proposed tax year of change determined without regard to any potential closing of the year under section 381(b)(1)?   X

   b If "Yes," for the items of income and expense that are the subject of this application, attach a statement identifying the methods of accounting used by the parties to the section 381(a) transaction immediately before the date of distribution or transfer and the method(s) that would be required by section 381(c)(4) or (c)(5) absent consent to the change(s) requested in this application.

16 Does the applicant request a **conference of right** with the IRS National Office if the IRS proposes an adverse response?.   X

17 If the applicant is changing to or from the cash method or changing its method of accounting under sections 263A, 448, 460, or 471, enter the gross receipts of the 3 tax years preceding the year of change.

1st preceding year ended: mo. yr.	2nd preceding year ended: mo. yr.	3rd preceding year ended: mo. yr. n/a
$	$	$

Part III	Information For Advance Consent Request n/a	Yes	No

18 Is the applicant's requested change described in any revenue procedure, revenue ruling, notice, regulation, or other published guidance as an automatic change request? . . . .

    If "Yes," attach an explanation describing why the applicant is submitting its request under advance consent request procedures.

19 Attach a full explanation of the legal basis supporting the proposed method for the item being changed. Include a detailed and complete description of the facts that explains how the law specifically applies to the applicant's situation and that demonstrates that the applicant is authorized to use the proposed method. Include all authority (statutes, regulations, published rulings, court cases, etc.) supporting the proposed method. The applicant should include a discussion of any authorities that may be contrary to its use of the proposed method.

20 Attach a copy of all documents related to the proposed change (see instructions).

21 Attach a statement of the applicant's reasons for the proposed change.

22 If the applicant is a member of a consolidated group for the year of change, do all other members of the consolidated group use the proposed method of accounting for the item being changed? . . . .

    If "No," attach an explanation.

23a Enter the amount of **user fee** attached to this application (see instructions). ▶ $ _____

   b If the applicant qualifies for a reduced user fee, attach the necessary information or certification required by Rev. Proc. 2003-1 (or its successor) (see instructions).

Part IV	Section 481(a) Adjustment	Yes	No

24 Do the procedures for the accounting method change being requested require the use of the cut-off method?   X

    If "Yes," do not complete lines 25, 26, and 27 below.

25 Enter the section 481(a) adjustment. Indicate whether the adjustment is an increase (+) or a decrease (-) in income. ▶ $ _(32,188)_   Attach a summary of the computation and an explanation of the methodology used to determine the section 481(a) adjustment. If it is based on more than one component, show the computation for each component. If more than one applicant is applying for the method change on the same application, attach a list of the name, identification number, principal business activity code (see instructions), and the amount of the section 481(a) adjustment attributable to each applicant.   **See Note ** Below**

26 If the section 481(a) adjustment is an increase to income of less than $25,000, does the applicant elect to take the entire amount of the adjustment into account in the year of change? . . . .   n/a

27 Is any part of the section 481(a) adjustment attributable to transactions between members of an affiliated group, a consolidated group, a controlled group, or other related parties?   X

    If "Yes," attach an explanation.

Form **3115** (Rev. 12-2003)

Note ** - See Tax Return Footnotes Attached

Figure 6.2b

Form 3115 (Rev. 12-2003)   Page **4**

Schedule A—Change in Overall Method of Accounting (If Schedule A applies, Part I below must be completed.)

Part I   Change in Overall Method (see instructions)

1   Enter the following amounts as of the close of the tax year preceding the year of change. If none, state "None." Also, attach a statement providing a breakdown of the amounts entered on lines 1a through 1g.

	Amount
a Income accrued but not received	$ None
b Income received or reported before it was earned. Attach a description of the income and the legal basis for the proposed method	None
c Expenses accrued but not paid	None
d Prepaid expenses previously deducted	None
e Supplies on hand previously deducted and/or not previously reported	None
f Inventory on hand previously deducted and/or not previously reported. Complete Schedule D, Part II	None
g Other amounts (specify) ▶ ....See Tax Return Footnotes Attached........	(32,188)
h Net section 481(a) adjustment (Combine lines 1a–1g.)	$ (32,188)

2   Is the applicant also requesting the recurring item exception under section 461(h)(3)? . . . . . . ☐ Yes ☒ No

3   Attach copies of the profit and loss statement (Schedule F (Form 1040) for farmers) and the balance sheet, if applicable, as of the close of the tax year preceding the year of change. On a separate sheet, state the accounting method used when preparing the balance sheet. If books of account are not kept, attach a copy of the business schedules submitted with the Federal income tax return or other return (e.g., tax-exempt organization returns) for that period. If the amounts in Part I, lines 1a through 1g, do not agree with those shown on both the profit and loss statement and the balance sheet, explain the differences on a separate sheet.   n/a

Part II   Change to the Cash Method For Advance Consent Request (see instructions)   n/a

Applicants requesting a change to the cash method must attach the following information:

1   A description of inventory items (items whose production, purchase, or sale is an income-producing factor) and materials and supplies used in carrying out the business.

2   An explanation as to whether the applicant is required to use the accrual method under any section of the Code or regulations.

Schedule B—Change in Reporting Advance Payments (see instructions)   n/a

1   If the applicant is requesting to defer advance payment for services under Rev. Proc. 71-21, 1971-2 C.B. 549, attach the following information:

a   Sample copies of all service agreements used by the applicant that are subject to the requested change in accounting method. Indicate the particular parts of the service agreement that require the taxpayer to perform services.

b   If any parts or materials are provided, explain whether the obligation to provide parts or materials is incidental (of minor or secondary importance) to an agreement providing for the performance of personal services.

c   If the change relates to contingent service contracts, explain how the contracts relate to merchandise that is sold, leased, installed, or constructed by the applicant and whether the applicant offers to sell, lease, install, or construct without the service agreement.

d   A description of the method the applicant will use to determine the amount of income earned each year on service contracts and why that method clearly reflects income earned and related expenses in each year.

e   An explanation of how the method the applicant will use to determine the amount of gross receipts each year will be no less than the amount included in gross receipts for purposes of its books and records. See section 3.11 of Rev. Proc. 71-21.

2   If the applicant is requesting a deferral of advance payments for goods under Regulations section 1.451-5, attach the following information:

a   Sample copies of all agreements for goods or items requiring advance payments used by the applicant that are subject to the requested change in accounting method. Indicate the particular parts of the agreement that require the applicant to provide goods or items.

b   A statement providing that the entire advance payment is for goods or items. If not entirely for goods or items, a statement that an amount equal to 95% of the total contract price is properly allocable to the obligation to provide activities described in Regulations section 1.451-5(a)(1)(i) or (ii) (including services as an integral part of those activities).

c   An explanation of how the method the applicant will use to determine the amount of gross receipts each year will be no less than the amount included in gross receipts for purposes of its books and records. See Regulations section 1.451-5(b)(1).

Form **3115** (Rev. 12-2003)

Figure 6.2c

Form **4797**	**Sales of Business Property**	OMB No. 1545-0184
Department of the Treasury Internal Revenue Service (99)	(Also Involuntary Conversions and Recapture Amounts Under Sections 179 and 280F(b)(2)) ► Attach to your tax return. ► See separate instructions.	**2003** 27

Name(s) shown on return	Identifying number
EX13 Fed-CA fulltime MTM, loss, 481 loss	111-11-1111

1 Enter the gross proceeds from sales or exchanges reported to you for 2003 on Form(s) 1099-B or 1099-S (or substitute statement) that you are including on line 2, 10, or 20 (see instructions) .... | **1** | 27,248,020.

Part I **Sales or Exchanges of Property Used in a Trade or Business and Involuntary Conversions From Other Than Casualty or Theft — Most Property Held More Than 1 Year** (See instructions.)

2 (a) Description of property	(b) Date acquired (month, day, year)	(c) Date sold (month, day, year)	(d) Gross sales price	(e) Depreciation allowed or allowable since acquisition	(f) Cost or other basis, plus improvements and expense of sale	(g) Gain or (loss) Subtract (f) from the sum of (d) and (e)	(h) Post-May 5, 2003, gain or (loss)* (see below)

3 Gain, if any, from Form 4684, line 39 .... | **3** |
4 Section 1231 gain from installment sales from Form 6252, line 26 or 37 .... | **4** |
5 Section 1231 gain or (loss) from like-kind exchanges from Form 8824 .... | **5** |
6 Gain, if any, from line 32, from other than casualty or theft .... | **6** |
7 Combine lines 2 through 6 in columns (g) and (h). Enter the gain or (loss) here and on the appropriate line as follows .... | **7** |

Partnerships (except electing large partnerships) and S corporations. Report the gain or (loss) following the instructions for Form 1065, Schedule K, line 6, or Form 1120S, Schedule K, line 5. Skip lines 8, 9, 11, and 12 below.

All others. If line 7, column (g) is zero or a loss, enter that amount on line 11 below and skip lines 8, 9, and 12. If line 7, column (g) is a gain and you did not have any prior year section 1231 losses, or they were recaptured in an earlier year, enter the gain or (loss) from column (g) as a long-term capital gain or (loss) on Schedule D and skip lines 8, 9, 11, and 12 below.

8 Nonrecaptured net section 1231 losses from prior years (see instructions) .... | **8** |
9 Subtract line 8 from line 7. If line 9, column (g) is zero or less, enter -0- in column (g). If line 9, column (g) is zero, enter the gain from line 7, column (g) on line 12 below. If line 9, column (g), is more than zero, enter the amount from line 8, column (g) on line 12 below and include the gain or (loss) in each column of line 9 as a long-term capital gain or (loss) on Schedule D (see instructions) .... | **9** |

*Corporations (other than S corporations) should not complete column (h). Partnerships and S corporations must complete column (h). All others must complete column (h) only if line 7, column (g), is a gain **and** the amount, if any, on line 8, column (g), does **not** equal or exceed the gain on line 7, column (g). Include in column (h) all gains and losses from column (g) from sales, exchanges, or conversions (including installment payments received) **after** May 5, 2003. However, do **not** include gain attributable to unrecaptured section 1250 gain.

Part II **Ordinary Gains and Losses**

10 Ordinary gains and losses not included on lines 11 through 17 (include property held 1 year or less):

See Statement 1						-213,504.	

11 Loss, if any, from line 7, column (g) .... | **11** |
12 Gain, if any, from line 7, column (g), or amount from line 8, column (g), if applicable .... | **12** |
13 Gain, if any, from line 31 .... | **13** |
14 Net gain or (loss) from Form 4684, lines 31 and 38a .... | **14** |
15 Ordinary gain from installment sales from Form 6252, line 25 or 36 .... | **15** |
16 Ordinary gain or (loss) from like-kind exchanges from Form 8824 .... | **16** |
17 Recapture of section 179 expense deduction for partners and S corporation shareholders for property dispositions from 2002-2003 fiscal year partnerships and S corporations (see instructions) .... | **17** |
18 Combine lines 10 through 17. Enter the gain or (loss) here and on the appropriate line as follows .... | **18** | -213,504. |
  a For all except individual returns. Enter the gain or (loss) from line 18 on the return being filed.
  b For individual returns:
    (1) If the loss on line 11 includes a loss from Form 4684, line 35, column (b)(ii), enter that part of the loss here. Enter the part of the loss from income-producing property on Schedule A (Form 1040), line 27, and the part of the loss from property used as an employee on Schedule A (Form 1040), line 22. Identify as from 'Form 4797, line 18b(1).' See instructions .... | **18b(1)** |
    (2) Redetermine the gain or (loss) on line 18 excluding the loss, if any, on line 18b(1). Enter here and on Form 1040, line 14 .... | **18b(2)** | -213,504. |

BAA For Paperwork Reduction Act Notice, see instructions.   FDIZ1001L 12/02/03   Form **4797** (2003)

Figure 6.3

Home-office deduction: The client used one bedroom in his apartment exclusively for his trading business. Form 8829 is used to report his home office deduction. Note that the client does not benefit from the home office deduction for this tax return year because he does not have trading gains. These trading gains would be transferred to Schedule C to zero out Schedule C. This process is explained elsewhere in our guide. The client may benefit in future years with the Form 8829 home office expense carried over to the following tax years.

Depreciation: Because this client has losses, he is unable to benefit from IRC Section 179 (100 percent depreciation up to $102,000 for 2004; $100,000 for 2003); instead, we used regular and special depreciation on Form 4562.

Federal net operating loss (NOL) tax return: This client is entitled to significant tax relief using a Form 1045 NOL carryback claim. For more information on NOLs, see an earlier part in our book.

Example 2: Profitable, Full-Time Securities Business MTM Trader

Trader elected mark-to-market accounting for 2003 with a positive and deferred section 481 adjustment.

Client facts: This client is single and he lives in California. He trades securities full-time and operates from his three-bedroom rental apartment. Even though he is full-time, he only had 1,000 round-trip trades. He traded every day the market was open, except when he was sick or on vacation. His trading business is his only means of making a living. On average, his holding periods are less than a few days. On most days, he spends the entire day in his trading business, executing and researching trades, and doing management activities. The client's securities proceeds total more than $27 million.

GTT trader tax status determination: Based on the preceding facts, GTT considers this trader to have trader tax status for the entire year; therefore, GTT prepared his return as a sole proprietor. We reported all this client's trading business expenses on Schedule C (Profit or Loss From Business), as shown in Figure 6.4. GTT reached this conclusion because the client was trading full time, made a sufficient number of round-trip trades, had short holding periods, spent sufficient time in the business, and had large proceeds. Equally important, the client mentioned to GTT that his intention was to operate a trading business on a frequent, continuous, and regular basis, and his objective was to profit from quick swings in price, not long term price appreciation.

Mark-to-market accounting process: Client elected mark-to-market (MTM) accounting (IRC § 475) for 2003 by the due date of April 15, 2003. See the Footnote (end) for a copy of the election that should be attached to this tax return. This election document completes the first part of the MTM process.

Filing of Form 3115: For the second step of completing the MTM election process, we attach a Form 3115 (Change of Accounting Method) to his 2003 tax return. We also file a duplicate copy of Form 3115 only to the IRS National Office. This filing needs to be done by the due date of this tax return, including extensions. We include the section 481 adjustment calculation on the Form 3115. See an example of Form 3115 in Figure 6.2.

Applying MTM: For the third and final step of completing the MTM election process, we make sure to mark all open trading positions at year-end to market prices. We also report MTM gains and losses on Form 4797 Part II, Ordinary Gain and Loss (see Figure 6.3).

Warning: If any of the preceding steps are done incorrectly or late (after the extended due date), the IRS can challenge this client's right to use MTM. This challenge can have serious consequences. Without

SCHEDULE C
(Form 1040)

Department of the Treasury
Internal Revenue Service (99)

Profit or Loss From Business
(Sole Proprietorship)

► Partnerships, joint ventures, etc, must file Form 1065 or 1065-B.
► Attach to Form 1040 or 1041. ► See Instructions for Schedule C (Form 1040).

OMB No. 1545-0074

2003

09

Name of proprietor

EX14 Fed-CA fulltime MTM, gain, 481 gain

Social security number (SSN)

111-11-1111

A Principal business or profession, including product or service (see instructions)

Trader in Securities - Mark-to-Market accounting

B Enter code from instructions

► 523110

C Business name. If no separate business name, leave blank.

D Employer ID number (EIN), if any

E Business address (including suite or room no.) ►
City, town or post office, state, and ZIP code

F Accounting method: (1) ☐ Cash (2) ☐ Accrual (3) ☒ Other (specify) ► Sec.475(f)-Note

G Did you 'materially participate' in the operation of this business during 2003? If 'No,' see instructions for limit on losses.... ☒ Yes ☐ No

H If you started or acquired this business during 2003, check here.. ► ☒

Part I Income

1	Gross receipts or sales. **Caution.** If this income was reported to you on Form W-2 and the 'Statutory employee' box on that form was checked, see the instructions and check here.......... ► ☐	1	
2	Returns and allowances...	2	
3	Subtract line 2 from line 1.	3	
4	Cost of goods sold (from line 42 on page 2)................................	4	
5	**Gross profit.** Subtract line 4 from line 3.................................	5	
6	Other income, including Federal and state gasoline or fuel tax credit or refund.......See.Statement..4	6	36,443.
7	**Gross income.** Add lines 5 and 6....................................... ►	7	36,443.

Part II Expenses. Enter expenses for business use of your home **only** on line 30.

8	Advertising.................	8		19	Pension and profit-sharing plans........	19	
9	Car and truck expenses (see instructions).............	9		20	Rent or lease (see instructions):		
10	Commissions and fees........	10		a	Vehicles, machinery, and equipment.....	20a	
11	Contract labor (see instructions)	11		b	Other business property..............	20b	
12	Depletion.................	12		21	Repairs and maintenance.............	21	
13	Depreciation and section 179 expense deduction (not included in Part III) (see instructions).............	13	4,195.	22	Supplies (not included in Part III).......	22	893.
				23	Taxes and licenses.................	23	
				24	Travel, meals, and entertainment:		
				a	Travel............................	24a	1,679.
14	Employee benefit programs (other than on line 19)........	14		b	Meals and entertainment....	2,345.	
15	Insurance (other than health)...	15		c	Enter nondeductible amount included on line 24b (see instrs)..	1,173.	
16	Interest:						
a	Mortgage (paid to banks, etc)....	16a		d	Subtract line 24c from line 24b..........	24d	1,172.
b	Other......................	16b	14,375.	25	Utilities..........................	25	
17	Legal & professional services...	17		26	Wages (less employment credits)........	26	
18	Office expense.............	18		27	Other expenses (from line 48 on page 2)...	27	10,310.
28	**Total expenses** before expenses for business use of home. Add lines 8 through 27 in columns....... ►					28	32,624.

29	Tentative profit (loss). Subtract line 28 from line 7...................................	29	3,819.
30	Expenses for business use of your home. Attach Form 8829.............................	30	3,819.
31	Net profit or (loss). Subtract line 30 from line 29.		

• If a profit, enter on **Form 1040, line 12,** and **also** on **Schedule SE, line 2** (statutory employees, see instructions). Estates and trusts, enter on Form 1041, line 3. | 31 | 0. |

• If a loss, you **must** go to line 32.

32 If you have a loss, check the box that describes your investment in this activity (see instructions).

• If you checked 32a, enter the loss on **Form 1040, line 12,** and **also** on **Schedule SE, line 2** (statutory employees, see instructions). Estates and trusts, enter on Form 1041, line 3.

32 a ☐ All investment is at risk.

32 b ☐ Some investment is not at risk.

• If you checked 32b, you **must** attach Form 6198.

BAA **For Paperwork Reduction Act Notice, see Form 1040 instructions.**

FDIZ0112L 10/14/03

Schedule **C** (Form 1040) 2003

Figure 6.4

Schedule **C** (Form 1040) 2003 EX14 Fed-CA fulltime MTM, gain, 481 gain   111-11-1111   Page **2**

Part III   **Cost of Goods Sold** (see instructions)

33	Method(s) used to value closing inventory: **a** ☐ Cost **b** ☐ Lower of cost or market **c** ☐ Other (attach explanation)		
34	Was there any change in determining quantities, costs, or valuations between opening and closing inventory? If 'Yes,' attach explanation.		☐ Yes ☐ No
35	Inventory at beginning of year. If different from last year's closing inventory, attach explanation	**35**	
36	Purchases less cost of items withdrawn for personal use	**36**	
37	Cost of labor. Do not include any amounts paid to yourself	**37**	
38	Materials and supplies	**38**	
39	Other costs	**39**	
40	Add lines 35 through 39	**40**	
41	Inventory at end of year	**41**	
42	**Cost of goods sold.** Subtract line 41 from line 40. Enter the result here and on page 1, line 4	**42**	

Part IV   **Information on Your Vehicle.** Complete this part **only** if you are claiming car or truck expenses on line 9 and are not required to file Form 4562 for this business. See the instructions for line 13 to find out if you must file Form 4562.

43 When did you place your vehicle in service for business purposes? (month, day, year) ▶ _ _ _ _ _ _ _ _ _ _ _ _ .

44 Of the total number of miles you drove your vehicle during 2003, enter the number of miles you used your vehicle for:

   a Business _ _ _ _ _ _ _ _ _ _ _   **b** Commuting _ _ _ _ _ _ _ _ _ _ _   **c** Other _ _ _ _ _ _ _ _ _ _ _

45	Do you (or your spouse) have another vehicle available for personal use?	☐ Yes ☐ No
46	Was your vehicle available for personal use during off-duty hours?	☐ Yes ☐ No
47a	Do you have evidence to support your deduction?	☐ Yes ☐ No
b	If 'Yes,' is the evidence written?	☐ Yes ☐ No

Part V   **Other Expenses.** List below business expenses not included on lines 8-26 or line 30.

Postage	195.
Trader tax and accounting	755.
Trading cable and internet service	652.
Trading chat room	1,350.
Trading newsletters and publications	1,145.
Trading online information services	2,988.
Trading seminars	3,225.
48 **Total other expenses.** Enter here and on page 1, line 27 **48**	10,310.

Schedule **C** (Form 1040) 2003

FDIZ0112L 10/14/03

Figure 6.4a

2003	Federal Statements	Page 1
Client EX14F-CA	EX14 Fed-CA fulltime MTM, gain, 481 gain	111-11-1111
8/04/04		12:34PM

Statement 1
Schedule A, Line 13
Investment Interest

.... $	796.
Total $	796.

Statement 2
Schedule A, Line 15
Contributions by Cash or Check

.... $	976.
Total $	976.

Statement 3
Schedule A, Line 16
Contributions Other than Cash

.... $	345.
Total $	345.

Statement 4 - Trader in Securities - Mark-to-Market accounting
Schedule C, Line 6
Other Income

Tsfr part of trading gain fr F4797-Note... $	36,443.
Total $	36,443.

Statement 5
Form 4797, Page 1, Part II
Ordinary Gains and Losses

Description of Property	Date Acquired	Date Sold	Sales Price	Depreciation Allowed	Cost or Basis	Gain or Loss
Cybertrader trading a/c (details avail) (Trader Transaction)						
	Various	Various	15,471,893.		15,339,352. $	132,541.
TerraNova trading a/c (details avail) (Trader Transaction)						
	Various	Various	11,642,914.		11,467,516.	175,398.
Sec. 481(a) adjustment-See Note (Trader Transaction)						
	Various	Various	975,998.		936,346.	39,652.
Sec. 481(a) prorate 4 years - See Note (Trader Transaction)						
	Various	Various			29,739.	-29,739.
Tsfr part trading gain to Sch C-See Note (Trader Transaction)						
	Various	Various			36,443.	-36,443.
					Total $	281,409.

Figure 6.4b

MTM, the IRS will require all capital gains to be reported on Schedule D. The client will be subject to wash sale loss and straddle loss deferral rules, a problem even when a trader is profitable.

Section 481 adjustment: Because the client elected MTM for 2003, the client had to calculate and report a section 481 adjustment. See the explanation of a section 481 adjustment and the related tax law in the Footnotes. The section 481 adjustment calculation was made by GTT TradeLog accounting software, and the calculation recap is reported on Form 4797, the Footnotes, and on Form 3115.

   Note: This client's section 481 adjustment is positive and more than $25,000. According to the tax law, we prorated the adjustment over four years, deferring three-fourth's of the adjustment income to the following three tax years as shown in Figure 6.4b, statement 5.

Home office deduction: The client used one bedroom in his apartment exclusively for his trading business. Form 8829 is used to report his home office deduction. Note that the client does benefit from the home office deduction in 2003 because he has trading gains. Sufficient trading gains are transferred from Form 4797 to Schedule C to zero out Schedule C as shown in Figure 6.4. This process is explained elsewhere in this book.

Depreciation: Because this client has gains, he is able to benefit from section 179 (100 percent depreciation up to $100,000 for 2003) in 2003. This depreciation is reported on Form 4562. All depreciation in excess of the section 179 cap is subject to regular depreciation.

Schedule C adjusted to zero: Notice the following key GTT tax filing strategy. All trading business expenses are reported on Schedule C. We used section 179 depreciation and home office expenses as well. It is important to note that section 179 depreciation expenses and home office expenses are only deductible on Schedule C in 2003 if sufficient net income is listed on Schedule C to cover these expenses. Otherwise, they must be carried over to 2004. Neither expense is permitted to generate a tax loss (except for the mortgage interest and real estate tax portion of home office expenses). The GTT filing strategy is to transfer sufficient trading gains (only) from Schedule D (cash method) or Form 4797 (mark-to-market method, which is the case here) to Schedule C to zero out Schedule C. Notice that we don't transfer too many trading gains to result in a Schedule C net income, which might invite the IRS to inquire about self-employment (SE) taxes. As indicated in the Footnotes, traders with or without MTM are exempt from SE taxes. This strategy is disclosed in the Footnotes.

Note: Not having a Schedule C loss helps reduce your chance of IRS questions. Having a Schedule C loss for trading business expenses, because you have trading losses, is fully acceptable and understandable. We advise you not to "short sell" yourself on your rightful trading business expenses. The Footnote explains this treatment and reduces the chance of IRS questions.

Alternative minimum tax (AMT): AMT is generated in this example because the client is over the AMT exemption threshold and his high-state income taxes paid are a preference item.

Note: Without trader tax status, the client would report all expenses as investment expenses. Besides being severely limited, these expenses are also preference items for AMT (meaning they are not AMT deductions). So, trader tax status saves this client a lot more money.

Estimated income taxes: For purposes of this example, assume the client had zero tax liability for 2002 and could therefore pay his entire federal 2003 tax liability by April 15, 2004. Otherwise, this client should have paid estimated taxes during 2003. For this example, the client paid his state tax liability on December 31, 2003, in order to get a state tax deduction. Notice that this contributed to the AMT. To avoid AMT, this client should have paid a few dollars less and paid the balance of state taxes due on April 15, 2004, as he is doing for the federal return.

California State Notes: California is one of many states that is not respecting all the federal tax law changes from the 2003 Tax Act. Specifically, California does not accept "bonus depreciation" and the increased Section 179 deduction, as stated previously. There is an adjustment on the California return, adding back the difference between bonus depreciation and regular depreciation.

Example 3: A Full-Time Securities Trader Treated as an Investor (Close Call).

This trader's activity fell short of qualifying for trader tax status in 2003. Each year is assessed on its own. We reelected MTM for 2004 in case his trading activity picks up again. A continuing MTM business trader does not need to reelect each year.

> *Client facts:* This client will be treated as an investor in 2003 and will reelect MTM for 2004.

> *History:* An MTM election was made for 2002 by April 15, 2002. This was the first MTM election, and this client was treated as a business trader for 2002. No section 481 adjustment proration was needed, and therefore exiting the trading business as described presents no concern.

> *Trader tax status review:* We reviewed the actual trades in his three trading accounts. They total 180 (90 round trips) for the year. This amount is much too low to qualify as a trader. He traded only

67 days out of a possible 250, and he went six months with only two or four trades. Although his proceeds might be sufficient (more than $1 million) and trading is his sole occupation, problems arise when you look at number of trades and days on which trading activity took place. He does not rise to the level of trader. Actual trades and days traded are too sporadic, and he does not meet the regular, continuous, or frequency tests. We know the IRS is attacking traders who trade sporadically, because the IRS feels case law is strong on this point. This change in classification from trader to investor does not hurt the client. He receives the same refund either way but with a lot less risk of a potential IRS challenge to a person whose trader tax status is a close call. The client agrees with our conservative approach and advice.

Trade accounting: We prepared our GTT worksheets using the cash basis for investors. No positions were open at year-end, and our accounting agrees with the client's numbers. We confirmed the client had no wash sales, since our worksheets do not account for wash sales (only our GTT TradeLog software does). The client did not have enough expenses, even investor expenses, to itemize. Because the client is filing as an investor, a footnote is not required with this tax return.

GTT observations: Filing as an investor rather than a business trader did not cost this client any additional taxes. The investor status is correct, and it's less risky with the IRS.

Example 4: Part-Year Trader and Reentered Trading Business with MTM

Engineer for first part of year and then became a full-time securities business trader with mark-to-market accounting. He has MTM trading gains and an office in his Illinois home that he owns.

Client facts: Client made the 2003 mark-to-market IRC § 475(f) accounting election by April 15, 2003. We prepared Form 3115 (Change of Accounting Method) to go along with the tax return and sent a second copy directly to the IRS. Taxpayer does not have a section 481 adjustment on this Form 3115 and Form 4797.

Trader tax status analysis: Total round-trip stock and option trades are 866 from March to December, and total trading proceeds are more than $11 million. The average daily time spent on trading is nine hours, and the average round-trip trades per day are more than six. We reviewed the days the client was available to trade compared to the days he actually traded and found no sporadic lapses in trading. He traded every day from March to December 2003. His total proceeds, number of trades, time spent on business, average number of trades per day and daily trading activity are all sufficient for qualifying for trader tax status. See Figure 6.5. The client is still trading in 2004 and making more than five round-trip trades per day. Plus, he is profitable. His intention is to continue this trading business for the future.

Trader accounting: We reviewed the client-prepared GTT Inventory Approach Worksheets using MTM accounting, and all appears to be correct, including open short sales and so on. Both realized and unrealized trading gains and losses are being reported, with the straddles marked to market at year-end. The client purchased GTT TradeLog after year-end and downloaded his 2003 trades. The GTT TradeLog Form 4797 gains and losses report agrees with his worksheets results.

Home office: We apportioned taxpayer's expenses between two home office schedules: one for the consulting business earlier in the year and one for trading. We also apportioned depreciation as well between two Schedule Cs based on number of months (two months for consulting and ten months for trading). Expenses reported on

SCHEDULE C	**Profit or Loss From Business**	OMB No. 1545-0074
(Form 1040)	(Sole Proprietorship)	**2003**
Department of the Treasury Internal Revenue Service (99)	► Partnerships, joint ventures, etc., must file Form 1065 or 1065-B. ► Attach to Form 1040 or 1041. ► See Instructions for Schedule C (Form 1040).	09

Name of proprietor
EX17F-IL part year trader with MTM loss

Social security number (SSN)
999-99-9999

A Principal business or profession, including product or service (see instructions)
Trader in Securities-Mark-to-Market (03/01/03 to 12/31/03)

B Enter code from instructions
► 523110

C Business name. If no separate business name, leave blank.

D Employer ID number (EIN), if any

E Business address (including suite or room no.) ►
   City, town or post office, state, and ZIP code

F Accounting method: **(1)** ☐ Cash **(2)** ☐ Accrual **(3)** ☒ Other (specify) ► Sec.475(f)-Note

G Did you 'materially participate' in the operation of this business during 2003? If 'No,' see instructions for limit on losses..... ☒ Yes ☐ No
   ►

H If you started or acquired this business during 2003, check here ....

Part I   Income

1	Gross receipts or sales. **Caution.** If this income was reported to you on Form W-2 and the 'Statutory employee' box on that form was checked, see the instructions and check here.......... ► ☐		1	
2	Returns and allowances..		2	
3	Subtract line 2 from line 1...		3	
4	Cost of goods sold (from line 42 on page 2)...		4	
5	**Gross profit.** Subtract line 4 from line 3...		5	
6	Other income, including Federal and state gasoline or fuel tax credit or refund.......See Statement 3		6	13,767.
7	**Gross income.** Add lines 5 and 6... ►		7	13,767.

Part II   Expenses. Enter expenses for business use of your home **only** on line 30.

8	Advertising..................	8		19	Pension and profit-sharing plans..........	19	
9	Car and truck expenses (see instructions)............	9		20	Rent or lease (see instructions):		
				a	Vehicles, machinery, and equipment.....	20a	
10	Commissions and fees........	10		**b**	Other business property................	20b	
11	Contract labor (see instructions)	11		21	Repairs and maintenance..............	21	
12	Depletion...................	12		22	Supplies (not included in Part III)........	22	541.
13	Depreciation and section 179 expense deduction (not included in Part III) (see instructions).............	13	705.	23	Taxes and licenses....................	23	
				24	Travel, meals, and entertainment:		
				a	Travel...............................	24a	664.
14	Employee benefit programs (other than on line 19)........	14		**b**	Meals and entertainment.... 367.		
15	Insurance (other than health)...	15		**c**	Enter nondeductible amount included on line 24b (see instrs).. 184.		
16	Interest:			**d**	Subtract line 24c from line 24b........	24d	183.
a	Mortgage (paid to banks, etc)....	16a		25	Utilities..............................	25	
b	Other.......................	16b	1,566.	26	Wages (less employment credits)........	26	
17	Legal & professional services...	17		27	Other expenses (from line 48 on page 2)...	27	8,159.
18	Office expense..............	18					
28	**Total expenses** before expenses for business use of home. Add lines 8 through 27 in columns............ ►					28	11,818.

29	Tentative profit (loss). Subtract line 28 from line 7..	29	1,949.
30	Expenses for business use of your home. Attach **Form 8829**.............................	30	1,949.
31	**Net profit or (loss).** Subtract line 30 from line 29.		
	● If a profit, enter on **Form 1040, line 12,** and also on **Schedule SE, line 2** (statutory employees, see instructions). Estates and trusts, enter on Form 1041, line 3.	31	0.
	● If a loss, you **must** go to line 32.		
32	If you have a loss, check the box that describes your investment in this activity (see instructions).		
	● If you checked 32a, enter the loss on **Form 1040, line 12,** and also on **Schedule SE, line 2** (statutory employees, see instructions). Estates and trusts, enter on Form 1041, line 3.	32a ☐	All investment is at risk.
	● If you checked 32b, you **must** attach **Form 6198.**	32b ☐	Some investment is not at risk.

BAA For Paperwork Reduction Act Notice, see Form 1040 instructions.   Schedule **C** (Form 1040) 2003

FDIZ0112L 10/14/03

Figure 6.5

```
┌─────────────────────────────────────────────────────────────────────────┐
│ 2003                        Federal Statements                    Page 1  │
├─────────────────────────────────────────────────────────────────────────┤
│ Client EX17F-IL        EX17F-IL part year trader with MTM loss  999-99-9999│
│ 8/04/04                                                          12:54PM   │
│                                                                            │
│   Statement 1                                                             │
│   Schedule A, Line 10                                                     │
│   Home Mortgage Interest Reported on Form 1098                            │
│                                                                            │
│   Home Office Nonbusiness Allocation.......................  $   15,173.  │
│                                                  Total $        15,173.   │
└─────────────────────────────────────────────────────────────────────────┘
```

Statement 1
Schedule A, Line 10
Home Mortgage Interest Reported on Form 1098

Home Office Nonbusiness Allocation	$	15,173.
Total	$	15,173.

Statement 2
Schedule A, Line 15
Contributions by Cash or Check

Jersey Village Church of Christ	$	855.
Total	$	855.

Statement 3 - Trader in Securities-Mark-to-Market (03/01/03 to 12/31/03)
Schedule C, Line 6
Other Income

Tsfr part trading gains from F4797-Note	$	13,767.
Total	$	13,767.

Statement 4 - Trader in Securities-Mark-to-Market (03/01/03 to 12/31/03)
Schedule C, Part V
Other Expenses

Bank Charges	$	108.
Business accessories		591.
Dues and Subscriptions		204.
Trader tax and accounting		984.
Trading backup services		221.
Trading cable data and internet service		1,355.
Trading communication		407.
Trading data/chart services		2,577.
Trading publications		657.
Trading research		1,055.
Total	$	8,159.

Statement 5
Form 4797, Page 1, Part II
Ordinary Gains and Losses

Description of Property	Date Acquired	Date Sold	Sales Price	Depreciation Allowed	Cost or Basis	Gain or Loss
CyberTrader trading ac (details availabl (Trader Transaction)						
	Various	Various	3,455,877.		3,441,070. $	14,807.
TerraNova trading ac (details available) (Trader Transaction)						
	Various	Various	7,899,546.		7,881,892.	17,654.
Tsfr trading gains to Sch C - see note (Trader Transaction)						
	Various	Various			13,767.	-13,767.
					Total $	18,694.

Figure 6.5a

his engineering Schedule C reduce SE tax, whereas expenses on his trading business Schedule C do not reduce SE tax.

AGI Deductions: Client received earned income from engineering business Schedule C only. The trading business is not an earned income activity. The engineering business Schedule C is subject to the SE tax and serves as the basis of earned income used for retirement accounts as shown in Figure 6.6. With this earned income, the taxpayer also has an AGI deduction for health insurance premiums (100 percent in 2003). The client set up a Mini 401(k) plan before year-end and we made the maximum allowable contribution ($12,000 elective deferral plus 20 percent after-tax profit-sharing plan).

Entry/Exit issues: Taxpayer was in the trading business in 2002 and he duly elected and used mark-to-market (MTM) accounting until he exited the trading business in May 2002. Exiting the trading business negates the opportunity to use MTM accounting and requires the acceleration of any deferred positive prorated section 481 adjustments. When taxpayer reentered the trading business in March 2003, he was required to reelect MTM accounting (duly done) and file another Form 3115 with section 481 adjustment. The date of adjustment is March 1, 2003. Taxpayer's trading activity before March 2003 is not subject to MTM accounting and is reported on Schedule D.

Example 5: Part-Time Trader and Full-time Other Job

Client has MTM trading gains and an office in his Georgia home that he owns.

Client facts: Client is a part-time trader and computer specialist at a bank. (The IRS could consider it a full-time job). Client made the

SCHEDULE C
(Form 1040)

Department of the Treasury
Internal Revenue Service   (99)

Profit or Loss From Business
(Sole Proprietorship)

▶ **Partnerships, joint ventures, etc, must file Form 1065 or 1065-B.**
▶ **Attach to Form 1040 or 1041.** ▶ **See Instructions for Schedule C (Form 1040).**

OMB No. 1545-0074

2003

09

Name of proprietor	Social security number (SSN)
EX17F-IL part year trader with MTM loss	999-99-9999

A Principal business or profession, including product or service (see instructions)
    Engineering (01/01/03 to 02/28/03)

B Enter code from instructions
  ▶ 541330

C Business name. If no separate business name, leave blank.

D Employer ID number (EIN), if any

E Business address (including suite or room no.) ▶
   City, town or post office, state, and ZIP code

F Accounting method: (1) [X] Cash (2) [ ] Accrual (3) [ ] Other (specify) ▶
G Did you 'materially participate' in the operation of this business during 2003? If 'No,' see instructions for limit on losses. [X] Yes [ ] No
H If you started or acquired this business during 2003, check here .... ▶ [ ]

Part I   Income

1	Gross receipts or sales. **Caution.** If this income was reported to you on Form W-2 and the 'Statutory employee' box on that form was checked, see the instructions and check here.......... ▶ [ ]	1	42,555.
2	Returns and allowances	2	
3	Subtract line 2 from line 1...	3	42,555.
4	Cost of goods sold (from line 42 on page 2).................................	4	
5	**Gross profit.** Subtract line 4 from line 3...................................	5	42,555.
6	Other income, including Federal and state gasoline or fuel tax credit or refund............	6	
7	**Gross income.** Add lines 5 and 6 .... ▶	7	42,555.

Part II   Expenses. Enter expenses for business use of your home **only** on line 30.

8	Advertising..................	8		19	Pension and profit-sharing plans..........	19	
9	Car and truck expenses (see instructions)	9		20	Rent or lease (see instructions):		
10	Commissions and fees	10			a Vehicles, machinery, and equipment.....	20a	
11	Contract labor (see instructions)	11			b Other business property...............	20b	
12	Depletion	12		21	Repairs and maintenance..............	21	
13	Depreciation and section 179 expense deduction (not included in Part III) (see instructions)	13		22	Supplies (not included in Part III)	22	244.
				23	Taxes and licenses..................	23	
				24	Travel, meals, and entertainment:		
					a Travel............................	24a	677.
14	Employee benefit programs (other than on line 19)...	14			b Meals and entertainment....		
15	Insurance (other than health)...	15					
16	Interest:				c Enter nondeductible amount included on line 24b (see instrs)..		
	a Mortgage (paid to banks, etc)..	16a					
	b Other......................	16b			d Subtract line 24c from line 24b..........	24d	194.
17	Legal & professional services..	17	488.	25	Utilities...........................	25	
18	Office expense..............	18		26	Wages (less employment credits)........	26	
				27	Other expenses (from line 48 on page 2)....	27	1,219.

(Meals and entertainment: 389.   Enter nondeductible amount: 195.)

28	**Total expenses** before expenses for business use of home. Add lines 8 through 27 in columns............ ▶	28	2,822.
29	Tentative profit (loss). Subtract line 28 from line 7..	29	39,733.
30	Expenses for business use of your home. Attach **Form 8829**............................	30	294.
31	**Net profit or (loss).** Subtract line 30 from line 29.		
	• If a profit, enter on **Form 1040, line 12,** and **also** on **Schedule SE, line 2** (statutory employees, see instructions). Estates and trusts, enter on Form 1041, line 3.	31	39,439.
	• If a loss, you **must** go to line 32.		
32	If you have a loss, check the box that describes your investment in this activity (see instructions).		
	• If you checked 32a, enter the loss on **Form 1040, line 12,** and **also** on **Schedule SE, line 2** (statutory employees, see instructions). Estates and trusts, enter on Form 1041, line 3.	32a [ ]	All investment is at risk.
	• If you checked 32b, you must attach Form 6198.	32b [ ]	Some investment is not at risk.

BAA For Paperwork Reduction Act Notice, see Form 1040 instructions.

FDIZ0112L 10/14/03

Schedule **C** (Form 1040) 2003

Figure 6.6

2003 mark-to-market accounting (MTM) election by April 15, 2003, the due date for a 2003 election. We prepared a Form 3115 (Change of Accounting Method). Client has a section 481 adjustment that is more than $25,000, so we prorate it over four years.

Trader tax status analysis: Total trading proceeds are more than $12 million, and his GTT TradeLog reports indicate he had more than 1,000 total round-trip trades. The client traded all day, every day. Although client is located on East Coast and could not trade in the mornings before work (as West Coast clients can), the client was able to trade throughout the day at his bank job. The client had no sporadic lapses in trading. Most of the client's trades are day trades, and rarely does he keep a position open overnight—and even then, usually only one day. The client's banking job involves computer support, and he is mostly on call to deal with infrequent problems. Hence, he has free time to trade at work during the day. The taxpayer spends more than six hours per day in the trading business, he makes trades at work, and spends plenty of time on research and management, before and after the bank hours and on weekends. The positive factors meet the requirements of IRS Publication 550; therefore, this part-time trader has trader tax status.

Trade accounting: We reviewed the client-prepared GTT TradeLog data files and reports showing MTM accounting and section 481 adjustment. We checked his stock proceeds totals and reconciled them to GTT TradeLog.

Example 6: Sole Proprietor Versus a Single-Member LLC Trader

Both sole proprietor and single-member LLC (SMLLC) business traders can deduct all possible trading business expenses on Schedule C (see Figures 6.7a,b,c and 6.8) and elect mark-to-market (MTM) accounting for

SCHEDULE C
(Form 1040)

Department of the Treasury
Internal Revenue Service   (99)

Profit or Loss From Business
(Sole Proprietorship)

► Partnerships, joint ventures, etc., must file Form 1065 or 1065-B.
► Attach to Form 1040 or 1041.   ► See Instructions for Schedule C (Form 1040).

OMB No. 1545-0074

2003

09

Name of proprietor	Social security number (SSN)
Joe Trader Single Member LLC	111-11-1111

A Principal business or profession, including product or service (see instructions)
Trader in Securities - Mark-to-Market Accounting

B Enter code from instructions
► 523110

C Business name. If no separate business name, leave blank.

D Employer ID number (EIN), if any

E Business address (including suite or room no.) ►
City, town or post office, state, and ZIP code

F Accounting method: (1) ☐ Cash (2) ☐ Accrual (3) ☒ Other (specify) ► Sec. 475(f) - Note

G Did you 'materially participate' in the operation of this business during 2003? If 'No,' see instructions for limit on losses.... ☒ Yes ☐ No

H If you started or acquired this business during 2003, check here .... ► ☒

Part I   Income

1	Gross receipts or sales. **Caution.** If this income was reported to you on Form W-2 and the 'Statutory employee' box on that form was checked, see the instructions and check here .... ► ☐	1
2	Returns and allowances...	2
3	Subtract line 2 from line 1..	3
4	Cost of goods sold (from line 42 on page 2)..	4
5	**Gross profit.** Subtract line 4 from line 3..	5
6	Other income, including Federal and state gasoline or fuel tax credit or refund ......See Statement 1	6	192,073.
7	**Gross income.** Add lines 5 and 6... ►	7	192,073.

Part II   Expenses. Enter expenses for business use of your home **only** on line 30.

8	Advertising.................	8	19	Pension and profit-sharing plans....	19
9	Car and truck expenses (see instructions).........	9	20	Rent or lease (see instructions):	
10	Commissions and fees........	10		a Vehicles, machinery, and equipment.....	20a
11	Contract labor (see instructions).........	11		b Other business property.............	20b
12	Depletion....................	12	21	Repairs and maintenance..............	21
13	Depreciation and section 179 expense deduction (not included in Part III) (see instructions)............	13	7,866.	22	Supplies (not included in Part III)....	22	943.
			23	Taxes and licenses..................	23
			24	Travel, meals, and entertainment:	
			a	Travel..........................	24a	2,466.
14	Employee benefit programs (other than on line 19)........	14	b	Meals and entertainment....	1,325.	
15	Insurance (other than health)...	15		c Enter nondeductible amount included on line 24b (see instrs). 663.	
16	Interest:				
a	Mortgage (paid to banks, etc.)........	16a	d	Subtract line 24c from line 24b..........	24d	662.
b	Other......................	16b	15,752.	25	Utilities.............................	25
17	Legal & professional services..	17	147,366.	26	Wages (less employment credits)....	26
18	Office expense...............	18		27	Other expenses (from line 48 on page 2)..........	27	9,074.
28	**Total expenses** before expenses for business use of home. Add lines 8 through 27 in columns............. ►				28	184,129.

29	Tentative profit (loss). Subtract line 28 from line 7..	29	7,944.
30	Expenses for business use of your home. Attach **Form 8829**	30	7,944.
31	Net profit or (loss). Subtract line 30 from line 29.		
	• If a profit, enter on **Form 1040, line 12,** and also on **Schedule SE, line 2** (statutory employees, see instructions). Estates and trusts, enter on Form 1041, line 3.	31	0.
	• If a loss, you **must** go to line 32.		
32	If you have a loss, check the box that describes your investment in this activity (see instructions).		
	• If you checked 32a, enter the loss on **Form 1040, line 12,** and **also** on **Schedule SE, line 2** (statutory employees, see instructions). Estates and trusts, enter on Form 1041, line 3.	32a ☐	All investment is at risk.
	• If you checked 32b, you **must** attach Form 6198.	32b ☐	Some investment is not at risk.

BAA   For Paperwork Reduction Act Notice, see Form 1040 instructions.

FDIZ0112L 10/14/03

Schedule **C** (Form 1040) 2003

Figure 6.7a

Schedule **C** (Form 1040) 2003 Joe Trader Single Member LLC   111-11-1111   Page **2**

Part III   **Cost of Goods Sold** (see instructions)

33	Method(s) used to value closing inventory: **a** ☐ Cost **b** ☐ Lower of cost or market **c** ☐ Other (attach explanation)	
34	Was there any change in determining quantities, costs, or valuations between opening and closing inventory? If 'Yes,' attach explanation.	☐ Yes ☐ No
35	Inventory at beginning of year. If different from last year's closing inventory, attach explanation	**35**
36	Purchases less cost of items withdrawn for personal use	**36**
37	Cost of labor. Do not include any amounts paid to yourself	**37**
38	Materials and supplies	**38**
39	Other costs	**39**
40	Add lines 35 through 39	**40**
41	Inventory at end of year	**41**
42	**Cost of goods sold.** Subtract line 41 from line 40. Enter the result here and on page 1, line 4.	**42**

Part IV   **Information on Your Vehicle.** Complete this part **only** if you are claiming car or truck expenses on line 9 and are not required to file Form 4562 for this business. See the instructions for line 13 to find out if you must file Form 4562.

43 When did you place your vehicle in service for business purposes? (month, day, year)   ▸ _ _ _ _ _ _ _ _ _ _ _ .

44 Of the total number of miles you drove your vehicle during 2003, enter the number of miles you used your vehicle for:

  a Business _ _ _ _ _ _ _ _ _ _ _   **b** Commuting _ _ _ _ _ _ _ _ _ _ _   **c** Other _ _ _ _ _ _ _ _ _ _ _

45 Do you (or your spouse) have another vehicle available for personal use? .... ☐ Yes ☐ No

46 Was your vehicle available for personal use during off-duty hours? .... ☐ Yes ☐ No

47a Do you have evidence to support your deduction? .... ☐ Yes ☐ No

  b If 'Yes,' is the evidence written? .... ☐ Yes ☐ No

Part V   **Other Expenses.** List below business expenses not included on lines 8-26 or line 30.

Postage	199.
Seminars taken after trading started	2,685.
Telephone	660.
Trader tax & accounting services	750.
Trading chat rooms	1,349.
Trading internet service provider cable	540.
Trading online information services	1,852.
Trading publications and books	1,039.
48 Total other expenses. Enter here and on page 1, line 27. .... **48**	9,074.

Schedule **C** (Form 1040) 2003

FDIZ0112L 10/14/03

Figure 6.7b

SCHEDULE C	**Profit or Loss From Business**	OMB No. 1545-0074
(Form 1040)	(Sole Proprietorship)	**2003**
Department of the Treasury Internal Revenue Service (99)	► **Partnerships, joint ventures, etc., must file Form 1065 or 1065-B.** ► **Attach to Form 1040 or 1041.** ► **See Instructions for Schedule C (Form 1040).**	09

Name of proprietor	Social security number (SSN)
Joe Trader Single Member LLC	111-11-1111

A Principal business or profession, including product or service (see instructions)	B Enter code from instructions
Administration	► 561900

C Business name. If no separate business name, leave blank.	D Employer ID number (EIN), if any

E Business address (including suite or room no.) ► _
  City, town or post office, state, and ZIP code

F Accounting method: (1) [X] Cash (2) [ ] Accrual (3) [ ] Other (specify) ► _

G Did you 'materially participate' in the operation of this business during 2003? If 'No,' see instructions for limit on losses.... [X] Yes [ ] No

H If you started or acquired this business during 2003, check here .... ► [X]

Part I Income

1	Gross receipts or sales. **Caution.** If this income was reported to you on Form W-2 and the 'Statutory employee' box on that form was checked, see the instructions and check here .... ► [ ]	1	147,366.
2	Returns and allowances	2	
3	Subtract line 2 from line 1	3	147,366.
4	Cost of goods sold (from line 42 on page 2)	4	
5	**Gross profit.** Subtract line 4 from line 3	5	147,366.
6	Other income, including Federal and state gasoline or fuel tax credit or refund	6	
7	**Gross income.** Add lines 5 and 6 .... ►	7	147,366.

Part II Expenses. Enter expenses for business use of your home only on line 30.

8	Advertising...................	8		19	Pension and profit-sharing plans	19	
9	Car and truck expenses (see instructions)	9		20	Rent or lease (see instructions):		
				a	Vehicles, machinery, and equipment.....	20a	
10	Commissions and fees........	10		b	Other business property	20b	
11	Contract labor (see instructions)	11		21	Repairs and maintenance...............	21	
				22	Supplies (not included in Part III)........	22	
12	Depletion...................	12		23	Taxes and licenses....................	23	
13	Depreciation and section 179 expense deduction (not included in Part III) (see instructions).............	13		24	Travel, meals, and entertainment:		
				a	Travel	24a	
14	Employee benefit programs (other than on line 19)........	14		b	Meals and entertainment		
15	Insurance (other than health) ...	15		c	Enter nondeductible amount included on line 24b (see instrs)...		
16	Interest:						
a	Mortgage (paid to banks, etc)........	16a		d	Subtract line 24c from line 24b	24d	
b	Other........................	16b		25	Utilities	25	
17	Legal & professional services ..	17		26	Wages (less employment credits)........	26	
18	Office expense...............	18		27	Other expenses (from line 48 on page 2)....	27	

28	**Total expenses** before expenses for business use of home. Add lines 8 through 27 in columns............. ►	28	
29	Tentative profit (loss). Subtract line 28 from line 7	29	147,366.
30	Expenses for business use of your home. Attach **Form 8829**	30	
31	Net profit or **(loss).** Subtract line 30 from line 29.		
	• If a profit, enter on **Form 1040, line 12,** and also on **Schedule SE, line 2** (statutory employees, see instructions). Estates and trusts, enter on Form 1041, line 3.	31	147,366.
	• If a loss, you **must** go to line 32.		

32 If you have a loss, check the box that describes your investment in this activity (see instructions).

	• If you checked 32a, enter the loss on **Form 1040, line 12,** and **also** on **Schedule SE, line 2** (statutory employees, see instructions). Estates and trusts, enter on Form 1041, line 3.	32a [ ]	All investment is at risk.
	• If you checked 32b, you **must** attach **Form 6198.**	32b [ ]	Some investment is not at risk.

BAA For Paperwork Reduction Act Notice, see Form 1040 instructions.   Schedule **C** (Form 1040) 2003

FDIZ0112L 10/14/03

Figure 6.7c

SCHEDULE C	**Profit or Loss From Business**	OMB No. 1545-0074
(Form 1040)	(Sole Proprietorship)	**2003**
Department of the Treasury Internal Revenue Service (99)	▶ Partnerships, joint ventures, etc., must file Form 1065 or 1065-B. ▶ Attach to Form 1040 or 1041. ▶ See Instructions for Schedule C (Form 1040).	09

Name of proprietor: Joe Trader Sole Proprietor

Social security number (SSN): 111-11-1111

A Principal business or profession, including product or service (see instructions)
Trader in Securities - Mark-to-Market Accounting

B Enter code from instructions ▶ 523110

C Business name. If no separate business name, leave blank.

D Employer ID number (EIN), if any

E Business address (including suite or room no.)▶
City, town or post office, state, and ZIP code

F Accounting method: (1) ☐ Cash (2) ☐ Accrual (3) ☒ Other (specify) ▶ Sec. 475(f) - Note

G Did you 'materially participate' in the operation of this business during 2003? If 'No,' see instructions for limit on losses.... ☒ Yes ☐ No

H If you started or acquired this business during 2003, check here... ▶ ☒

Part I Income

1	Gross receipts or sales. **Caution.** If this income was reported to you on Form W-2 and the 'Statutory employee' box on that form was checked, see the instructions and check here..... ▶ ☐	1	
2	Returns and allowances..	2	
3	Subtract line 2 from line 1...	3	
4	Cost of goods sold (from line 42 on page 2).......................................	4	
5	**Gross profit.** Subtract line 4 from line 3...	5	
6	Other income, including Federal and state gasoline or fuel tax credit or refund ...... See Statement 1	6	44,707.
7	**Gross income.** Add lines 5 and 6.. ▶	7	44,707.

Part II Expenses. Enter expenses for business use of your home **only** on line 30.

8	Advertising...............	8		19 Pension and profit-sharing plans........	19		
9	Car and truck expenses (see instructions)	9		20 Rent or lease (see instructions): a Vehicles, machinery, and equipment....	20a		
10	Commissions and fees	10		b Other business property..............	20b		
11	Contract labor (see instructions)	11		21 Repairs and maintenance..............	21		
12	Depletion..................	12		22 Supplies (not included in Part III).......	22	943.	
13	Depreciation and section 179 expense deduction (not included in Part III) (see instructions)............	13	7,866.	23 Taxes and licenses....................	23		
14	Employee benefit programs (other than on line 19)..........	14		24 Travel, meals, and entertainment: a Travel..............................	24a	2,466.	
15	Insurance (other than health)...	15		b Meals and entertainment.... 1,325.			
16	Interest:			c Enter nondeductible amount included on line 24b (see instrs)... 663.			
	a Mortgage (paid to banks, etc)........	16a		d Subtract line 24c from line 24b.......	24d	662.	
	b Other.......................	16b	15,752.	25 Utilities.............................	25		
17	Legal & professional services ...	17		26 Wages (less employment credits).......	26		
18	Office expense...............	18		27 Other expenses (from line 48 on page 2)...	27	9,074.	
28	**Total expenses** before expenses for business use of home. Add lines 8 through 27 in columns............. ▶				28	36,763.	

29	Tentative profit (loss). Subtract line 28 from line 7.......................................	29	7,944.
30	Expenses for business use of your home. Attach **Form 8829**.................................	30	7,944.
31	**Net profit or (loss).** Subtract line 30 from line 29.		
	• If a profit, enter on **Form 1040, line 12**, and also on **Schedule SE, line 2** (statutory employees, see instructions). Estates and trusts. enter on **Form 1041, line 3**. • If a loss, you **must** go to line 32.	31	0.
32	If you have a loss, check the box that describes your investment in this activity (see instructions). • If you checked 32a, enter the loss on **Form 1040, line 12**, and also on **Schedule SE, line 2** (statutory employees, see instructions). Estates and trusts, enter on **Form 1041, line 3**. • If you checked 32b, you **must** attach **Form 6198**.	32a ☐ All investment is at risk. 32b ☐ Some investment is not at risk.	

BAA   For Paperwork Reduction Act Notice, see Form 1040 instructions.   Schedule **C** (Form 1040) 2003

FDIZ0112L 10/14/03

Figure 6.8

ordinary gain or loss treatment (tax loss insurance if you have losses). However, only a SMLLC trader can deduct health insurance premiums and contribute to a tax-deductible retirement plan.

> *Filing of Form 3115:* When you change your method of accounting for trading gains and losses from the default cash method to the MTM method (IRC § 475), you are required to file a Form 3115 (Change of Accounting Method). The one exception is if you are a new taxpayer (you never filed a tax return before as an individual, or if you are a new entity that has never filed a return before), then you can skip filing Form 3115. Electing MTM accounting is a three-step process. First, you elect MTM by April 15, 2003, for 2003. Next, you must properly report MTM on your 2003 tax return, and then you file your Form 3115 by the due date of your 2003 tax return, including extensions.

Line-by-Line Guidance
(Based on 2003 tax forms, the latest available as of this writing)

Form 1040, page 2
On the bottom of Form 1040, page 2, under Occupation, enter "Trader in Securities" if you qualify for trader tax status.

Trading gains and losses

- Use Form 4797 for mark-to-market (IRC § 475) trading gains and losses.
- Use Schedule D for cash method trading gains and losses.

Home office deductions

- See our separate section on Form 8829 Home Office deductions.

Footnotes

- See our separate section on footnotes; every trader tax return should have one.

Schedule C

For purposes of this guidance, we refer to Example 2. Profitable, full-time securities business trader who elected mark-to-market accounting for 2003 with a positive and deferred section 481 adjustment. Home office for rental apartment. Includes federal and state returns for California. If you qualify for trader tax status—meaning your trading activity for 2003 rose to the level of trading as a business—then you should report all your trading business expenses on Schedule C. Traders may deduct unlimited amounts of their trading business expenses on Schedule C, without restrictions. A qualifying trader may use Schedule C whether or not they elect mark-to-market accounting. Even if you did not learn about trader tax status until the following year (2004), you can still file this Schedule C for 2003 (after the fact).

   Note: Mark-to-market accounting may not be elected after the fact; it must be elected by April 15th of the current tax year. Always attach a footnote to your Schedule C to explain your trader tax status and so on. See the Footnotes section.

Line A, Principle business
If you trade both securities and commodities, write "Trader in Securities and Commodities—See Note." If you elect MTM for securities only, then put "Trader in Securities—Mark-to-Market Accounting." To play it safe, just put "Trader—See Note."

Line B, Enter code
Trader in securities or commodities without mark-to-market accounting: 523900 for "Other financial investment activities."

Trader in securities with mark-to-market accounting: 523110 for "Investment bankers & securities dealers."

Trader in securities with MTM and trader in commodities without MTM: 523110 for "Investment bankers & securities dealers."

Trader in securities and commodities with mark-to-market accounting: 523130 for "Commodity contract dealers."

Lines C, D, and E, Business name, tax ID number, and address

Nothing is required on these lines. Some traders use an assumed name or a d/b/a (doing business as) name for their business. If that's the case, enter that name on line C. Some traders file an SS-4 to get a tax ID number for their d/b/a. In that case, enter this EIN on line D. You will need a business EIN if you have employees. If you have a separate address for your trading business—different from your home address—you can enter it here.

One Word of Caution: It might be better to omit your business address if you want to reduce the chances of the IRS questioning your home office expense (assuming you have one).

Line F, Accounting method

Schedule C businesses by default use the cash method of accounting, as opposed to the accrual method. Both methods are listed on Line F; "Other" is also listed. If you use mark-to-market accounting for securities, check Other and enter: IRC § 475(f)(1). 475(f)(1) is for securities and 475(f)(2) is for commodities. You can elect both or just one alone. If you do not use mark-to-market accounting for securities or commodities, check the cash method. If you want the accrual method for your business expenses, then check accrual method.

Line G, Material participation

Check the Yes box to indicate that you did materially participate in your trading business. If you check No, then you don't qualify to use a trading business Schedule C.

Line H, Started business in 2003
Check the box if you started your trading business in 2003.

Part I, income
No entries are made on lines 1 to 5, because you do not have revenues, inventory, or cost of goods sold in this trading business.

Line 6, Other income
For line 6—Other income (loss)—If you receive commission rebates from your broker reported on Form 1099-Misc, those should be reported here. Then, report a negative amount to zero out your rebate, and transfer the amount to your trading gains and losses cost basis. This amount is not income, but rather a cost basis adjustment. (See Line 11.) Note that commissions are not business expenses (on Schedule C) but are part of your trading gains and losses reported on Schedule D (cash method) or Form 4797 (MTM method).

Transfer income from Form 4797 or Schedule D
Schedule C is adjusted to zero by an entry on line 6. Notice the following key GTT tax filing strategy. All trading business expenses are reported on Schedule C. We used section 179 depreciation and home office expenses as well. It is important to note that section 179 depreciation expenses and home office expenses are deductible on Schedule C in 2003 if sufficient net income is entered on Schedule C to cover these expenses. Otherwise, they must be carried over to 2004. Neither expense can generate a tax loss (except for the mortgage interest and real estate tax portion of home office expenses). The GTT filing strategy is to transfer sufficient trading gains (only), not gains on segregated investment positions, from Schedule D (cash method) or Form 4797 (mark-to-market method, which is the case here) to Schedule C to zero out Schedule C. Notice that we don't transfer too many trading gains to result in a Schedule C net income, which might invite the IRS to inquire about self-employment taxes. As indicated in the Footnotes, traders with or without MTM are exempt from SE taxes. This strategy is disclosed in the Footnotes.

Note: Not having a Schedule C loss helps reduce your chance of IRS questions. Having a Schedule C loss for trading business expenses, because you have trading losses, is fully acceptable and understandable. We advise you not to short sell yourself on your rightful trading business expenses. The Footnote explains this treatment and reduces the chance of IRS questions.

Part II, Expenses

Choose the cash or accrual method of accounting for business expenses. Don't confuse your expense method of accounting with your trading gains and loss method of accounting (cash or MTM). Here are some tax planning ideas that point out the advantage of accrual method accounting for expenses: Business traders accelerate expenses into 2003 for lower 2003 tax liabilities. The cardinal rule of year-end tax planning is to accelerate business deductions and losses into the current tax year and defer income and gains into the following tax year.

Deferring income taxes until the following tax years benefits the taxpayer by allowing the use of this tax money during the current and following tax year. These benefits are referred to as *timing* rather than *permanent* tax benefits. As a default method of accounting, business traders use the cash method of accounting for both business expenses and trading gains and losses, meaning business expenses are deductible when paid, as opposed to when incurred. For example, if a cash method business trader attends a seminar on December 28, 2003, but pays the bill on January 4, 2004, it is a 2004 business expense. A business trader may also elect to use the accrual method of accounting, which means that expenses are deductible when incurred (in 2003), not when paid (in 2004).

A business trader may also elect to use IRC § 475 mark-to-market accounting for trading gains and losses. This MTM election must be filed with the IRS by April 15 of the current tax year. Otherwise, the cash method of capital gains and losses applies for the entire tax year. (See the following chapter on tax planning moves related to trading gains and losses.)

Because trading gains and losses are treated separately from expenses and business traders don't have other forms of income, most business traders would be better served taxwise to use the accrual method of accounting for business expenses. However, this approach may be more trouble accounting-wise. For cash method business traders, the easiest way to accelerate deductions is to pay all bills early, before the end of the year. Remember that a prepayment of 2004 expenses will not give rise to a 2003 tax deduction.

Credit card charges are treated like payments of cash or check. It does not matter when you pay the credit card bill. For example, if you charge your credit card for a new computer on December 31, 2003, it is a 2003 tax deduction under the cash method. It does not matter that the computer is listed on your January credit card statement. If you plan to upgrade your computers, equipment, or furniture and fixtures soon, it's better to do it before year-end than early the next year. Each tax year, a business taxpayer is allowed 100 percent (IRC § 179) depreciation up to the first $100,000 of depreciable assets ($102,000 for 2004). Excess amounts are subject to the normal rules of depreciation (over the useful life of the asset).

Line 8, Advertising

Most traders don't advertise because they don't have customers as dealers do.

Line 9, Bad debts

If you loaned money to another trader for business reasons, and he or she defaulted on paying it back, you may deduct the entire amount of the debt on Line 9. However, you need to first bring or otherwise threaten legal action against the debtor. Don't play around with this situation. Nonbusiness bad debts can be deducted as capital losses on Schedule D. Proprietary traders may write off lost deposits (with proprietary trading firms) as business bad debts.

Line 10, Car expenses

Most traders don't use a car for business. The nature of trading online involves trading from an office at home. If you trade at home and also trade in a trading office outside the home (and qualify for a home office deduction), then traveling from your home office to your other daytime trading office may qualify as travel expenses. Otherwise, if you don't have a home office, travel to and from that office is nondeductible commuting expenses. Anyway, we don't suggest entering this type of expense here. Instead, enter it on line 24a, travel expense.

Line 11, Commissions and fees

Trading commissions are not recorded on Schedule C. Rather, all trading commissions are recorded as part of trading transactions on Schedule D and Form 4797. Commissions on purchases of securities are added to your cost basis and commissions on sales of securities are subtracted from proceeds. Your broker reports commissions in this manner on each confirmation and on your statements. Be careful in reading your broker's year-end reporting of net commissions on their website. Some brokerage firms separate commissions from profit and loss in their online reports, so be sure to ask your broker.

Some traders receive rebates on commissions. These amounts are usually not reflected on your confirmations, your statements, or Form 1099. Some traders do receive a Form 1099-Misc for commission rebates, but many traders don't realize that these amounts should be reported as a negative adjustment to cost basis reported on your Schedule D or Form 4797. Don't try to omit this income from your tax returns as it will lead to trouble.

Line 13, Depreciation

Traders use plenty of computers, equipment and furniture, and fixtures. Enter these costs on Form 4562 and choose the correct depreciation method. Form 4562 depreciation amounts are then transferred to this line.

Some notes about depreciation: These costs are depreciable whether you buy the item in 2003 or in a prior year and then convert it to business use in 2003. Don't short-change yourself here. Make a list of every item of technology, equipment, and furniture in your home office and in your trading business.

Fixed assets are depreciated, expenses are expensed. When you purchase an asset, you need to make a decision about whether that asset is going to help you earn income in future years. If the answer is Yes, then it is called a *fixed asset* and you must depreciate it over its useful life. The IRS has schedules for different types of fixed assets and provides different methods for depreciating fixed assets over their designated useful lives. Computers and equipment are depreciated over five years and office furniture is seven years. Take note of bonus depreciation and accelerated methods allowed.

Section 179 Depreciation

Section 179 allows you to deduct 100 percent of your fixed asset cost up to $100,000 for 2003 ($102,000 for 2004) as a current expense for qualifying property purchased and placed in service during 2003. This property would otherwise have to be depreciated. You can only deduct section 179 depreciation if you have net income from wages and other business activities (let your tax software handle this calculation).

If trading is your only business or job activity, then this requires that you be a profitable trader and that you follow our suggested strategy of transferring sufficient trading gains to Schedule C, line 6 from Schedule D or Form 4797. If you have trading losses, and no income, then we suggest that you skip section 179 depreciation and take regular and bonus depreciation. This option would allow you to get some depreciation rather than none (carrying over your section 179 depreciation to the following tax year).

Form 4562 for your Schedule C

All depreciation is first entered on Form 4562. Section 179 depreciation is entered on the top of Part I, special bonus depreciation in Part II, and regular depreciation is entered in Part III. You should file a separate Form 4562 for each different business activity. You file one Form 4562 for your trading business Schedule C.

Software is an intangible asset, and it is amortized on Form 4562, page 2, Part VI. The depreciation method is three years straight-line. Starting in 2003, software may now be included with section 179 depreciable property or be included with bonus depreciation.

Line 14, Employee benefit programs

If you have employees, you enter the amounts of payroll taxes and other employee benefits here. If you have employees, you need to file payroll tax returns and issue all employees Form W-2s. You also have to withhold and remit payroll taxes. See the IRS Publications for Employers.

Sole proprietors, unlike single member LLCs, are not allowed to pay themselves a W-2 salary and then set up a retirement plan on that earned income. Trading income is not "earned income," and sole proprietors are not entitled to contribute to retirement plans on this income. You need to form a separate business entity to pay yourself a fee or a salary in order to have a retirement plan.

Line 15, Insurance

Taxpayers without earned income, including business traders, may not deduct health insurance premiums from adjusted gross income. Other types of sole proprietors have earned income, and they can deduct health insurance premiums. This line 15 is for other types of insurance like business liability insurance, which few traders have. Home insurance is reported with other home office expenses on Form 8829.

Line 16b, Interest expense

If you have margin interest expense on your trading accounts, enter it here. Do not enter margin interest for investment positions or investment accounts. Investment interest expenses go on Form 4952 and deductions are limited to investment income. If you margin investment positions to purchase trading positions, that interest may be deemed business interest.

Line 17, Legal and professional fees

Legal fees for operations or business tax advice are deductible. Legal fees for asset acquisition are added to the cost basis of the asset. Legal fees for personal reasons are not deductible. Fees paid to your trader tax business preparer may be deducted here or on line 27, other expenses.

Line 18, Office expense

If you have an office in your home, don't use this line. Instead, use Form 8829 (Expenses for the business use of your home). **Note:** New IRS regulations further liberalize home office deductions by allowing taxpayers to protect more of their gain exclusion on sale of their principal residence, by not allocating the home office gain to the overall home gain (providing your office is in your home and not a separate structure). This rule is intended to help more taxpayers by not making them afraid to take this deduction and home depreciation in fear of losing their exclusion. The only recapture in many sales will be depreciation taken to date. That is not a lost benefit, but rather a timing difference (you pick up income later for what you deduct now). Note that depreciation is "allowed" or "allowable," which means you are treated by the IRS as taking this depreciation whether you did or not. So you may as well take it and receive the related tax benefits.

Line 19, Pension and profit-sharing plans

As previously stated, sole proprietor traders do not have earned income and they may not contribute to pension or profit-sharing retirement plans. Traders can contribute to tax-deductible retirement plans by creating an entity for their trading business and then paying themselves a salary or fee from that entity. If your Schedule C business has employees and you have a retirement plan for them, you would use this line.

Line 20a, Rent or lease

Enter operating lease payments on trading equipment here. Note that some leases should be capitalized and then depreciated on Form 4562.

Line 20b, Other business property

If you have a trading office outside your home, enter any rent you pay for that office on this line.

Line 21, Repairs and maintenance

If you have repairs or have done maintenance on either your trading business equipment or your home office assets, enter those expenses on this line. General home repairs and maintenance are reported on Form 8829 (home office expenses).

Line 22, Supplies

Traders use a great deal of supplies. Enter supplies expenses on this line. Remember, the home office form is for indirect home costs, not specific trading business expenses such as supplies.

Line 23, Taxes and licenses

Some traders also get security industry licenses. The cost of those can be deducted here. Some states or cities (such as New York City) charge stealth taxes on unincorporated businesses. In most cases, these taxes won't apply to Schedule Cs, because Schedule Cs for traders always show either zero net income or a large loss (if you don't transfer any gains; see the line 6 explanation). Furthermore, trading gains are usually not subject to NYC unincorporated business tax (UBT). For a regular NYC business, they would deduct their NYC UBT tax here. State and local income taxes, real estate taxes, and personal property taxes are itemized deductions reported on Schedule A. Real estate taxes may instead be reported on Form 8829, for better tax results.

Line 24a , Travel expenses

Many traders working from a home office do not have large travel expenses. Traders don't usually visit the companies they trade in. Online traders don't usually visit their brokerage firms, professional advisors, or others. Traders don't have clients to visit either. (See line 10, Car expenses.)

Traders do travel for seminars, conferences, and meetings. The travel portion of these expenses can be taken as travel or combined with seminar costs. Some traders travel with other traders for trading seminars or conferences. Even if you all go on a ski trip/conference or seminar, these expenses can be deductible if you follow the rules on travel business expenses closely.

- The actual costs of travel (e.g., plane fare, cab to airport, etc.) are deductible for out-of-town business trips. Additionally—and this aspect is significant—you are also allowed to deduct the cost of meals and lodging. Your meals are deductible even if they are "personal" (i.e., not directly connected with the out-of-town business) although, as with all deductible meals, only 50 percent of the cost is allowed. Also, no deduction will be allowed for meals or lodging to the extent the expense is "lavish or extravagant." Although this term is not defined in the tax rules, it has been interpreted to mean "unreasonable."

- Personal entertainment costs on the trip aren't deductible, but business-related costs such as for dry-cleaning, phone calls, and computer rentals are.

- Some allocations may be required if the trip is a combined business/pleasure trip. For example, if you fly to a location for five days of business meetings and stay on for an additional period of vacation, only the cost of meals, lodging, and so on for the business days—not for the personal vacation days—are deductible.

- On the other hand, with respect to the cost of travel itself (plane fare, etc.), if the trip is "primarily" business, it can be deducted in its entirety and no allocation is required. Conversely, if the trip is primarily personal, none of the travel costs are deductible. An important factor in determining if the trip is primarily business or personal is the amount of time spent on each, although this factor isn't the sole consideration.

- If the trip doesn't involve the actual conduct of business but is for the purpose of attending a convention, seminar, or similar event, the IRS checks the nature of the meetings carefully to make sure they are not vacations in disguise. Be careful to save all material helpful in establishing the business or professional nature of this travel.

- The rules on deducting the costs for a spouse who accompanies you on a business trip are restrictive. No deduction is allowed unless the spouse is an employee of yours or your company and traveling for a business purpose.

Line 24b, Meals and entertainment
Many traders have meals with other traders to discuss their respective trading businesses. These traders seek ideas for improvement, research, trading ideas, and advice. In most cases, these meals qualify for this deduction.

Line 24c, Nondeductible amount
Fifty percent of meals and entertainment are not deductible, per IRS rules.

Line 25, Utilities
These expenses are usually included with indirect expenses allocated for the home office on Form 8829. If you have a separate meter for your business usage, then enter that amount on this line. Do not use this line for your phone and communications. Enter your communication costs on Part V where you list your Other Expenses.

Line 27, Other expenses, Schedule C, page 2, Part V
Here is where you list all your other actual trading business product and service expenses.

We include a partial list here:

- Internet access providers used for business exclusively. If combined with personal use, then report them as indirect expenses on Form 8829 for your home office.
- Trading market information online services.
- Trading research products and services.
- Trading print publications and subscriptions.
- Trading gifts to other traders, brokers, and other business related persons (limited to $25 per person per year).
- Trading communication services (phone, fax, dial-up).
- Trading accessories not depreciated (small items less than $100).
- Training and seminars for trading after getting started in the business. Education, training, and seminars before you commence business operations (trader tax status) are either start-up

costs (IRC § 195), investment expenses, or personal nonde-
ductible expenses. See more guidance below.
- Trading chat room expenses.
- Trading tax and accounting fees. If you lack trader tax status,
  these expenses are reported as miscellaneous expenses on
  Schedule A (Itemized Deductions).
- Trading books.
- Trading miscellaneous expenses.
- Education expenses related to trading. Be careful with education
  expenses. If you incur education expenses to learn the trading business before you start trading, those expenses may not be deductible
  as education expenses. On the other hand, if you start your trading
  business and then take courses, training, and seminars, you may
  deduct these expenses on your Schedule C.

Here are the rules: A deduction is available if the education
maintains or improves the skills related to your trade or business.
Educational costs are also deductible if the education is required
(e.g., by law or an employer) to keep your position or job.
Conversely, educational costs are not deductible if the education
is required to get a new field (as opposed to staying in a new
field) or qualifies you for a new trade or business.

Observation: Most traders are not required to take trading seminars or other education courses. Some proprietary traders are
required to take some training before being allowed to trade the
firm's capital, so their education is deductible. A retail trader is
his/her own employer (self-employed). Strictly speaking, a retail
trader's educational costs do not meet the spirit of the tax law for
not allowing a deduction. In most cases, a trader takes these
courses to "improve trading skills," not to qualify to enter the business. Take note that in the future, the SEC may require day traders
to qualify to enter the business, and they may require a minimum
of educational courses. That requirement would change things
here and perhaps disallow the current allowed deductions.

Line 28, Total expenses
Just total up all expenses. **Note:** this amount is before your home office deduction on line 30.

Line 29, Tentative profit (loss)
See our transfer income strategies in line 6.

Line 30, Business use of the home
Expenses are listed here if you have net income. Otherwise, all except mortgage interest and real estate taxes remain a carryover to 2004 listed on Form 8829, home office.

Line 31, Net profit (loss)
Just do the calculations on the form. In all cases, you should break even for profitable traders (because you transferred sufficient trading gains from Schedule D or Form 4797 to break even), or end up with a loss for your trading business expenses. You should never end up with a net income on Schedule C. Make sure to cover your entire home office deduction and section 179 depreciation deductions, if you have sufficient trading gains.

Line 32a
If you have a loss, check this box showing that "All your investment is at risk" in this trading business. Otherwise, leave blank.

Trading gains and losses
Use Form 4797 for mark-to-market IRC § 475 trading gains and losses.
    Use Schedule D for cash method trading gains and losses (not needed in this book, since standard rules apply).

Form 4797, Part II (Ordinary gains and losses)

Traders with mark-to-market (MTM) accounting report their trading gains and losses on Form 4797, Part II—Ordinary Gains and Losses.

Form 4797 instruction excerpts:

Traders Who Made a Mark-to-Market Election A trader in securities or commodities may elect under section 475(f) to use the mark-to-market method to account for securities or commodities held in connection with a trading business. Under this method of accounting, any security or commodity held at the end of the tax year is treated as sold (and reacquired) at its FMV on the last business day of that year.

Unless you are a new taxpayer, the election must be made by the due date (not including extensions) of the tax return for the year prior to the year for which the election becomes effective.

If you are a trader in securities or commodities with a mark-to-market election under section 475(f) in effect for the tax year, the following special rules apply.

Gains and losses from all securities or commodities held in connection with your trading business (including those marked to market) are treated as ordinary income and losses, instead of capital gains and losses. As a result, the lower capital gain tax rates and the limitation on capital losses do not apply.

The gain or loss from each security or commodity held in connection with your trading business (including those marked to market) is reported on Form 4797, line 10 (see the instructions for line 10).

The wash sale rule does not apply to securities or commodities held in connection with your trading business.

For more details on the mark-to-market election and how to make it, see Pub. 550; Rev. Proc. 99-17, 1999-7 I.R.B. 52; and sections 475(e) and 475(f). Form 4797 Instructions for line 10 on page 4.

Part II

If a transaction is not reportable in Part I or Part III and the property is not a capital asset reportable on Schedule D, report the transaction in Part II.

Line 10

Report other ordinary gains and losses, including gains and losses from property held one year or less, on this line.

Securities or commodities held by a
trader who made a mark-to-market election

On line 10, report all gains and losses from sales and dispositions of securities or commodities held in connection with your trading business, including gains and losses from marking to market securities and commodities held at the end of the tax year (see "Traders Who Made a Mark-to-Market Election" on page 2).

Attach a statement to your tax return using the same format as line 10 showing the details of each transaction. Separately show and identify securities or commodities held and marked to market at the end of the year. On line 10, enter "Trader—see attached" in column (a) and the totals from the statement in columns (d), (f), and (g). Also, see the instructions for line 1 on page 3.

Observation: For the past twenty years we have followed a widely accepted practice of reporting one line item per brokerage account. All our example tax returns use this strategy on Form 4797 or Schedule D.

Form 4797 Instructions for line 1

Enter on line 1 the total gross proceeds from:

- Sales or exchanges of real estate reported to you for 2003 on Form(s) 1099-S (or substitute statement) that you are including on line 2, 10, or 20 and
- Sales of securities reported to you for 2003 on Forms 1099-B (or substitute statements) that you are including on line 10 because you are a trader with a mark-to-market election under section 475(f) in effect for the tax year. See "Traders Who Made a Mark-to-Market Election" on page 2 and the instructions for line 10 on page 4.

Traders with mark-to-market (MTM) accounting report their trading gains and losses on Form 4797 Part II—Ordinary Gains and Losses.

Tax Return Footnotes

The following excerpts come from our 2004 GTT Guides.

In our companion guides, in each of the example tax returns, several pages are titled "Supplemental Information" at the end of the federal return (the PDF file) and before the state return. The first few supplemental information pages are marked "Tax Return Footnotes," and just after them are "Client Notes—for Internal Use Only."

Tax return footnotes: These footnotes are included with your tax return and help explain your complex tax status to the IRS. Some accountants advocate no footnotes, but we strongly believe that trader tax status is too complex. To prevent IRS questions and exams, we have had great success in using footnotes for our clients. The footnotes explain trader tax laws, your status, and the trader tax treatment used on the return.

Client notes—For internal use only: Do not file this section with your tax return. These notes are for internal use only. The notes are intended to explain to you how we prepared these example tax returns. We include guidance, notes, warnings, strategies, tips, and form references.

COMMODITY EXAMPLES

Comparing the Tax Return Examples

For examples 7 through 11, we used the same amounts for portfolio income, trading gains or losses, trading expenses, and itemized deductions, except that examples 7 and 8 have the same numbers, including the same amount of commodities trading gains, but example 7 uses MTM IRC § 475 and example 8 does not. Examples 10 and 11 replace commodities trading gains with commodities trading losses.

Example 7

In example 7, Joe qualifies as a "trader in commodities" (i.e., he has trader tax status), so he reports all his trading business expenses on Schedule C (Business Profit and Loss) as in Figure 6.9. Notice that no limitation is placed on these ordinary trading expenses. In order to deduct home office expenses and section 179 depreciation expenses, Joe transferred trading gains from Form 6781 to Schedule C to have them result in zero net income or loss. Home office and section 179 depreciations are only deductible to the extent you have business income. This transfer is discussed in the tax return footnote. Without a transfer, Joe would carry over these expenses to the following tax year, or choose normal depreciation. Trader tax status alone (without MTM) saves Joe a significant amount of taxes, because of the Schedule C deductions.

Commodity trading gains and losses are reported on Form 6781. Because Joe elected mark-to-market accounting on his commodities trading, he reports his commodities trading gains first on Form 6781 and then transfers the net Form 6781 amount to Form 4797, Part II—Ordinary gains and losses.

Joe has commodity trading gains, so he pays a higher tax for electing MTM IRC § 475. See Example 8.

Example 8

In this example, Joe was wise; he was profitable trading commodities for the year as of April 15, 2003, and he decided to not elect mark-to-market accounting for 2003. If he had decided to, the election would have been

SCHEDULE C (Form 1040)	**Profit or Loss From Business** (Sole Proprietorship)	OMB No. 1545-0074

Department of the Treasury Internal Revenue Service (99)

► Partnerships, joint ventures, etc, must file Form 1065 or 1065-B.
► Attach to Form 1040 or 1041. ► See Instructions for Schedule C (Form 1040).

2003

09

Name of proprietor: Joe Trader MTM Comm Gains Ex 7

Social security number (SSN): 111-11-1111

A Principal business or profession, including product or service (see instructions): Trader in Commodities - Mark-to-Market accounting

B Enter code from instructions ► 523130

C Business name. If no separate business name, leave blank.

D Employer ID number (EIN), if any

E Business address (including suite or room no.)► City, town or post office, state, and ZIP code

F Accounting method: (1) ☐ Cash (2) ☐ Accrual (3) ☒ Other (specify) ► Sec 475(f)(2)-Note

G Did you 'materially participate' in the operation of this business during 2003? If 'No,' see instructions for limit on losses. . . . ☒ Yes ☐ No

H If you started or acquired this business during 2003, check here . . . . ►

Part I Income

1 Gross receipts or sales. **Caution.** If this income was reported to you on Form W-2 and the 'Statutory employee' box on that form was checked, see the instructions and check here . . . . . . ► ☐	1	
2 Returns and allowances	2	
3 Subtract line 2 from line 1	3	
4 Cost of goods sold (from line 42 on page 2)	4	
5 **Gross profit.** Subtract line 4 from line 3	5	
6 Other income, including Federal and state gasoline or fuel tax credit or refund . . . . . . See Statement 4	6	46,147.
7 **Gross income.** Add lines 5 and 6 . . . . ►	7	46,147.

Part II Expenses. Enter expenses for business use of your home **only** on line 30.

8 Advertising	8		19 Pension and profit-sharing plans	19	
9 Car and truck expenses (see instructions)	9		20 Rent or lease (see instructions):		
10 Commissions and fees	10		a Vehicles, machinery, and equipment	20a	
11 Contract labor (see instructions)	11		b Other business property	20b	
12 Depletion	12		21 Repairs and maintenance	21	
13 Depreciation and section 179 expense deduction (not included in Part III) (see instructions)	13	7,865.	22 Supplies (not included in Part III)	22	953.
			23 Taxes and licenses.	23	
			24 Travel, meals, and entertainment:		
14 Employee benefit programs (other than on line 19).	14		a Travel.	24a	1,855.
15 Insurance (other than health). . .	15		b Meals and entertainment. . . .	2,654.	
16 Interest:			c Enter nondeductible amount included on line 24b (see instrs). .	1,327.	
a Mortgage (paid to banks, etc)	16a		d Subtract line 24c from line 24b.	24d	1,327.
b Other	16b	16,299.	25 Utilities.	25	
17 Legal & professional services . .	17		26 Wages (less employment credits)	26	
18 Office expense	18		27 Other expenses (from line 48 on page 2)	27	10,612.
28 **Total expenses** before expenses for business use of home. Add lines 8 through 27 in columns . . . . ►				28	38,911.

29 Tentative profit (loss). Subtract line 28 from line 7	29	7,236.
30 Expenses for business use of your home. Attach **Form 8829**	30	7,236.
31 **Net profit or (loss).** Subtract line 30 from line 29.		

• If a profit, enter on **Form 1040, line 12,** and **also** on **Schedule SE, line 2** (statutory employees, see instructions). Estates and trusts, enter on Form 1041, line 3.

31	0.

• If a loss, you **must** go to line 32.

32 If you have a loss, check the box that describes your investment in this activity (see instructions).

• If you checked 32a, enter the loss on **Form 1040, line 12,** and **also** on **Schedule SE, line 2** (statutory employees, see instructions). Estates and trusts, enter on Form 1041, line 3.

32a ☐ All investment is at risk.

• If you checked 32b, you **must** attach **Form 6198.**

32b ☐ Some investment is not at risk.

BAA For Paperwork Reduction Act Notice, see Form 1040 instructions.

Schedule **C** (Form 1040) 2003

FDIZ0112L 10/14/03

Figure 6.9

due by April 15, 2003. Joe understood that electing MTM would convert his commodities capital gains and losses to ordinary gains and losses, and he did not want to forgo the 60 percent long-term capital gains rate benefit on commodities gains (see full discussion of this benefit on our Form 6781 earlier in this book). Without MTM IRC § 475, Joe saved a considerable amount of federal taxes versus Example 7.

Note: Had Joe ended the year with commodities trading losses, he would have been much better off having elected MTM IRC § 475. See discussion of this difference on the Loss Examples page.

One important note about transferring gains from Form 6781 to Schedule C to "zero out": If a taxpayer does not elect IRC § 475 on commodities, then consider that transferring gains from Form 6781 to Schedule C (to zero it out) and unlocking section 179 depreciation and home office expenses (which require income on the tax return from any business or wage activity) may not be tax-beneficial in all cases. Be aware that this transfer will unlock those Schedule C benefits, but on the other hand it will also reduce a taxpayer's 60 percent long-term capital gains rate tax benefit. For our clients, we run the numbers both ways to see which is preferable taxwise. Showing a Schedule C loss and gains on Form 6781 is fine, it's more an issue of taking home office and 179 depreciation deductions.

Example 8(b) is the same as example 8, except no transfer of gains is made from Form 6781 to Schedule C. Notice in Figure 6.10 how Joe is better off taxwise with the transfer in that he wants to benefit from his home office expenses in 2003 and not carry them over to 2004. Keep in mind, if Joe exits the trading business in 2003, he may not be able to use carryover home office expenses. He prefers example 8 over example 8(b) without the transfer of trading gains from Form 6781.

Example 9

In example 9, Joe doesn't qualify for trader tax status, so he is forced to report as a normal investor. Therefore, Joe may not report his trading business expenses on Schedule C. Instead, Joe must report these expenses as

SCHEDULE C
(Form 1040)

Department of the Treasury
Internal Revenue Service   (99)

Profit or Loss From Business
(Sole Proprietorship)

► Partnerships, joint ventures, etc, must file Form 1065 or 1065-B.
► Attach to Form 1040 or 1041.   ► See Instructions for Schedule C (Form 1040).

OMB No. 1545-0074

2003
09

Name of proprietor	Social security number (SSN)
Joe Trader no MTM CommGain Ex8B	111-11-1111

A Principal business or profession, including product or service (see instructions)
    Trader in Commodities - See Note

B Enter code from instructions
  ► 523900

C Business name. If no separate business name, leave blank.

D Employer ID number (EIN), If any

E Business address (including suite or room no.) ►
   City, town or post office, state, and ZIP code

F Accounting method: (1) [X] Cash (2) [ ] Accrual (3) [ ] Other (specify) ►

G Did you 'materially participate' in the operation of this business during 2003? If 'No,' see instructions for limit on losses. . . . [X] Yes   [ ] No

H If you started or acquired this business during 2003, check here . . . . ►

Part I   Income

1	Gross receipts or sales. **Caution.** If this income was reported to you on Form W-2 and the 'Statutory employee' box on that form was checked, see the instructions and check here . . . . ►[ ]	1	
2	Returns and allowances	2	
3	Subtract line 2 from line 1	3	
4	Cost of goods sold (from line 42 on page 2)	4	
5	**Gross profit.** Subtract line 4 from line 3	5	
6	Other income, including Federal and state gasoline or fuel tax credit or refund	6	
7	**Gross income.** Add lines 5 and 6 . . . . ►	7	

Part II   Expenses. Enter expenses for business use of your home **only** on line 30.

8	Advertising	8		19	Pension and profit-sharing plans	19	
9	Car and truck expenses (see instructions)	9		20	Rent or lease (see instructions):		
					a Vehicles, machinery, and equipment	20a	
10	Commissions and fees	10			b Other business property	20b	
11	Contract labor (see instructions)	11		21	Repairs and maintenance	21	
				22	Supplies (not included in Part III)	22	953.
12	Depletion	12		23	Taxes and licenses	23	
13	Depreciation and section 179 expense deduction (not included in Part III) (see instructions) . .	13	3,188.	24	Travel, meals, and entertainment:		
					a Travel	24a	1,855.
14	Employee benefit programs (other than on line 19)	14			b Meals and entertainment . . . . 2,654.		
15	Insurance (other than health) . .	15			c Enter nondeductible amount included on line 24b (see instrs). . . . 1,327.		
16	Interest:						
	a Mortgage (paid to banks, etc).	16a			d Subtract line 24c from line 24b	24d	1,327.
	b Other	16b	16,299.	25	Utilities	25	
17	Legal & professional services . .	17		26	Wages (less employment credits)	26	
18	Office expense	18		27	Other expenses (from line 48 on page 2)	27	10,612.
28	**Total expenses** before expenses for business use of home. Add lines 8 through 27 in columns . . . . ►					28	34,234.

29	Tentative profit (loss). Subtract line 28 from line 7	29	-34,234.
30	Expenses for business use of your home. Attach **Form 8829**	30	
31	**Net profit or (loss).** Subtract line 30 from line 29.		

• If a profit, enter on **Form 1040, line 12,** and **also** on **Schedule SE, line 2** (statutory employees, see instructions). Estates and trusts, enter on Form 1041, line 3.

• If a loss, you **must** go to line 32.

	31	-34,234.

32 If you have a loss, check the box that describes your investment in this activity (see instructions).

• If you checked 32a, enter the loss on **Form 1040, line 12,** and also on **Schedule SE, line 2** (statutory employees, see instructions). Estates and trusts, enter on Form 1041, line 3.

• If you checked 32b, you **must** attach **Form 6198.**

32a [X] All investment is at risk.
32b [ ] Some investment is not at risk.

BAA For Paperwork Reduction Act Notice, see Form 1040 instructions.

Schedule **C** (Form 1040) 2003

FDIZ0112L 10/14/03

Figure 6.10

itemized deductions on Schedule A. Investment interest expenses are limited on Form 4952 (not in this case, because Joe has investment income) and investment expenses are subject to "Miscellaneous Itemized Deduction" limitations.

Take note of the other nasty surprise for Joe: he triggered the nasty alternative minimum tax (AMT). When a taxpayer has a significant long-term capital gain (60 percent of Joe's gains are taxed at the long-term capital gains rate) plus large miscellaneous itemized deductions and state taxes (both are not deductible for AMT tax), a taxpayer can oftentimes trigger the AMT tax.

The Bottom Line: Trader tax status always saves a trader a meaningful amount of taxes.

We don't recommend MTM IRC § 475 for commodities traders because they forgo the 60 percent long-term capital gains rate benefit. However, if you have large commodities trading losses for 2003 as of April 15, 2003, and you might exit the commodities trading business, we suggest you do elect MTM IRC § 475 for 2003. This election will allow you to convert your commodities trading losses to ordinary loss treatment. Otherwise, you will be stuck with a capital loss limitation of $3,000. Commodities traders are entitled to a three-year carryback of losses from section 1256 contracts, but only applied against commodities trading gains in those years.

Commodities Trader with Trading Losses

Joe Trader is single. He traded commodities as a business from his home office in Los Angeles for all of 2003. His tax matters are fairly simple. He has two brokerage accounts: a commodities trading account at Interactive Brokers, and a segregated securities account (i.e., he trades from the account but also has long-term investment positions) at Schwab. He elected MTM IRC § 475 accounting on commodities for tax year 2003 when he filed his 2002 federal tax return by April 15, 2003. Joe is not registered with an exchange as a commodities dealer, so he is exempt from self-employment taxation.

For examples 10 and 11, Joe qualifies as a trader in commodities (i.e., he has trader tax status), so he reports all his trading business expenses on Schedule C (Business Profit and Loss). Notice it places no limitation on these ordinary trading expenses. However, Joe's home office expenses are carried over to 2004, because Joe does not have trading gains from Form 6781 as he did in examples 7 and 8.

Joe does receive significant tax savings from reporting these large Schedule C expenses. Note that he used a regular depreciation method rather than section 179 depreciation, because he needs income to deduct section 179 depreciation (without income, section 179 depreciation is carried over to 2004).

Example 10

In example 10, because Joe elected MTM IRC § 475 accounting on his commodities trading, he reports his commodities losses first on Form 6781 and then he transfers the net Form 6781 amounts to Form 4797 Part II—Ordinary gains and losses.

Joe has commodities trading losses, so he benefits greatly from having elected MTM. Joe was wise: He was losing on his commodities trading as of April 15, 2003, for tax year 2003, so he decided to elect mark-to-market accounting for 2003. The 2003 MTM was due by April 15, 2003.

Joe understood that electing MTM would convert his capital gains and losses on commodities trading into ordinary gains and losses. Joe wisely exchanged the 60 percent long-term capital gains rate benefit on commodities trading gains in exchange for the important loss insurance of Form 4797 (ordinary gain or loss treatment). With MTM, Joe saved a considerable amount of federal and state taxes by utilizing his net operating loss for immediate tax refunds.

Net Operating Losses: Joe has an NOL in connection with trader tax status. His NOL is comprised of his Schedule C trading business expenses plus his large Form 4797 trading losses, shown in Figure 6.11.

SCHEDULE C (Form 1040)	**Profit or Loss From Business** (Sole Proprietorship)	OMB No. 1545-0074 **2003**
Department of the Treasury Internal Revenue Service (99)	▶ Partnerships, joint ventures, etc., must file Form 1065 or 1065-B. ▶ Attach to Form 1040 or 1041. ▶ See Instructions for Schedule C (Form 1040).	09

Name of proprietor: Joe Trader MTM Comm Loss Ex 10 — Social security number (SSN): 111-11-1111

A Principal business or profession, including product or service (see instructions): Trader in Commodities - Mark-to-Market accounting

B Enter code from instructions ▶ 523130

C Business name. If no separate business name, leave blank.

D Employer ID number (EIN), if any

E Business address (including suite or room no.) ▶ City, town or post office, state, and ZIP code

F Accounting method: (1) ☐ Cash (2) ☐ Accrual (3) ☒ Other (specify) ▶ Sec 475(f)(2)-Note

G Did you 'materially participate' in the operation of this business during 2003? If 'No,' see instructions for limit on losses.... ☒ Yes ☐ No

H If you started or acquired this business during 2003, check here .... ▶

Part I Income

1 Gross receipts or sales. Caution. If this income was reported to you on Form W-2 and the 'Statutory employee' box on that form was checked, see the instructions and check here ...... ▶ ☐	1	
2 Returns and allowances	2	
3 Subtract line 2 from line 1	3	
4 Cost of goods sold (from line 42 on page 2)	4	
5 Gross profit. Subtract line 4 from line 3	5	
6 Other income, including Federal and state gasoline or fuel tax credit or refund	6	
7 Gross income. Add lines 5 and 6 ▶	7	

Part II Expenses. Enter expenses for business use of your home only on line 30.

8 Advertising	8		19 Pension and profit-sharing plans	19	
9 Car and truck expenses (see instructions)	9		20 Rent or lease (see instructions): a Vehicles, machinery, and equipment	20a	
10 Commissions and fees	10		b Other business property	20b	
11 Contract labor (see instructions)	11		21 Repairs and maintenance	21	
12 Depletion	12		22 Supplies (not included in Part III)	22	953.
13 Depreciation and section 179 expense deduction (not included in Part III) (see instructions)	13	3,983.	23 Taxes and licenses	23	
14 Employee benefit programs (other than on line 19)	14		24 Travel, meals, and entertainment: a Travel	24a	1,855.
15 Insurance (other than health)	15		b Meals and entertainment 2,654.		
16 Interest: a Mortgage (paid to banks, etc)	16a		c Enter nondeductible amount included on line 24b (see instrs) 1,327.		
b Other	16b		d Subtract line 24c from line 24b	24d	1,327.
17 Legal & professional services	17		25 Utilities	25	
18 Office expense	18		26 Wages (less employment credits)	26	
			27 Other expenses (from line 48 on page 2)	27	10,612.
28 Total expenses before expenses for business use of home. Add lines 8 through 27 in columns ▶				28	18,730.

29 Tentative profit (loss). Subtract line 28 from line 7	29	-18,730.
30 Expenses for business use of your home. Attach Form 8829	30	
31 Net profit or (loss). Subtract line 30 from line 29. • If a profit, enter on Form 1040, line 12, and also on Schedule SE, line 2 (statutory employees, see instructions). Estates and trusts, enter on Form 1041, line 3. • If a loss, you must go to line 32.	31	-18,730.

32 If you have a loss, check the box that describes your investment in this activity (see instructions).
• If you checked 32a, enter the loss on Form 1040, line 12, and also on Schedule SE, line 2 (statutory employees, see instructions). Estates and trusts, enter on Form 1041, line 3.   32a ☒ All investment is at risk.
• If you checked 32b, you must attach Form 6198.   32b ☐ Some investment is not at risk.

BAA For Paperwork Reduction Act Notice, see Form 1040 instructions.   Schedule C (Form 1040) 2003

FDIZ0112L 10/14/03

Figure 6.11a

Form **4797**	**Sales of Business Property**	OMB No. 1545-0184
	(Also Involuntary Conversions and Recapture Amounts Under Sections 179 and 280F(b)(2))	**2003**
Department of the Treasury Internal Revenue Service (99)	▶ Attach to your tax return. ▶ See separate instructions.	27

Name(s) shown on return: Joe Trader MTM Comm Loss Ex 10   Identifying number: 111-11-1111

1 Enter the gross proceeds from sales or exchanges reported to you for 2003 on Form(s) 1099-B or 1099-S (or substitute statement) that you are including on line 2, 10, or 20 (see instructions) ... | 1 |

Part I Sales or Exchanges of Property Used in a Trade or Business and Involuntary Conversions From Other Than Casualty or Theft — Most Property Held More Than 1 Year (See instructions.)

2 (a) Description of property	(b) Date acquired (month, day, year)	(c) Date sold (month, day, year)	(d) Gross sales price	(e) Depreciation allowed or allowable since acquisition	(f) Cost or other basis, plus improvements and expense of sale	(g) Gain or (loss) Subtract (f) from the sum of (d) and (e)	(h) Post-May 5, 2003, gain or (loss)* (see below)

3 Gain, if any, from Form 4684, line 39 ... | 3 |
4 Section 1231 gain from installment sales from Form 6252, line 26 or 37 ... | 4 |
5 Section 1231 gain or (loss) from like-kind exchanges from Form 8824 ... | 5 |
6 Gain, if any, from line 32, from other than casualty or theft ... | 6 |
7 Combine lines 2 through 6 in columns (g) and (h). Enter the gain or (loss) here and on the appropriate line as follows ... | 7 |

Partnerships (except electing large partnerships) and S corporations. Report the gain or (loss) following the instructions for Form 1065, Schedule K, line 6, or Form 1120S, Schedule K, line 5. Skip lines 8, 9, 11, and 12 below.

All others. If line 7, column (g) is zero or a loss, enter that amount on line 11 below and skip lines 8, 9, and 12. If line 7, column (g) is a gain and you did not have any prior year section 1231 losses, or they were recaptured in an earlier year, enter the gain or (loss) in each column as a long-term capital gain or (loss) on Schedule D and skip lines 8, 9, 11, and 12 below.

8 Nonrecaptured net section 1231 losses from prior years (see instructions) ... | 8 |
9 Subtract line 8 from line 7. If line 9, column (g) is zero or less, enter -0- in column (g). If line 9, column (g) is zero, enter the gain from line 7, column (g) on line 12 below. If line 9, column (g), is more than zero, enter the amount from line 8, column (g) on line 12 below and include the gain or (loss) in each column of line 9 as a long-term capital gain or (loss) on Schedule D (see instructions) ... | 9 |

*Corporations (other than S corporations) should not complete column (h). Partnerships and S corporations must complete column (h). All others must complete column (h) only if line 7, column (g), is a gain and the amount, if any, on line 8, column (g), does **not** equal or exceed the gain on line 7, column (g). Include in column (h) all gains and losses from column (g) from sales, exchanges, or conversions (including installment payments received) **after** May 5, 2003. However, do **not** include gain attributable to unrecaptured section 1250 gain.

Part II Ordinary Gains and Losses

10 Ordinary gains and losses not included on lines 11 through 17 (include property held 1 year or less):

| Trnsfer Form 6781 loss fr Form 4797-Note (Trader Transaction) | | | | | | 79,186. | -79,186. |
| Various | Various | | | | | | |

11 Loss, if any, from line 7, column (g) ... | 11 |
12 Gain, if any, from line 7, column (g), or amount from line 8, column (g), if applicable ... | 12 |
13 Gain, if any, from line 31 ... | 13 |
14 Net gain or (loss) from Form 4684, lines 31 and 38a ... | 14 |
15 Ordinary gain from installment sales from Form 6252, line 25 or 36 ... | 15 |
16 Ordinary gain or (loss) from like-kind exchanges from Form 8824 ... | 16 |
17 Recapture of section 179 expense deduction for partners and S corporation shareholders for property dispositions from 2002-2003 fiscal year partnerships and S corporations (see instructions) ... | 17 |
18 Combine lines 10 through 17. Enter the gain or (loss) here and on the appropriate line as follows ... | 18 | -79,186. |

a For all except individual returns. Enter the gain from line 18 on the return being filed.
b For individual returns:
(1) If the loss on line 11 includes a loss from Form 4684, line 35, column (b)(ii), enter that part of the loss here. Enter the part of the loss from income-producing property on Schedule A (Form 1040), line 27, and the part of the loss from property used as an employee on Schedule A (Form 1040), line 22. Identify as from 'Form 4797, line 18b(1).' See instructions ... | 18b (1) |
(2) Redetermine the gain or (loss) on line 18 excluding the loss, if any, on line 18b(1). Enter here and on Form 1040, line 14 ... | 18b (2) | -79,186. |

BAA For Paperwork Reduction Act Notice, see instructions.   FDIZ1001L 12/02/03   Form **4797** (2003)

Figure 6.11b

Form 1045: Joe is ready to consult with GTT about filing a Form 1045 NOL refund claim. We will show him exactly how to get a quick NOL refund without problems (and avoid the many pitfalls here). If you have a large NOL and a large refund coming, we suggest you engage a professional to prepare your tax return with Form 1045 carrybacks. We have done many of these returns with great success. We also have heard horror stories about people who tried this on their own or with another firm that was less than expert. (E-mail info@greencompany.com.)

Joe may elect to carry back his 2003 NOL two years, or he may elect to carry forward the NOL instead to future tax years up to twenty years.

Note: It does not matter whether Joe was a trader in any of the prior or future carryback or forward years. Starting in 2003, the NOL carryback period reverts to only two years (the law was temporarily changed to allow two or five year carry backs for 2001 and 2002 only).

Example 11

In example 11, without MTM IRC § 475, Joe is really hurt. He is stuck with a capital loss limitation of $3,000 and a large capital loss carryover to 2004. Joe does benefit from having an NOL from his Schedule C business expenses, shown in Figure 6.11.

Note About Form 6781 Carrybacks: Joe may carry back his Form 6781 (Section 1256 contract) losses three tax years but only to be applied to Form 6781 gains in those prior three years. This topic is included in this tax guide. Our firm generally does not recommend IRC § 475 MTM accounting for commodity traders because they lose the 60/40 tax benefit and also they have a built-in carryback rule (only on Form 6781) any way. This Form 6781 carryback rule applies to business traders and investors (who don't have trader tax status), so it helps Joe in Example 12 as well.

Example 12

When Joe doesn't qualify for trader tax status, he is forced to file as a normal investor. Therefore, Joe may not report his trading business expenses on Schedule C. Instead, he must report these expenses as itemized deductions on Schedule A. Investment interest expenses are limited on Form 4952 and investment expenses are subject to "Miscellaneous Itemized Deduction" limitations.

Joe has negative taxable income, so his trading business expenses are entirely wasted for this year or any other year. Joe does have a carryover of his investment interest expense. See note in Example 11 about Form 6781 carrybacks. This rules applies to investors as well.

The Bottom Line: Trader tax status always saves a trader a meaningful amount of money. We don't recommend MTM IRC § 475 for successful commodities traders because they forgo the 60 percent long-term capital gains rate benefit (and if you have losses you can carry them back three years against Form 6781 gains only). However, if you have large commodities trading losses for 2004 as of April 15, 2004, and you might exit the commodities trading business, we suggest you do elect MTM for 2004. This election will allow you to convert your commodities trading losses to ordinary loss treatment. Otherwise, you will be stuck with a capital loss limitation of $3,000.

Line-by-Line Guidance

Form 1040, page 2
Where it says "Occupation," enter "Trader in Commodities" if you qualify for trader tax status.

Trading expenses
If you qualify for trader tax status, you should report all your trading expenses on Schedule C (Profit or Loss From Business).

Trading gains and losses
Commodity trading gains and losses are reported on Form 6781 (Gains and Losses from Section 1256 Contracts and Straddles).

If you elected IRC § 475(f)(2)—the MTM commonly used by securities traders—for commodities (or use it from the prior year), transfer your Form 6781 commodities trading gains and losses to Form 4797 (Sale of Business Property—Part II, Ordinary Gains and Losses).

Change of Accounting Method
If you elected IRC § 475(f)(2) mark-to-market accounting for 2003 by April 15, 2003, file a Form 3115 with your 2003 tax return. Notice a copy of your election is included in the following footnote.

Home office deductions
If you have an office in your home, file a Form 8829 (Expenses for Business Use of Your Home).

Footnotes
All trader tax returns should include a footnote to explain trader tax status and how you reported your trading business activity.

Schedule C

For purposes of this guidance, we refer to Joe Trader example 7.

If you qualify for trader tax status—meaning your trading activity for 2003 rose to the level of a business—then you should report all your trading business expenses on Schedule C.

Traders may deduct unlimited amounts of their trading business expenses on Schedule C; there are no restrictions. A qualifying trader may use Schedule C whether or not they elect mark-to-market accounting IRC § 475. Even if you did not learn about trader tax status until 2004, you can still file this Schedule C for 2003.

Always attach a footnote to your Schedule C to explain your trader tax status. (See our Footnotes section.)

Line A, Principle business
If you trade commodities with MTM IRC § 475, write "Trader in Commodities—Mark-to-Market accounting—See Note." in line A.

Line B, Enter code
Trader in commodities without mark-to-market accounting: 523900 for "Other financial investment activities."

Trader in commodities with mark-to-market accounting: 523130 for "Commodity contract dealers."

Trader in commodities and securities with mark-to-market accounting: 523130 for "Commodity contract dealers."

Lines C, D, and E, Business name, tax ID number, and address
Nothing is required on these lines. Some traders use an assumed name or a d/b/a (doing business as) name for their business. If that is the case, you can enter that name on line C.

Some traders file an SS-4 to get a tax ID number for their d/b/a. If that is the case, you can enter the EIN on line D. You will need a business EIN if you have employees.

If you have a separate address for your trading business, different from your home address, you can enter it here. **One note of caution:** It might be better to omit this address if you want to reduce chances of the IRS questioning your home office expense (if you have one).

Line F, Accounting method
Schedule C businesses by default use the cash method of accounting as opposed to the accrual method. Both methods are listed on line F, but "Other" is also listed.

If you use mark-to-market accounting for commodities, check "Other" and enter: IRC Sec 475(f)(2). 475(f)(1) is for securities and 475(f)(2) is for commodities. You can elect both or just one alone.

If you do not use mark-to-market accounting for commodities, check the cash method. If you want the accrual method for your business expenses, then check accrual method.

Line G, Material participation
Check the Yes box indicating that you did materially participate in your trading business. If you check No, then you don't qualify to use a trading business Schedule C.

Line H, Started business in 2003
Check the box if you started your trading business in 2003.

Part I, Income
No entries are made on lines 1 to 5, because you do not have revenues, inventory, or cost of goods sold in this trading business.

Line 6, Other income (loss)
Transfer income from Form 6781. See the Joe Trader example 7 Footnote section titled "SPECIAL NOTES." If the taxpayer has net trading gains, sufficient trading gains can be transferred from Form 6781 to Schedule C to cover taxpayer's related trading business expenses. This transfer is made because Schedule C business expenses relate to taxpayer's trading gains.

See the Joe Trader example 8 section discussion on the tax consequences or benefits caused by transferring income on Form 6781 to Schedule C. You stand to lose some lower long-term capital gain rate benefits, as a trade-off to unlocking home office and 179 depreciation benefits. Also, see this same section of the securities examples area of this book.

Part II, Expenses
Choose the cash or accrual method of accounting for business expenses. Don't confuse your expense method of accounting with your trading gains and loss method of accounting (cash or MTM). Here are some tax planning ideas that point out the advantage of accrual method accounting for expenses: Business traders accelerate expenses into 2003 for lower 2003 tax

liabilities. The cardinal rule of year-end tax planning is to accelerate business deductions and losses into the current tax year and defer income and gains into the following tax year.

Deferring income taxes until the following tax years benefits the taxpayer by allowing the use of this tax money during the current and following tax year. These benefits are referred to as *timing* rather than *permanent* tax benefits. As a default method of accounting, business traders use the cash method of accounting for both business expenses and trading gains and losses, making business expenses deductible when paid, as opposed to when incurred. For example, if a cash method business trader attends a seminar on December 28, 2003, but pays the bill on January 4, 2004, it is a 2004 business expense. A business trader may also elect to use the accrual method of accounting, which means that expenses are deductible when incurred (in 2003), not when paid (in 2004).

A business trader may also elect to use IRC § 475 mark-to-market accounting for trading gains and losses. This MTM election must be filed with the IRS by April 15 of the current tax year. Otherwise, the cash method of capital gains and losses applies for the entire tax year. (See the following chapter on tax planning moves related to trading gains and losses.)

Because trading gains and losses are treated separately from expenses and business traders don't have other forms of income, most business traders would be better served taxwise to use the accrual method of accounting for business expenses. However, this approach may be more trouble accounting-wise. For cash method business traders, the easiest way to accelerate deductions is to pay all bills early, before the end of the year. Remember that a prepayment of 2004 expenses will not give rise to a 2003 tax deduction.

Credit card charges are treated like payments of cash or check. It does not matter when you pay the credit card bill. For example, if you charge your credit card for a new computer on December 31, 2003, it is a 2003 tax deduction under the cash method. It does not matter that the computer is listed on your January credit card statement. If you plan to upgrade your computers, equipment, or furniture and fixtures soon, it's better to do it before year-end than early the next year. Each tax year, a business taxpayer is allowed 100 percent (IRC § 179) depreciation up to the first $100,000 of depreciable assets ($102,000 for 2004). Excess amounts are subject to the normal rules of depreciation (over the useful life of the asset).

Line 8, Advertising
Most traders don't advertise because they don't have customers as dealers do.

Line 9, Bad debts
If you loaned money to another trader for business reasons, and he or she defaulted on paying it back, then you may deduct the entire business bad debt on line 9. However, you first need to bring legal action or threaten legal-type action against the debtor. Don't play around with this situation. Nonbusiness bad debts are deducted as capital losses on Schedule D. Proprietary traders may write off lost deposits (with proprietary trading loss) as business bad debts.

Line 10, Car expenses
Most traders don't use a car for business. The nature of trading online involves trading from an office at home. If you trade at home and also trade in a trading office outside the home (and qualify for a home office deduction), then traveling from your main home office to your other daytime trading office may qualify as a travel expense. Otherwise, if you don't have a home office, travel to and from that office is a nondeductible commuting expense. Anyway, we don't suggest entering this type of travel here (under Car), but rather we suggest entering it on line 24a, Travel expense.

Line 11, Commissions and fees
Trading commissions are not recorded here on Schedule C. Rather, all trading commissions are recorded as part of trading transactions on Form 6781. Commissions on purchases are added to your cost basis and commissions on sales are subtracted from proceeds. Your broker reports commissions in this manner on each confirmation and on your statements. Be careful in reading your year-end brokerage website reporting of net commissions. Some brokerage firms separate commissions from profit and loss

in their online reports. It is important that you ask your broker.

Caution: A few brokers report commissions separately from trading gains and losses on Form 1099. This practice is wrong, but needless to say you should not omit reporting both amounts. If you leave out commissions, then you will overstate your tax liability.

Some traders receive rebates of commissions. These amounts are usually not reflected on your confirmations, your statements, or Form 1099. Some traders do receive a Form 1099-Misc for commission rebates. Many traders don't realize that these amounts should be reported as additional commodity trading income on Form 6781. If the Form 1099 is a Form 1099-Misc, we suggest you first report it on Schedule C line 6 in Other Income and then transfer it to Form 6781. This way, the IRS has a trail. It is unusual for commodities traders to receive rebates, although stock traders do receive such rebates.

Line 13, Depreciation

Traders use plenty of computers, equipment and furniture, and fixtures. Enter these costs on Form 4562 and choose the correct depreciation method. Form 4562 depreciation amounts are then transferred to this line.

Some notes about depreciation: These costs are depreciable whether you buy the item in 2003 or in a prior year and then convert it to business use in 2003. Don't short-change yourself here. Make a list of every item of technology, equipment, and furniture in your home office and in your trading business.

Fixed assets are depreciated, expenses are expensed. When you purchase an asset, you need to make a decision about whether that asset is going to help you earn income in future years. If the answer is Yes, then it is called a "fixed asset" and you must depreciate it over its useful life. The IRS has schedules for different types of fixed assets and provides different methods for depreciating fixed assets over their designated useful lives. Computers and equipment are depreciated over five years and office furniture is seven years. Take note of bonus depreciation and accelerated methods allowed.

Section 179 Depreciation

Section 179 allows you to deduct 100 percent of your fixed asset cost up to $100,000 for 2003 ($102,000 for 2004) as a current expense for qualifying property purchased and placed in service during 2003. This property would otherwise have to be depreciated. You can only deduct section 179 depreciation if you have net income from wages and other business activities (let your tax software handle this calculation). If trading is your only business or job activity, then this requires that you be a profitable trader and that you follow our suggested strategy of transferring sufficient trading gains to Schedule C line 6 from Form 6781. If you have trading losses, and no income, then we suggest that you skip section 179 depreciation and take regular and bonus depreciation. This option would allow you to get some depreciation rather than none (carrying over your section 179 depreciation to the following tax year).

Form 4562 for your Schedule C

All depreciation is first entered on Form 4562. Section 179 depreciation is entered on the top of Part I, special bonus depreciation in Part II, and regular depreciation is entered in Part III. You should file a separate Form 4562 for each different business activity. You file one Form 4562 for your trading business Schedule C.

Software is an intangible asset and it is amortized on Form 4562, page 2, Part VI. The depreciation method is three years straight-line. Starting in 2003, software may now be included with section 179 depreciable property or be included with bonus depreciation.

Line 14, Employee benefit programs

If you have employees, you enter the amounts of payroll taxes and other employee benefits here. If you have employees, you need to file payroll tax returns and issue all employees Form W-2s. You also have to withhold and remit payroll taxes. See the IRS Publications for Employers.

Sole proprietors, unlike single member LLCs, are not allowed to pay themselves a W-2 salary and then set up a retirement plan on that earned income. Trading income is not "earned income," and sole proprietors are not entitled to contribute to retirement plans on this income. You need to form a separate business entity to pay yourself a fee or a salary in order to have a retirement plan.

Line 15, Insurance

Taxpayers without earned income, including business traders, may not deduct health insurance premiums from adjusted gross income. Other types of sole proprietors have earned income, and they can deduct health insurance premiums. This line 15 is for other types of insurance like business liability insurance, which few traders have. Home insurance is reported with other home office expenses on Form 8829.

Line 16b, Interest expense

If you have margin interest expense on your trading accounts, enter that amount here. Do not enter margin interest for investment positions or investment accounts; investment interest expenses go on Form 4952 and deductions are limited to investment income.

Line 17, Legal and professional fees

Legal fees for operations or business tax advice are deductible. Legal fees for asset acquisition are added to the cost basis of the asset. Legal fees for personal reasons are not deductible. Fees paid to your trader tax business preparer may be deducted here or on line 27, other expenses.

Line 18, Office expense

If you have an office in your home, don't use this line. Instead, use Form 8829 (Expenses for the business use of your home). **Note:** New IRS regulations further liberalize home office deductions by allowing taxpayers to protect more of their gain exclusion on sale of their principal residence, by not allocating the home office gain to the overall home gain (providing your office is in your home and not a separate structure). This rule is intended to help more taxpayers by not making them afraid to take this deduction and home depreciation in fear of losing their exclusion. The only recapture in many sales will be depreciation taken to date. That is not a lost benefit, but rather a timing difference (you pick up income later for what you deduct now). Note that depreciation is "allowed" or "allowable," which means you are treated by the IRS as taking this depreciation whether you did or not. So you may as well take it and receive the related tax benefits.

Line 19, Pension and profit-sharing plans

Traders do not have earned income, and as a result they may not contribute to pension or profit-sharing retirement plans. Traders can set up retirement plans by creating an entity for their trading and then paying themselves a salary or fee from that entity.

If your Schedule C business has employees and you have a retirement plan for them, you would use this line.

Exception: If a trader in commodities is registered with an exchange as a dealer, then their trading gains and losses (with or without IRC § 475(f)(2)) are subject to self-employment taxation. In that case, the trader can have a retirement plan contribution, but it would be reported in the adjusted gross income area, not on this line.

Line 20a, Rent or lease

Enter operating lease payments on trading equipment here.

Note: Some leases should be capitalized and then depreciated on Form 4562.

Line 20b, Other business property

If you have a trading office outside your home, enter any rent you pay for that office here.

Line 21, Repairs and maintenance

If you have repairs or maintenance on trading business equipment, or your trading home office assets, enter those expenses here. General home repairs and maintenance are reported on Form 8829.

Line 22, Supplies

Traders use a great deal of supplies. Enter those supplies expenses here. Remember, the home office form is for indirect home costs, not specific trading business expenses such as supplies.

Line 23, Taxes and licenses

Some traders also get security industry licenses. The cost of those can be deducted here. Some states or cities (such as New York City) charge stealth taxes on unincorporated businesses. In most cases, these taxes won't apply to Schedule Cs, because Schedule Cs for traders always show either zero net income or a large loss (if you don't transfer any gains; see the line 6 explanation). Furthermore, trading gains are usually not subject to NYC unincorporated business tax (UBT). For a regular NYC business, they would deduct their NYC UBT tax here. State and local income taxes, real estate taxes, and personal property taxes are itemized deductions reported on Schedule A. Real estate taxes may instead be reported on Form 8829, for better tax results.

Line 24a, Travel expenses

Many traders working from a home office do not have large travel expenses. Traders don't usually visit the companies they trade in. Online traders don't usually visit their brokerage firms, professional advisors, or others. Traders don't have clients to visit either. (See line 10, Car expenses, for deductions that can be taken here.)

Traders do travel for seminars, conferences, and meetings. The travel portion of these expenses can be taken as a travel expense or combined with seminar costs. Some traders travel with other traders for trading seminars or conferences. Even if you all go to a conference or seminar that winds up doubling as a ski trip, these expenses can be deductible if you follow the rules on travel business expenses closely:

- The actual costs of travel (e.g., plane fare, cab to airport, etc.) are deductible for out-of-town business trips. More significant than that, however, is the fact that you are also allowed to deduct the cost of meals and lodging. Your meals are deductible even if they are personal (i.e., not connected with business), although as with all deductible meals, only 50 percent of the cost is deductible (55 percent for long-haul truckers, certain airline, train, and bus employees, and certain merchant mariners). Additionally, no deduction will be allowed for meals or lodging to the extent the expense is "lavish or extravagant." Although this term is not defined in the tax rules, it has been interpreted to mean "unreasonable."

- Personal entertainment costs on the trip aren't deductible, but business-related costs such as dry cleaning, phone calls, and computer rentals are.

- Some allocations may be required if the trip is a combined business/pleasure trip. For example, if you fly to a location for five days of business meetings and stay on for an additional period of vacation, only the cost of meals, lodging, and so on, for the business days are deductible. Any expenses accrued on the personal vacation days are not deductible.

- On the other hand, if the trip is "primarily" business, the cost of the trip itself (i.e., plane or bus fare, etc.) can be deducted in its entirety. No allocation is required. Conversely, if the trip is primarily personal, none of the travel costs are deductible. An important factor in determining whether the trip is primarily business or personal is the amount of time spent on each, although this factor isn't the sole consideration.

- If the trip doesn't involve the actual conduct of business but is for the purpose of attending a convention, seminar, or similar event, you might be able to deduct it. The IRS checks the nature of these meetings carefully to make sure they are not vacations in disguise. Be careful to save all material that will be helpful in establishing the business or professional nature of this travel.

- The rules on deducting the costs for a spouse who accompanies you on a business trip are restrictive. No deduction is allowed unless the spouse is an employee of yours or your company and is also traveling for a business purpose.

Line 24b, Meals and entertainment
Many traders have meals with other traders to discuss their respective trading businesses. These traders seek advice and ideas for improvement, research, and strategies. In most cases, these meals qualify for a deduction.

Line 24c, Nondeductible amount
Fifty percent of meals and entertainment are not deductible, per IRS rules.

Line 25, Utilities
These expenses are usually included with indirect expenses allocated for the home office Form 8829. If you have a separate meter for your business usage, enter that amount here. Do not use this line for your phone and communications. Enter your communication costs on Part V where you list your Other Expenses.

Line 27, Other expenses, schedule C, page 2, Part V
Here is where you list all your other actual trading business product and service expenses. A partial list of these would include:

- Internet access providers used for business exclusively. If combined with personal use, then report them as indirect expenses on Form 8829 for your home office.
- Trading market information online services.
- Trading research products and services.
- Trading print publications and subscriptions.
- Trading gifts to other traders, brokers, and other business related persons (limited to $25 per person per year).
- Trading communication services (phone, fax, dial-up).
- Trading accessories not depreciated (small items less than $100).
- Training and seminars for trading after getting started in the business. Education, training, and seminars before you commence business operations (trader tax status) are either start-up costs (IRC § 195), investment expenses, or personal nondeductible expenses. See more guidance below.

- Trading chat room expenses.
- Trading tax and accounting fees. If you lack trader tax status, these expenses are reported as miscellaneous expenses on Schedule A (Itemized Deductions).
- Trading books.
- Trading miscellaneous expenses.
- Education expenses related to trading.

Education expenses is a tricky area as far as deductions go. If you incur education expenses to learn the trading business before you start trading, those expenses may not be deductible as education expenses. On the other hand, if you start your trading business and then take courses and seminars, you may deduct these expenses on your Schedule C. Here are the rules: A deduction is available if the education maintains or improves the skills related to your trade or business. Educational costs are also deductible if the education is required (e.g., by law or an employer) to keep your position or job.

Conversely, educational costs are not deductible if the education is required to get into a new field (as opposed to staying in the field) or qualifies you for a new trade or business.

Observation: Most traders are not required by anyone to take trading seminars or other education courses. A trader is his/her own employer (i.e., he or she is self-employed). Strictly speaking, a trader's educational costs (even those incurred before a trader actually begins trading) do not meet the spirit of the tax law for not allowing a deduction. In most cases, a trader takes these courses to "improve trading skills," not to qualify to enter the business. Take note that in the future, the SEC or CFTC may require day traders to qualify to enter the business, and they may require a minimum of educational courses. That requirement would change things here and perhaps disallow the current allowed deductions.

Line 28, Total expenses
Just total up all expenses.

Note: This amount is before your home office deduction on line 30.

Line 29, Tentative profit (loss)
See our transfer income strategies in line 6.

Line 30, Business use of the home
Form 8829 home office expenses are listed here to the extent you have net income; otherwise all except mortgage interest and real estate taxes remain a carryover to 2004 and are listed on Form 8829.

Line 31, Net profit (loss)
Just do the calculations on the form. In all cases, profitable traders should break even (because sufficient trading gains have been transferred from Form 6781 or Form 4797), and other traders should end up with a loss. You should never end up with a net income on Schedule C.

Line 32a
If you have a loss, check this box if "All your investment is at risk" in your trading business. Otherwise, leave blank.

Form 6781

Form 6781 is for entering commodity transactions or section 1256 contracts (also see IRS Publication 550 Glossary). The new section 1256 laws effectively applied mark-to-market accounting to all section 1256 contracts. It closed the loophole, because taxpayers had to mark all open gain positions to market at year-end, thereby doing away with deferring the gain side of the straddle transaction.

Section 1256 mark-to-market laws should not be confused with the mark-to-market (MTM) accounting tax law section 475(f): (1) for securities and (2) for commodities.

Congress and the IRS take away the concept of unrealized gains and losses (MTM makes them realized) and instead allowed gains and losses on section 1256 contracts to be treated as 60 percent long-term capital gains and losses (a lower tax rate) and 40 percent short-term capital gains and losses. This treatment gives commodities traders a significant tax benefit versus securities traders.

Congress also realized that many commodities traders were operating businesses trading, so they require options. Congress also passed a special rule to treat their commodities trading gains as earned income for purposes of self-employment taxation and contributions for retirement plans (only for dealers registered on an exchange).

Trading Gains and Losses

If you elected IRC § 475(f)(2) MTM accounting for commodities (or use it from the prior year), transfer your Form 6781 commodities trading gains and losses to Form 4797 (Sale of Business Property—Part II Ordinary Gains and Losses).

Form 4797, Part II (Ordinary gains and losses)

Traders with MTM accounting (IRC 475(f)) report their trading gains and losses on Form 4797 Part II—Ordinary Gains and Losses. Form 4797 instruction excerpts:

Traders Who Made a Mark-to-Market Election

> A trader in securities or commodities may elect under section 475(f) to use the mark-to-market method to account for securities or commodities held in connection with a trading business. Under this method of accounting, any security or commodity held at the end of the tax year is treated as sold (and reacquired) at its FMV on the last business day of that year.

Observation: Commodity trading is already subject to mark-to-market provisions in accordance with IRC § 1256 contract rules. For commodities traders, when you transfer your Form 6781 gains and losses to Form 4797, you are not changing any amounts, because the amounts are already marked to market; you are only changing the character of the income or loss. Form 6781 amounts are capital gain or loss (when they are transferred by the default method) on Schedule D (Capital Gains and Losses). By transferring Form 6781 to Form 4797, you convert your commodity trading gains and losses from capital gain or loss treatment to ordinary gain or loss treatment.

Unless you are a new taxpayer, the IRC § 475(f) election must be made by the due date (not including extensions) of the tax return for the year prior to the year for which the election becomes effective.

If you are a trader in securities or commodities with a mark-to-market election under section 475(f) in effect for the tax year, the following special rules apply:

- Gains and losses from all securities or commodities held in connection with your trading business (including those marked to market) are treated as ordinary income and losses, instead of capital gains and losses. As a result, the lower capital gain tax rates and the limitation on capital losses do not apply.
- The gain or loss from each security or commodity held in connection with your trading business (including those marked to market) is reported on Form 4797, line 10 (see the instructions for line 10 on page 4).
- The wash sale rule does not apply to securities or commodities held in connection with your trading business. (Wash sales don't apply to commodities anyway, because all unrealized gains and losses are treated as realized at year-end.)

For more details on the mark-to-market election and how to make it, see Pub. 550; Rev. Proc. 99-17, 1999-7 I.R.B. 52; and sections 475(e) and 475(f).

Form 4797 Instructions for line 10 on page 4.

Part II

If a transaction is not reportable in Part I or Part III and the property is not a capital asset reportable on Schedule D, report the transaction in Part II.

Line 10

Report other ordinary gains and losses, including gains and losses from property held one year or less, on this line.

Securities or commodities held by a trader who made a mark-to-market election

Report on line 10 all gains and losses from sales and dispositions of securities or commodities held in connection with your trading business, including gains and losses from marking to market securities and commodities held at the end of the tax year (see Traders Who Made a Mark-to-Market Election on page 2).

Attach to your tax return a statement, using the same format as line 10, showing the details of each transaction. Separately show and identify securities or commodities held and marked to market at the end of the year. On line 10, enter "Trader—see attached" in column (a) and the totals from the statement in columns (d), (f) and (g). Also, see the instructions for line 1 on page 3.

Observation: For the past twenty years we have followed a widely accepted practice of reporting one line item per brokerage account. All our example tax returns use this strategy on Form 4797 or Schedule D. In this case, it is only one line as follows: "Transfer commodity trading gains and losses from Form 6781—see Note."

Form 4797 Instructions for line 1.

Line 1

Enter on line 1 the total gross proceeds from:

- Sales or exchanges of real estate reported to you for 2003 on Form(s) 1099-S (or substitute statement) that you are including on lines 2, 10, or 20.
- Sales of securities or commodities reported to you for 2003 on Forms 1099-B (or substitute statements) that you are including on line 10 because you are a trader with a mark-to-market election under section 475(f) in effect for the tax year. See Traders Who Made a Mark-to-Market Election on page 2 and the instructions for line 10 on page 4.

Form 3115 (Change of Accounting Method)

If you elected IRC § 475(f)(2) mark-to-market accounting for 2003 by April 15, 2003, file a Form 3115 with your 2003 tax return.

Unlike the Form 3115 for securities traders, the Form 3115 for commodities traders does not need a section 481 adjustment. Commodities are already marked to market in accordance with section 1256 contract law. Therefore, no amount is generated from this change of accounting method, which is what a section 481 adjustment is for. The Form 3115 already filled out by GTT in our companion guides can be used for all commodities traders, whether you have gains or losses. Simply add your name and address to page 1, top and bottom.

HOME OFFICE DEDUCTIONS FOR TRADERS

If you qualify as a trader and have a home office (most do), you can save lots of extra taxes each year by deducting a home office. Be careful, because the rules are complex.

Many traders work out of an office in their home, and they should know about the strict rules that govern whether they can deduct their home office expenses. In our firm's experience, the average trader saves more than $6,000 per year from deducting their home office expenses.

Many active traders qualify as being in the trading business. For purposes of this discussion, when we mention "trader(s)," we refer to active traders who qualify as being in the business of trading. Nonactive traders and investors are not allowed to take a home office tax deduction.

A home office tax deduction is especially valuable because you are not spending extra money to generate a deduction. Instead, you are converting personal expenses into tax deductions. The IRS liberalized the home office deduction rules for tax years 1999 and afterwards. It is easier to qualify, but you still must make sure you meet the specific requirements as set forth. You may deduct your home office expenses if you meet any of the following three tests:

1. *Separate Structure Test:* You are allowed a deduction for the costs of a separate, unattached structure on your property. To qualify, the separate structure must be used exclusively and on a regular basis in connection with your trading business.

2. *Office Used for Meeting Patients, Clients, or Customers Test:* This test is not applicable to most traders, because traders don't have clients or customers.

3. *Principal Place of Business Test:* This third test is the one that many online traders have the best chance of satisfying. If you use your home office, exclusively and on a regular basis, as your principal place of business, you meet this third test. Two subtests are used to determine whether your home office is your principal place of business: the management or administrative activities test, and the relative importance/time test. If your home office satisfies either of these two subtests, it will be treated as your principal place of business.

   ■ *Management or administrative activities test:* Many traders use their home office to conduct administrative or management activities. These traders also must not have another fixed location where they conduct substantial administrative or management activities for their trading business. The IRS has been quoted as requiring the home office to be used exclusively and on a regular basis for a taxpayer's business administration or management. If your trading home office is your only home office, then meeting this principal place of business test is easily satisfied. If you use two trading offices, one at a day trading firm and the second in your home, some questions arise. Consider this example. Most traders in a day trading office come to work just before the markets open for trading and they leave soon after the markets close. Many of these traders also regularly use a home office for managing and administering their trading businesses. They use their day trading office for trading during market hours, and they use their home office (early in the morning, at night, and on weekends) for managing and administering their trading business. A trading business requires several hours per day of management and administration including accounting for trading buy/sell transactions and trading business expenses; trading risk assessment; trading market research; trader tax and financial planning and preparation; and computer hardware/software set up and maintenance. A trader meeting the facts and circumstances of this example (two offices) qualifies to use the home office deduction because the trader meets the management and administration subtest (assuming the trader also uses his or her home office exclusively and regularly for the trading business).

- *Relative importance/time test:* Two factors determine a trader's principal place of business using this test. First is the relative importance of the trading activities performed at each of a trader's offices. Second is the amount of time a trader spends at each office. Notice that this test assumes a trader has an office outside home in addition to his or her home office. The IRS says that it will first apply the relative importance test by comparing the activities performed at home with those carried on in another office outside the home. For the example of a trader using a day trading firm office during the day and a home office at night, we believe most traders will not meet this test. We believe that the relative importance of trading (buys and sells) is more important than management and administration. In the example of a trader with two offices, the trader met the management and administration test, so they do not need to meet the relative importance/time test. If a trader passes this relative importance test (they usually will not), then the time test is not necessary. If the trader is not sure about the relative importance test, then the time test is necessary.

Exclusive and Regular Use Requirements

A trader's home office must be used exclusively and on a regular basis in connection with their trading business. Exclusive means that traders must use their trading home office area only for their trading business. Traders cannot use their trading home office area for family living purposes, as a guest room, a TV room, a playroom for children, or for other nonbusiness purposes. A trader's home office area can simply consist of desks, chairs, TV(s) (for market information), computer(s), office equipment, file cabinet(s), a couch, and so on. This setting sounds like a home office library or family room, but it is not. If you do not meet the exclusive test, try to remove your personal usage from your trading home office area so you can meet this subtest. This requirement is not easy for traders living in expensive, big city apartments, like in New York City, where space is limited.

Regular use means that a trader must use a home office for his or her trading business on a continuous, ongoing, or recurring basis. Traders usually easily meet this test because they must spend many hours per day and every day in their trading business (to qualify for trader tax status in the first place). Most traders that use a day trading firm office also still spend several hours per day on management and administration activities in their home office.

Other tax benefits are connected to the home office deduction.

- *Travel expenses:* A trader with a home office may deduct travel expenses to (and from) a day trading firm office and other trading business destinations. Without a qualified home office, those travel expenses are treated as nondeductible commuting expenses.

Your home office expenses include the following:

- Direct expenses specifically traced to your trading home office, including painting, trading office build-ins, and repairs for your home office.
- Indirect expenses not specifically traced to your trading home office, including your general electric, oil and gas, water, sewer, lawn care, cleaning, insurance, and other home expenses including depreciation.

  The home office tax form (Form 8829) prorate these general home expenses based on square footage of your home office versus your total home. Your mortgage interest expenses and real estate taxes are included in these allocated indirect expenses. The amount of mortgage interest and real estate taxes not allocated to your home office is then deducted as itemized deductions on Schedule A.

Limitations on Home Office Deductions

You may deduct your home office expenses up to the amount of your net trading business income. Therefore, if you have a net trading loss for the tax year, you will not be allowed a home office deduction. Instead, you will be allowed to carry forward your home office expense to the following tax year. If you have sufficient trading business income the following year, you will be able to utilize your entire carry forward amount.

Home office expenses are reported on IRS Form 8829 (Expenses for Business Use of Your Home). Form 8829 calculates the allocated indirect expenses plus the direct expenses. Your net home office expenses are then transferred to your trading business Schedule C. If you don't have sufficient Schedule C net income, then the excess home office expense amount is reported on Form 8829 in the carry forward section. **Important:** For Schedule C and home office expense tax reporting strategy, see the Line-by-Line Guidance of Schedule C about the transfer of income strategy to drive the home office deduction.

Transfer income from Form 4797, Schedule D or Form 6781

If taxpayer has net trading gains, sufficient trading gains are transferred from Form 4797 Part II (or from Schedule D if not MTM or from Form 6781 for commodities traders) to Schedule C to cover the taxpayer's related trading expenses. This approach is used because Schedule C business expenses relate to trading gains. No change to the tax liability occurs as a result of this transfer for securities traders. Commodities traders can lose some 60/40 tax benefits as a trade-off to unlocking home office deductions.

For securities traders, we recommend this transfer to reduce the chance of the IRS questioning your Schedule C losses. If you have trading losses, obviously you can't do this transfer. If your trading gains are less than your trading expenses, transfer all your trading gains.

Note: Transfer enough gains to cover your Schedule C expenses including home office and section 179 depreciation. These amounts are only deductible to the extent you have income.

Effect of Home Office Deductions on Later Sales of Your Principal Residence

New IRS regulations further liberalize home office deductions by allowing taxpayers to protect more of their gain exclusion on sale of their residence by not allocating the home office gain to the overall home gain (providing your office is in your home and not a separate structure). This rule is intended to help more taxpayers by not making them afraid to take this deduction and home depreciation in fear of losing their exclusion. The only recapture in many sales will be depreciation taken to date. That is not a lost benefit, but rather a timing difference (you pick up income later for what you deduct now).

The Bottom Line: Most traders can qualify for a home office deduction by meeting the principal place of business test (subtests: management or administrative activities test, exclusive use test, and regular use test).

Under a 1997 law, homeowners who sell their homes can exclude as much as $250,000 (or $500,000 if you are married and filing jointly) of the gain from their federal taxable income.

To qualify for this full exclusion, you must have owned your home and lived in it as your primary residence for at least two of the five years before the sale. But if you used part of your home for business during the two-year ownership-and-use periods, the exclusion generally applied only to the gain attributable to the nonbusiness portion of your home. The new rule says homeowners don't have to allocate the gain between business and personal use, as long as the office was within their residence. However, as in the past, they still "must pay tax on the gain equal to the total depreciation they took after May 6, 1997," the IRS says.

Example: Suppose a lawyer bought a home in 1999 and sells it this year for a $13,000 profit. The lawyer used part of the house as his law office. He claimed depreciation deductions of $2,000 during those years. Under the new rules, the IRS says $11,000 of the gain would be tax-free. Only the $2,000 of the gain equal to the depreciation deductions would be taxable (at a maximum rate of 25 percent). Note that depreciation is "allowed" or "allowable," which means you are treated by the IRS as taking this depreciation whether you did or not. So you may as well take it and receive the related tax benefits.

This rule represents a big change from the old rules. The new regulations "can be applied retroactively," meaning that "taxpayers can go back and amend returns for any open years—typically within three years from the time the return was filed," and take advantage of the new rules. Some taxpayers still may decide not to claim the deduction because of fears it will trigger an IRS audit. Those fears probably are overblown, as long as you follow the rules carefully. Business traders, more than most taxpayers, really have a legitimate home office, and they should use this excellent tax deduction.

CHAPTER 7

Tax Planning for Traders

Wise taxpayers do tax planning before year-end. Traders have special circumstances that make year-end tax planning even more paramount. Certain moves can save you a fortune for next April 15.

YEAR-END TAX PLANNING STRATEGIES FOR TRADERS

Investors and active traders have tax-savings opportunities at year-end. Many investors sell losing positions toward the end of the year to lower their capital gains income and capital gains taxes (known as "tax loss selling").

Business traders with mark-to-market (MTM) accounting (IRC § 475) report unrealized gains and losses at year-end, so it's not necessary for them to exit their losing positions to gain tax savings. Traders have plenty of things they can do just before year-end to improve their tax situation, but it all depends on a trader's tax status.

Investors and active traders use the default cash method of accounting, which means they report realized gains and losses, and not open positions (unrealized gains and losses), at year-end. Cash method accounting also includes the dreaded wash sale and straddle loss deferral rules; certain realized losses are not allowed to be deducted on your current year's tax return; instead, they are carried over (deferred) to the following tax year, potentially raising your tax bill for the current year.

The most dreaded part of cash method accounting is the onerous excess capital loss limitation rules. Congress allows taxpayers to deduct a maximum loss of $3,000 per year, and the balance may be carried forward to future tax years (commodities and futures section 1256 contracts losses may also be carried *back* three tax years, although they can only be applied against section 1256 contract gains).

Many business traders elected MTM for securities only (because MTM is not beneficial for commodities) and thereby get around the less desirable aspects of cash method accounting. MTM business traders are exempt from the onerous wash sale and straddle loss deferral rules, and all losses are deductible as ordinary losses without any capital loss limitations. Many traders use the cash method for the current year and want to elect MTM in the following year, which raises further complications and requires other strategies.

Find Your Tax Status and Act Accordingly

Your first order of business in late November or early December is to determine what your tax status is for the current tax year. Did you rise to the level of business status (trader tax status) for the entire year, or a portion of the year? Will that portion of the year include the year-end?

Did you elect MTM IRC § 475 on time in the current tax year, or carry over that election from the prior tax year? Existing taxpayers must elect MTM by April 15 of the current tax year by attaching an election statement to their prior year tax return or extension. New taxpayers don't have a prior tax return, so they can elect internally (in their own books and records), within seventy-five days of inception.

Some taxpayers miss the MTM election filing and later realize they qualify as a de facto husband-wife general partnership because they have joint trading accounts and both worked as traders. Perhaps their de facto partnership made the necessary new taxpayer internal election with a verbal resolution. If you think you may qualify for a de facto partnership and need to use MTM accounting to deduct large losses in the current year, consult with a proven trader tax expert. Our firm handles many husband/wife trading partnerships.

If you elected MTM but don't qualify for trader tax status at year-end, you must use the cash method at year-end (and for any other portion of the year you did not qualify for trader tax status). If you are a business trader without MTM, you must use the cash method like any other investor. You can still take advantage of many business tax breaks, some of which require action before year-end.

Cash Method Accounting Trading Strategies to Lower Your Taxes at Year-end

If you are an active trader but don't qualify for business treatment (trader tax status)—or you do qualify but did not elect MTM IRC § 475—you must use the default cash method of accounting. Here are some tips for lowering your taxes at year-end:

- Manage your portfolio at year-end to defer unrealized capital gains and realize capital losses, which lowers your capital gains taxes.
- Hold investment securities positions for twelve months to avoid short-term capital gains (which are taxed at ordinary tax rates up to 35 percent) in order to benefit from long-term capital gains (which are capped at a 15 percent tax rate). The 2003 Tax Act lowered both rates, but it also widened the difference, making this strategy more beneficial than in prior years.
- Avoid wash sale and straddle loss deferrals by reentering similar, rather than identical, positions within thirty days. Sometimes wash sales are good; see below.
- Avoid purchasing mutual funds just after dividend declaration dates, which usually occur around the end of the year. Price often drops after dividends.

- Avoid capital loss carryovers. Don't exceed the $3,000 capital loss carryover. This carryover creates "tax baggage" for business traders.
- When planning for capital loss limitations and estimated taxes, anticipate mutual fund capital gain distributions.
- Avoid investment interest carryovers and investment expense limitations.
- Find out whether your hedge fund or investment company Form K-1s will report trading gains and losses using the cash or MTM methods of accounting (trader tax status and this accounting election is on the entity level).
- Consider allocating some of your taxable portfolio to tax-free investments and tax-free retirement accounts (with tax deductible or nondeductible contributions).
- Consider shifting income to other family members. Children younger than 14 are subject to the "kiddie tax" rules, which allow lower tax rates on the first $1,600 (for 2004) of unearned income (the excess is taxed at the parents' tax rates). Children 14 or older are exempt from the kiddie tax rules. Consider paying children wages to help in your trading business; you both are exempt from payroll taxes, and can benefit from the child's lower tax bracket rates. You can also set up fringe benefit plans for family members.
- Contribute appreciated securities to charity. You get a tax deductible contribution at the higher fair market value (FMV). You are exempt from capital gains taxes on the increase of FMV over purchase price. This approach is wiser than paying capital gains taxes and then contributing cash to the charity.
- Commodities and futures traders (with or without trader tax status) are automatically subject to another type of mark-to-market accounting, IRC section 1256. They report "economic" gains and losses and can't manage their income with some of the preceding strategies. Commodities losses can be carried back three tax years against commodities gains, so plan accordingly.
- If you are in low tax brackets in the current year and expect higher income and to be in high tax brackets the following year, you may want to reverse some of these strategies.

- Lower 2003 Tax Act rates apply for qualifying dividends and long-term capital gains.
- Arrange your investments to take advantage of the new lower tax rates on qualifying dividends, paid by domestic and qualifying foreign corporations. Pay careful attention to the detailed rules; most traders won't get these benefits, except on their segregated investment accounts.
- Dividends from money market funds, life insurance policies, real estate investment trusts (REITS, 90 percent portion), and some mutual funds do not qualify. Many mutual funds invest in bonds, currencies and other instruments that do not have qualifying corporate earnings and profit taxes.
- The holding period for qualifying dividends is 60 of 120 days beginning 60 days before the ex-dividend date, which will ruin this benefit for many traders (those who don't hold positions that long).
- The "effective date" for lower long-term capital gains rates is May 5, 2003.
- Shift investment income to children (with annual gift limits) to take advantage of the two lowest tax brackets (5 percent) on long-term capital gains.
- MTM traders can't manage trading gains and losses, but they have many other tax-saving opportunities, including net operating losses (NOL). Unlike traders who use the default cash method of accounting, MTM business traders (and all commodities and futures traders) report both realized and unrealized gains and losses at year-end.
- MTM business traders may not defer capital gains on trading positions, but can on segregated investment positions; segregated investments are not subjected to MTM.
- MTM business traders are not penalized with the onerous wash sale and straddle loss deferral rules and capital loss limitations; all realized and unrealized trading losses are deductible in the current tax year in full as ordinary losses (not capital losses).
- MTM business traders can have negative taxable income and carry back net operating losses (NOLs—the business portion of

trading expenses and trading losses) two tax years (or five years for 2001 and 2002 only).

- Carefully plan your NOLs in advance in order to receive immediate tax refund relief for prior years in which you have taxable income taxed at higher marginal rates. For example, if you have significant taxable income in 2001 but losses in 2002, try to increase your 2003 NOL so you can carry the NOL back to 2001. You won't be able to carry back a 2004 NOL for any benefit in 2002 and 2003 because you have losses in those carryback years. Instead, you can carry forward your 2004 NOL to 2005 and beyond (up to twenty years).

- Traders without MTM can still generate a NOL with their trading business expenses.

- MTM traders don't need to worry about tax loss selling. They can take profits early and not worry about trying to defer capital gains. They also don't have to worry about rushing to sell a losing position to lock in the tax loss; it is already locked in with MTM.

Switching to MTM from Cash Method Accounting Is Difficult If You Have Tax Baggage

Business traders may face complex issues when they consider switching to MTM from the default cash method (capital gains and losses). The most important issue concerns capital loss carryovers if you have any.

- Capital loss carryovers are the main culprit for putting traders out of business. Not being able to deduct your trading losses because of capital loss limitation and wash sale rules denies you the opportunity to get tax refunds from the IRS and your state to replenish your trading capital. It can accelerate your exit from a trading business.

- It's unwise not to obtain exemption from the capital loss limitation rules on securities if you are a business trader. What is nec-

essary is a little free education about how and when to elect
MTM IRC § 475. You can't tell the IRS later on to allow you to
use MTM. The IRS is strict about no late MTM elections.

- Many traders skip the MTM election when they start their trading business because they don't know about it, get the wrong
advice, or make the wrong decision about it. The latter is certainly the case if they get stuck with capital loss carryovers.

- You can carry back MTM losses for immediate tax refunds to
replenish your trading accounts rather than having carried-over
capital losses suspended to future years. Many traders never cash
in on those capital loss carryovers after having to exit a trading
business. They simply have no or little money left to invest for
capital gains, and the tax deductions are wasted.

- These non-MTM traders fall into the following tax trap, because
you can't have it both ways. If you have trading gains in the
following year, you want to keep the cash method to offset new
trading capital gains with capital loss carryovers. If you have
trading losses, you want to have MTM for ordinary loss treatment, as it's adding fuel to your fire to add to your capital
loss carryovers.

- If you have large trading losses by April 15, the election deadline,
it's probably safer to elect MTM to insure ordinary loss treatment.
Conversely, if you have large trading gains, it may be okay to skip
the MTM election and gamble on having net trading gains for the
year (and using your capital loss carryovers). If you have small
gains or losses, your MTM election decision is a gamble.

- Consider electing MTM on securities only (not commodities)
and utilizing other ways to generate capital gains to use up your
capital loss carryovers.

- Use up capital loss carryovers by trading commodities such as
the E-Minis, which may be similar to securities products you trade.
E-Minis and other commodities will not be subject to MTM
IRC § 475 treatment (unless you also elect MTM IRC § 475 on
commodities) and will instead generate capital gains and losses.

- Your first set of commodities gains will be tax-free because you will offset them with your capital loss carryovers. Afterwards, you will benefit from the lower tax rates on commodities: 60 percent is long-term capital gains (capped at a 15 percent tax rates) and 40 percent is short-term capital gains (which are taxed at up to 35 percent). Those rates translate to a maximum blended rate of 23 percent on commodities versus a maximum rate of 35 percent on short-term securities trading. Instead of trading the QQQ, an exchange-traded fund taxed as a security, trade the E-Mini, a similar market risk instrument taxed as a commodity.

- Traders have a large variety of new financial products to trade: ETFs, E-Minis, single-stock futures, plenty of new indexes, and options and futures on almost everything. Learn how all these new products are taxed—as securities or commodities—and consider that commodities have lower tax rates. This is covered in an earlier section of this book.

- Another way to use up capital loss carryovers is to segregate some securities as investment positions, not subject to MTM. For starters, until you use up your capital loss carryovers. their capital gains are tax-free. Afterwards, if you hold them for twelve months, the capital gains are taxed at the lower long-term capital gains rates. If you believe the markets are trending higher, this strategy may be timely.

- Limit capital losses and then convert some into wash sales for ordinary loss treatment with MTM next year. The higher your capital loss carryovers, the harder it is for you to make the switch to MTM. First, try to limit the amount of your capital loss carryovers.

- If you already reached the capital loss limitation, sell profitable positions and keep open losing positions. Hedge accordingly. Don't sell any additional losing positions. More losses won't benefit your current year's taxes, and they will make your MTM election in the following year a tougher decision to make.

- If you do sell losing positions that generate a capital loss carryover, consider reentering the position within thirty days to create a beneficial wash sale condition (in all other cases, wash sales are not beneficial). If you elect MTM in the following year, wash sale loss deferrals are better than capital loss carryovers because wash sales can be converted into ordinary losses (with an MTM election the following year), whereas capital loss carryovers may never be converted into ordinary losses (and remain as your tax baggage).

Pay Your Bills Early for Additional Tax Savings, Providing You Don't Trigger AMT Taxes and AGI Limitations

- Most taxpayers should consider paying more bills early before year-end to maximize current year tax deductions.
- Taxpayers and most sole proprietor business traders use the cash method of accounting rather than the accrual method of accounting. This treatment is different from the cash versus MTM methods of accounting. Those methods apply to trading gains and losses. Cash accounting is when bills are paid; accrual accounting is when expenses are incurred. Credit card purchases are cash items on the date purchased, not when the credit card bill is paid.
- Normal taxpayers and investors may want to consider "bunching" their itemized deductions into the current year and then taking a standard deduction in the following year. The point is to avoid coming up short on the standard deduction every year and wasting some itemized deductions such as charitable contributions.
- Again, watch out for that dreaded alternative minimum tax (AMT), because many itemized deductions are not deductible for AMT (including investment interest, all taxes, and miscellaneous itemized deductions).
- Calculate whether your adjusted gross income (AGI) will be significantly lower in the following tax year. Many itemized deductions and other tax breaks are limited by AGI levels. Medical expenses

are deductible in excess of 7.5 percent of your AGI. Miscellaneous itemized deductions, including nonreimbursed employee business expenses, job-hunting expenses, education expenses (except business traders), and investment expenses are only deductible in excess of 2 percent of AGI. Also beware of casualty losses.

■ Business expenses are not added back for AMT tax calculations, so business traders should lower their AGI to unlock tax breaks. Business traders should accelerate expenses for two good reasons:

> (1) Additional business expenses lower your taxable income, which lowers your tax bill. If you have a net operating loss, additional expenses increase your NOL and related NOL tax refunds. The sooner the better when it comes to NOLs, because you can only go back two tax years.
> (2) A business trader should know about many special tax breaks that are based on lower AGI levels. These breaks are "phased out" at higher levels of AGI.

■ A business trader's AGI can significantly fluctuate from year to year. One year their AGI may be high and most tax breaks are phased out. In other years, they have low AGI and their window opens to put in place many special tax breaks. For example, if your AGI is less than $100,000, you can convert a taxable retirement plan into a Roth IRA, which can convert "timing" tax-free buildup into "permanent" tax-free buildup (every trader's dream scenario). More details on this strategy follow.

Here are some other tax breaks limited to certain AGI levels: IRA contributions, Roth IRA conversions, education credits, Coverdell education savings accounts, interest on student loans, exemptions for children, earned income credit, real estate passive activity losses, and social security income exclusions, to name a few. Read about them and the phase-out amounts at www.irs.gov.

Buy More Equipment Before Year-End

If you have trading gains in excess of your trading business expenses, accelerate fixed asset purchases before year-end to maximize IRC section 179 (100 percent) depreciation. IRC § 179 depreciation requires income; otherwise you must carry it over to the following year. Section 179 depreciation limits are $102,000 for 2004 (raised from $100,000 in 2003). If you don't have income, opt for accelerated bonus depreciation instead.

Deduct Health Insurance Premiums and Retirement Plans to Lower AGI

AGI deductions for sole proprietor businesses (Schedule C) include, but are not limited to, retirement plan deductions, health insurance premiums, and 50 percent of self-employment taxes. The problem for traders is that, unlike other sole proprietor businesses, they may not take these AGI deductions unless they create some earned income. Trading gains with or without MTM IRC § 475 are not earned income. Traders can form an entity for their trading business and have their entity pay them, as owner/manager, a fee.

This administration fee is reported on a Schedule C, which is earned income subject to self-employment taxes and which can drive a health insurance premium deduction and contribution to a tax-deductible retirement plan.

Alternatively, a trader can pay a spouse a fee for helping them administer the trading business, with the requirement that the spouse not be an owner of the trading business. A Schedule C owner may not pay himself or herself a fee or salary.

If the husband and wife are both owners, then they cannot file a Schedule C. Instead, they are a de facto general partnership and must file a partnership tax return. A guaranteed payment can then be declared in lieu of a fee to accomplish the same earned income result.

If you paid your spouse money during the year and he or she did help you in your trading business, you may be able to structure this arrangement all at year-end or early in the following year. Consult with a trader tax expert if you have further questions. It can be well worth it.

Paying fees to your children over age fourteen also lowers your AGI.

Establish Favorable Mini 401(k) Retirement Plans Before Year-End

Establish a Mini 401(k) retirement plan for you and/or your spouse before year-end with nominal funds. The balance of your tax deductible contribution can be calculated and paid after year-end.

All qualified retirement plans must be established before year-end, including 401(k) plans, Mini 401(k) plans, profit-sharing plans, and defined benefit plans. Qualified plans must be fully funded for annual contributions by the due date of your tax return, including extensions (up to October 15 of the following year).

IRA and Roth IRA plans must be established and contributions must be made by April 15 of the following year. SEP IRA plans, another type of profit-sharing plan for business owners, may be both established and funded up until the due date of your tax return, including extensions. If you miss the Mini 401(k) plan setup before year-end, use a SEP IRA instead.

Otherwise, Mini 401(k) plans are the most attractive for traders. You need fee income rather than trading income to fund a retirement plan. Therefore, owners/managers need a trading or investment entity such as a general partnership, LLC, or S-corporation to pay them a fee or salary before year-end.

Recent tax law changes increased the annual profit-sharing contribution limit from $40,000 for 2003 to $41,000 for 2004.

Make Use of Roth IRAs

Roth IRAs are especially attractive for traders. Their main tax features are permanent tax-free savings on portfolio income, and traders know how to maximize portfolio savings. Roth IRA contributions (limited to $3,000 per year) are not tax deductible, but the corresponding good news is that distributions in retirement are not taxable.

Traditional IRA contributions (limited to $3,000 per year) are tax deductible (up to certain AGI levels), but the corresponding bad news is that distributions in retirement are taxable at the higher ordinary income tax rates (up to 35 percent).

Roth IRAs provide for permanent tax savings on the portfolio income buildup, whereas traditional IRAs (and qualified retirement plans) only provide temporary tax savings. Traditional IRAs may not be attractive for traders.

It might be a better idea to buy and hold securities in taxable accounts for the long term—no tax is due until sale of the securities and lower long-term capital gains tax rates (up to 15 percent) apply.

A Note of Caution: If you operate a business (trading or otherwise) in a retirement account, the IRS may classify it as a prohibited transaction which makes you subject to penalties. See our earlier section on Trading Your Retirement Funds.

Note: All retirement plan contributions require earned income.

Get More from a Roth IRA Conversion

Roth IRAs are ideal for traders, but many traders can't accumulate a sizeable account with a small $3,000 nondeductible contribution per year, which you can make even if you have other retirement plans. As a better solution, you may convert an existing retirement plan into a Roth IRA. The one caveat is that you must pay all income taxes on the ordinary income portion of the conversion in the year of conversion. The requirement is that your modified AGI is less than $100,000 in the year of conversion, before the converted income is added in. The conversion rules are complex, so visit www.irs.gov to learn more. You may only convert from an IRA to a Roth IRA, so if you have a qualified retirement plan, do a rollover IRA direct transfer first. The IRS treats the Roth-converted amount as ordinary income (an early withdrawal), but you are exempt from the additional normal early withdrawal excise tax penalties of 10 percent. Not included in ordinary income are nondeductible contributions (and certain employer matched contributions in 401(k) plans).

If your existing retirement plans have been battered by the markets, it's an ideal time to consider this conversion. You will have lower conversion income taxed at ordinary rates and the recovery of these assets will be tax-free. So if you had a low income year in 2004, it can be worth your while to make this conversion. Rather than carry back a NOL, which can lead to questions from the IRS (which you don't want if you are a close call on trader tax status), do a Roth conversion to use up your losses. Don't just stop at zero taxable income, consider taking advantage of the lower tax brackets with some positive taxable income. You can stop wherever you like by only converting a portion of your retirement plans to the Roth IRA.

Use Fringe Benefits Plans and Flexible Spending Accounts

If you are interested in opportunities to convert more of your non-deductible family expenses into deductible business expenses, you should learn about fringe benefit plans. Most small businesses, including trading businesses, overlook fringe benefit plans; many larger companies rely on fringe benefit plans to attract and retain employees.

Fringe benefits, commonly known as "perks," include retirement plans; health, life, and disability insurance; education, dependent care, and adoption assistance; meals, lodging, and parking; and many other types of plans. Self-employed individuals (and pass-through entity owner/employees) who want to benefit from fringe benefit plans can do so if their spouses work for the business. By covering employees and spouses, they become entitled to benefits by virtue of being the spouse of an employee. Learn more in an earlier section on Fringe Benefit Plans.

Choose the Right Entity Early

You still may have time before year-end to choose the right entity for your trading business to provide the tax benefits you need (retirement plans, health insurance premiums, and fringe benefit plans among them) for the current tax year. If you want to use your entity for the following year, it's beneficial to form the entity just before year-end and to commence its operations on January 1 of the following year.

If you commence your business operations after the start of the tax year, you will have a more complex tax filing for the following year; with sole proprietor operations for the first part of the year and the entity operations for the balance of the tax year.

Traders prefer pass-through entities to avoid double taxation in a C-corporation; on both the entity level (up to a 35 percent tax rate) and again on the individual level (up to 15 percent, if there are qualifying dividends). Pass-through entities have single taxation on only the individual level (rates up to 35 percent).

Traders also prefer pass-through entities to utilize ordinary losses on their individual tax returns, which allows them to offset other types of income and to get NOL carryback tax refunds. Losses are often trapped in C-corporations for many years to come.

Plan Your Business Start-up, Suspension, and Exit Well

Many important tax-planning issues need to be considered when you start up your trading business, when you suspend it, and when you exit it. The key in all cases is to maximize your business expenses and to use MTM accounting during the period of business activity (not before or after it). Expenses paid outside the period of business activity may be start-up expenses, investment expenses (restricted and limited), or nondeductible expenses.

Trading losses outside the period of business activity may not utilize MTM accounting, meaning those capital losses will be subject to the capital loss limitation.

If the business activity stops before year-end, the trader must deal with the onerous wash sale and straddle loss deferral rules at year-end. Before year-end, if you believe you are falling short of qualification, try to increase your trading activity by trading tiny amounts or taking small risks. Commissions are low enough these days to make this strategy worthwhile.

If you know you are exiting your trading business, make sure to pay all your business expenses before you close your trading accounts (or slow the activity to a point you no longer qualify). If you use MTM, you can mark all open positions to market on the date of exit and start with that market value for cash accounting going forward. Play it safer and sell all open positions before you exit the trading business. However, most traders don't know they exited until after the fact.

If you exit your trading business and have an open section 481 adjustment, you will have to report the remaining deferred income in the year of exit (and it may trigger estimated taxes in the quarter you exit). It may pay to try to continue to qualify through year-end to defer a section 481 adjustment one more year.

If you stop trading for awhile but plan to resume soon, you are in a complex situation without much guidance from the IRS. It's wise to reelect MTM in the following year in case the IRS considers you to have exited and then reentered a trading business. You should consult with a proven trader tax expert.

Consider Start-up Expenses

In general, your costs for acquiring a capital asset, including the start of a business, are added to the cost basis of your asset and not deducted until the business is sold or closed.

With a special rule for start-up expenses (IRC § 195), you may amortize these expenses over not less than sixty months on a straight-line basis. Start-up expenses must meet three requirements: (1) expenses must be paid in connection with investigating the creation of your trading business (easy for traders); (2) they must be a normal expense of the business (also easy for traders); and (3) they must not be interest, taxes, or research and development, each of which has its own tax treatment.

Many traders spend considerable funds before entering a trading business. They attend seminars, educational programs, buy computers, and start using trading tools for mock trading. Later, when they see success from simulated trading, they open a brokerage account and start their actual trading activity. It's wise to open your trading account early and trade small sums with small risk before you pay for many business expenses. That avoids start-up expense complications and deferred deductions.

Pay Education Expenses After You Start Trading

Education expenses are only deductible as business expenses after you start your trading business. If you are already in a trading-related profession or business, such as a stock broker, then it's deductible for "maintaining and improving your job or business skills."

Education expenses may not be lumped in with start-up expenses. Investors can not deduct education expenses, even after trading (because they don't have business status). Education expenses for qualifying institutions (undergraduate or post-graduate school) can be utilized for education credits.

Trading schools are not qualifying institutions, but room for interpretation may allow you to aggressively consider trading schools as a way to investigate a trading business and then include these expenses as amortizable start-up expenses.

Make Timely Tax Payments to Avoid Penalties and Interest

Trading and investment income is subject to the estimated tax payment rules. This income is not part of an employee W-2; therefore no employer withheld your taxes. If you are late with estimated tax payments, consider asking your employer (if you have one) to withhold additional amounts from your paycheck at year-end. A tax loophole treats all W-2 tax withholding as being ratably done throughout the tax year.

Estimated tax payment rules call for paying your tax obligations on a quarterly basis. Read about these rules at www.irs.gov. Read about the "safe harbor" rules, which provide for paying a lower amount based on your prior year's taxes. In general, these rules work as follows: You may owe an underestimated tax penalty for the current year if the total of your withholding and estimated tax payments did not equal at least the smaller of 90 percent of your current year tax liability, or 100 percent of your prior year tax liability (the "safe harbor rule"). If your adjusted gross income (AGI) for the prior year was more than $150,000 ($75,000 if your filing status is married filing a separate return), substitute 110 percent for 100 percent.

Estimated tax payment rules are not a good match for trading businesses and provide headaches for many traders who face the following problem: They may have large trading gains in the first quarter only to lose some or all of it in the later quarters. If they pay Q1 estimated taxes, then they must wait until the following tax year to file their tax returns and get these refunds back. One could argue that if you lost money in the later quarters, it was safer to leave some capital with the IRS rather than in your trading account.

Some traders consider the underestimated nondeductible tax penalty of 5 percent per annum an attractive "margin loan" rate. The IRS changes the rate often, and the current rate is fairly low. Five percent is the published rate for April 16, 2004 through June 30, 2004. Even if you want to borrow from the IRS as long as possible (until April 15, the tax return due date) when you have to pay 90 percent of your taxes or be subject to additional penalties and interest), it's a good idea to pay some or all of your state taxes before year-end to maximize your itemized deductions for additional tax savings.

Note: State taxes are not deductible for alternative minimum tax (AMT), so you gain nothing from paying early if you don't get a tax benefit. Learn more about AMT taxes at www.irs.gov.

Get an Extension of Time to File, But Not to Pay

Trader tax law is complex, so if you aren't finished with your tax preparation on time (by April 15), don't panic, you are entitled to a six-month extension of time to file your actual tax return. This extension only applies to filing your actual tax return; it does not apply to paying what you owe in taxes.

The IRS and states want full payment of your taxes, based upon your best estimate, by the original due date of April 15. When you file after April 15, if you don't pay 90 percent or more of your actual tax liability with your timely extension, the IRS and most states treat the extension as invalid, rendering your returns late and subject to late filing and late payment penalties (5 percent per month up to five months for 25 percent total penalties). You are also subject to interest expense on all tax payments made after April 15, whether your extension is valid or not.

Example of Year-End Tax Planning for a Trader

Joe Trader converts unutilized unrealized capital losses from the current year into fully deductible ordinary losses in the following year. Joe Trader is a cash method (non-MTM) securities trader. On December 1 of the current tax year, Joe calculates current year-to-date net capital losses in the amount of $25,000. On the same day, Joe also calculates net unrealized trading losses on his open trading positions in the amount of $50,000. As a cash method trader, he is limited to a net capital loss deduction of $3,000 for the current tax year.

Joe plans to elect MTM for the following year, by April 15, so his following year securities trading gains and losses will be ordinary and not capital. Joe is happy to avoid the prospect of increasing his already unutilized capital loss carryovers.

Joe does not have a quality trade accounting program, and he is not certain of his wash sales and straddles. He figures he can skip this headache because he can't imagine that his deductible capital loss would end up being less than his capital loss limitation of $3,000.

Joe should know that a wash sale or straddle loss deferral may be better taxwise than a capital loss carryover, because he is electing MTM for the following year. In most cases, wash sale and straddle loss deferrals become part of a section 481(a) ordinary loss adjustment the following year. However, a capital loss carryover can never be recovered as an ordinary loss. Joe should calculate his proper wash sale and straddle loss deferrals to take advantage of this tax benefit. Our GTT TradeLog software program calculates wash sales and 481(a) adjustments.

When thinking about his open positions in December, Joe figures his current year-to-date capital losses already far surpass the $3,000 capital loss limitation, so why take more capital losses before year-end? They won't help lower his current year tax liability.

Joe further figures that capital loss carryovers are harder to utilize in the following year because he will be generating ordinary rather than capital gains from trading with MTM, and he will have few segregated investment positions to generate capital gains.

The smart move for Joe in December is to not sell his open losing positions and instead try to hold them through year-end. If the market risk is too great, Joe can hedge the open positions with indexes. In this way, Joe will convert unutilized current year unrealized capital loss carryovers into a negative section 481(a) adjustment that is an ordinary loss in the following year.

Joe solved two prolems with one move. He lowered his capital loss carryover, and he also increased his ordinary tax loss in the following year.

Joe can be even more clever by selling open unrealized gain positions before year-end. That action will reduce his capital-loss carryover and increase his section 481(a) adjustments, respectively.

Note: If Joe had the reverse fact pattern and had net unrealized capital gains instead of unrealized capital losses, it would be imperative for Joe to sell all those unrealized capital gains before year-end to offset his $25,000 of realized capital losses to date.

The Bottom Line: The tax code is complex for all taxpayers. For traders it's even more complex, with the myriad of investment rules and complexities of trader tax status. To make things even more difficult, the tax code has different breaks for different income levels, and traders move quickly between these levels. How can a trader keep one eye on the markets and another on mastering the tax code? The answer is they can't, so they need a trader tax expert to help. A general checkup is most effective just before the end of the year.

CHAPTER SUMMARY

Taxes are never an easy thing, but the more you can do before the tax year is over, the more time and money you will save when April 15 rolls around. Divide your tax planning into pre- and post-April 15 responsibilities, and it will make your life easier.

CHAPTER 8

Extensions

Extensions are always a good idea. Tax issues are complex, and the more time you have to deal with them, the better chance you have of making sure you get all the tax benefits coming to you. On or before April 15, you should file an extension, which gives you an additional six months to file (the extension actually expires on August 15, but a second extension will give you until October 15).

FILING AN EXTENSION

An extension gives you extra time to file, but not to pay. If you don't pay at least 90 percent of what taxes you owe when you file your extension, your extension will be designated invalid, meaning your return will be considered late and subject to late filing and late payment penalties (5 percent per month up to five months). You are also subject to interest expense on all tax payments made after April 15, whether your extension is valid or not.

Play it safe and pay 100 to 125 percent of your estimated liability. Why pay extra? This amount gives you a cushion for errors in trade accounting, and any overpayment can be applied to current-year estimated income taxes (especially if you are profitable in the first quarter of the following year). A good rule of thumb for traders is to pay your taxes on a conservative basis (to avoid interest and penalties) but file your tax returns on an aggressive basis (because that's where the real savings are).

First Automatic Extension

If you are not ready to file your individual income tax return by April 15, the due date, you are entitled to file a federal automatic extension by April 15. The application is made on Form 4868 (Application for Automatic Extension of Time to File U.S. Individual Income Tax Return). Some states accept the federal extension but most require their own form.

Filing valid extensions by April 15 automatically changes your tax return due date to August 15. A valid extension means that you must pay a minimum of 90 percent of your tax liability (for federal liability; some states differ) with the extension filing. This is not an extension to pay your tax, it is only an extension to file the tax return.

Remember to attach your MTM IRC § 475 election statement to your federal extension filed by April 15, the election due date. See Chapter 2 to learn more.

Second Extension

If you are still not ready to file your individual income tax return by August 15, the first extended due date, you are entitled to file a federal second extension by August 15. Some states accept the federal extension but most require their own form. A granted second extension changes your tax return due date to October 15. The second extension is not automatic (unlike the first extension), and you need to receive it back from the IRS marked "Granted."

The second extension is filed on an IRS Form 2688, and it must be postmarked by August 15. This filing assumes, of course, that you already filed a valid first extension by April 15, and that you properly paid your taxes with the first extension.

When you file the second extension form, you need to include a reason for the extension. The reason can be something such as, "taxpayer is awaiting additional expense documentation and a complete and accurate tax return can not be filed at this time." For all practical purposes, these extensions are automatic. We have never had one not granted in more than twenty years of CPA tax practice.

Why First and Second Extensions Are Recommended

With the first extension, you get an additional four months to work on your tax return. With the second extension, you get an additional two months. This additional time helps make sure tax returns are accurate and have the best tax savings results.

Many traders have trading losses in a given year. Many of these traders with mark-to-market (MTM) accounting will be entitled to file a net operating loss carryback refund claim on Form 1045. Filing a Form 1045 refund claim is tantamount to filing amended tax returns for your prior two tax years. This process takes time and requires care. Additionally, the IRS will review these Form 1045 refund claims, and we believe you are better off waiting until after April 15, when fewer agents are around to look over returns. This same concept works for all taxpayers. Technically, a Form 1045 return is not filed with your Form 1040, but it's wise to prepare them together.

Most traders have complex tax files because they have trader tax status. Traders usually don't complete their own trade accounting and record organization until the middle of March. If traders use a tax preparation firm, they don't receive your tax information until March. They then have only one month to complete your tax return. Oftentimes, additional information is needed. For example, if you have elected MTM, you might not have handled the opening and closing MTM values correctly. If you are cash basis (i.e., you haven't elected MTM), you might not have handled wash sales correctly.

Maybe you have not taken full advantage of home office deductions and all the expenses you are entitled to. More time is needed to get it all right and prepare the return that is most advantageous to you.

Many traders elected MTM accounting for the first time. This election requires additional work because a Form 3115 must be prepared.

The key is knowing whether you may owe money with the extension. Traders with large losses are surely in refund situations, and filing the extension is easy. Traders with large gains owe money, and most of the tax return needs to be prepared to see what you owe.

The other key decision to make by April 15 is whether or not you are electing MTM § 475 for the current tax year, the election statement of which must be attached to your first automatic extension.

New Reasons Why an Extension Is Wise

In 2004, the IRS announced significant new exam targets, policies, and procedures—random audits (exams), more audits of high net-worth taxpayers, and more. The IRS needs to help balance the government's budget, so suffice to say, it is back in the exam business with new support from Congress. When it comes to traders, the IRS is more interested in examining business traders, part-time traders, and money-losing traders.

Considering these developments, it is more prudent than ever to file extensions and mark-to-market (MTM) elections by April 15. Such a move will then allow traders to file their actual tax returns in the summer months or even as late as October 15. It's wise to be conservative on tax payments or refunds and aggressive with your tax return filings.

Filing your tax return after April 15 may significantly reduce your chance of triggering one of the previously stated IRS audit initiatives.

Many advantages and few disadvantages come from using extensions. One possible disadvantage is delaying a refund.

For traders with large losses and carryback refunds, be patient and file in May or June, which offers several advantages:

- You have more time to file and work out a better and more accurate tax return.
- You can consider your activity for the year and how it may affect your tax-filing strategy. For example, if you start to generate large income in an existing year, you might want to be more aggressive in the previous year.

Waiting may lessen your chance of being audited by the IRS or your state tax authority. Many IRS examinations are selected before you file, and many IRS agents are reassigned for training or other duties after the tax-filing season crunch ends on April 15. Most sophisticated taxpayers and wealthy individuals always file close to the last possible day, when the second extension is due October 15.

Read newspapers such as *The Wall Street Journal* near April 15 and August 15. They will provide stories about the many advantages of extensions. The early bird gets the worm, but you are the worm and the IRS is the bird. Patience is a virtue, which does not mean laziness, however, so get your numbers together and file an accurate extension.

Extension Filing Strategies

Some traders owe estimated taxes for the first quarter of the current year. With an extension filing, you can skip the first quarter estimated tax payment and instead pay an extra amount with your extension for the previous tax year.

When you file your previous year's return, you can apply the overpayment credit toward the current year's estimated taxes.

This strategy solves two problems with one move. You overpay previous year taxes to give yourself a cushion against inaccurate estimates (or changing your mind about being aggressive on expense deductions or other tax-savings strategies) and/or you pay your current year first-quarter estimates.

If it turns out you have little or no credit toward the current year, you just pay more estimated taxes for June 15 or September 15. Your tax return looks better showing a credit applied rather than a refund requested.

Consequences of Not Filing a
Valid Extension and Filing a Late Tax Return

If you file your tax return late (i.e., after the valid extension due date or without a valid extension), you will be subject to tax penalties and interest assessed on the amount of taxes you owe.

Penalties and Problems Caused by Paying Taxes Late

We strongly advise you to pay at least 90 percent of your tax liabilities by April 15. This payment will ensure that your extensions are valid and the penalties don't apply.

If you can't pay what you owe, it may be a better idea to file on time to avoid late-filing penalties. See the following.

IRS NOTICES AND BILLS,
PENALTIES, AND INTEREST CHARGES

The following is from the Payment Plan/Installment Agreement information on the IRS website.

April 15 is the deadline for most people to file their 2003 individual income tax return and pay any tax owed. During processing, the return is checked for mathematical accuracy, and the tax due is compared to all amounts paid. If there is any money owed, you will be sent a bill. There are several important things you should know about collection notices and bills. Generally, interest is charged on any unpaid tax from the due

date of the return until the date of payment. The interest rate is determined every three months and is the federal short-term rate plus
3 percent. Interest is compounded daily. If you file on time but don't pay
all amounts due on time, you'll generally have to pay a late payment
penalty of one-half of one percent of the tax owed for each month, or
part of a month, that the tax remains unpaid from the due date, up to
25 percent. The one-half of one percent rate increases to one percent if the
tax remains unpaid ten days after the IRS issues a notice of intent to levy.

If you owe tax and don't file on time, the total late payment penalty is
usually five percent of the tax owed for each month, or part of a month,
that your return is late and the tax is unpaid, up to five months. The late
file penalty continues at ½ percent a month up to 25 percent on unpaid
amounts. If your return is over sixty days late, the minimum penalty for
late filing is the smaller of $100 or 100 percent of the tax owed.

You must file your return and pay your tax by the due date to avoid
interest and penalty charges. Often the funds necessary to pay your tax
can be borrowed at a lower effective rate than the combined IRS interest and penalty rate.

To ensure your payment on a bill for tax is credited properly, be sure
to return the tear-off stub on your bill and use our return envelope.
Please make your check or money order payable to the United States
Treasury. Enter the primary social security number or employer identification number, the tax year and form number and your telephone number on your check or money order, and send it to the address provided.

The penalties for filing late and paying late may be abated if you
have reasonable cause for being late. If you're billed for either penalty
and feel you have reasonable cause, send your explanation along with
the bill to your service center, or call the IRS at (800) 829-1040 for
assistance. Generally, interest charges may not be waived; they continue
to accrue until all assessed tax, penalties, and interest are paid in full.
Also, any reasonable cause exception to the penalty for failure to pay tax
cannot be determined until the tax is first paid in full.

If you believe there is an error on your notice or bill, write to the IRS
office that sent it to you within the time frame given. You should provide

photocopies of any records that may help correct the error. Also, you may call (800) 829-1040 for assistance. If you are correct, we will make the necessary adjustment to your account and send you a corrected notice.

For more information about IRS notices and bills, refer to Publication 594, Understanding the Collection Process. More information about penalty and interest charges is contained in Publication 17, Your Federal Income Tax.

Just Pay It

Some traders know they owe money but don't pay, preferring to use the money to trade. They consider it a "margin loan" from the government.

When it comes to estimated taxes, due on a quarterly basis throughout the year, this strategy may work well for some traders—they may lose money later in the year, and those tax liabilities may disappear.

However, for annual taxes, this strategy can lead to disaster. The prior tax year liabilities do not disappear, and many traders wind up losing their tax money in the markets just after April 15. Be wise and pay what you owe on April 15.

If you can't pay what you owe, pay as much as you can (keeping money in the market is not a reasonable excuse to not pay). While you will still have an invalid extension, you have a chance at penalty abatement because you made a good-faith efffort to pay what you owed.

The worst thing you can do is ignore it. If the IRS contacts you before they receive a payment, you don't stand a very good chance of gaining penalty abatement.

Of course if you lost money, you merely need to file an extension.

Extensions of Time to Make MTM Elections

A large number of traders missed the MTM election for IRC § 475(f) by the due date of April 15 of the current tax year (e.g., April 15, 2004, for tax year 2004). Without MTM, a trader is stuck with capital loss treatment and cannot deduct trading losses as ordinary losses. This limitation significantly reduces the trader's opportunity for net operating loss refunds.

Late MTM Elections

If you act by October 15, you may be able to receive an extension of time to file your MTM election. Section 301.9100-1 of the IRC, "Extensions of time to make elections," provides relief for late elections. Note the maximum extension period is six months. One serious drawback is you must seek this relief with a private letter ruling.

Private Letter Rulings

The Private Letter Ruling (PLR) procedure is painstaking and expensive, and for traders seeking relief to use MTM (the six month MTM extension relief), the chance of success is extremely small.

As of this writing, the IRS website had published only four PLRs for traders seeking to use MTM, and all were denied.

Here are the four PLR rulings:

1. www.irs.gov/pub/irs-wd/0209052.pdf
2. www.irs.gov/pub/irs-wd/0209053.pdf
3. www.irs.gov/pub/irs-wd/0209054.pdf
4. www.irs.gov/pub/irs-wd/0304006.pdf

It is useful to read the IRS rulings in all four cases. In each case, the IRS discussed Reg § 301.9100-1 "Extensions of time to make elections." The trader did not qualify for Reg § 301.9100-1 relief.

CHAPTER 9

Proprietary Trading

Proprietary trading firm agreements and tax issues come in all forms and sizes, with a variety of tax, legal, and risk issues. Proprietary trading offers greater leverage than what is available to retail traders. That leverage is a double-edged sword, though. Leverage has an upside to greater and faster profits, but the downside is more risk, more costs, and pitfalls. Before you leap to "take the money and run," become an educated consumer first.

In addition to this chapter, there is more tax information for proprietary traders in Chapter 1.

Currently, many of the proprietary trading firms use the limited liability company (LLC) model, inviting you to join the firm as an LLC member. Some firms also offer to hire you as either independent contractors or employees. Other firms will allow you to trade with them as customers just like other retail traders, but then you don't get additional leverage over the pattern day trader rules (currently 4:1 leverage). If the firm is a broker dealer or a member of an exchange, you are required to have a brokerage license.

Before you leap into one of these deals, read the fine print of the agreements and see how they stack up.

A Note of Caution: WorldCo, during the bull market one of the largest and most successful proprietary trading firms, recently went out of business. Many of their prop traders got burned (they did not get their capital back). Recent rumors claim the SEC is looking closer at the proprietary trading firms, and that they are forcing some changes. Now is a good time to ask your firm questions, get better educated on the legal and tax issues, and reevaluate your situation.

LOOK CLOSELY AT AGREEMENTS

When you take a job or position with a proprietary trading firm (which allows you to trade the firm's capital), it's important to read the fine print of the agreements and policies and understand what you are signing.

Many firms ask you to deposit money up front, to be responsible for your trading losses, and some even ask you to indemnify the firm for losses in excess of your deposit amount. Most firms have a laundry list of expenses they will charge your account and restrictive policies for how you may trade (no overnight positions and much more). Take careful note of their margin and lending policies.

A proprietary trading opportunity may suit your needs, predominantly by giving you access to much greater trading capital than you have available or are prepared to risk in your own trading business. Pattern day traders with "customer accounts" may only have margin up to 4 to 1, whereas proprietary traders may have margin of 10 or 20 to 1 within a firm (even though the firm itself is limited to less margin overall). Your margin is not supposed to be directly connected to your deposit, but it often is, in an unofficial manner.

A day trading business is a high-risk activity to begin with. and proprietary trading with far greater leverage can be even more risky. Prop trading firms explain the point that they are on the hook for your losses, but they can control your trading and risk and usually make sure to limit your losses to the extent of your deposit, which most can ask you to replenish after a draw down.

Proprietary trading firms (PTFs) offer three types of agreements:

- Employment contracts or deals without signed contracts
- Independent contractor agreements or deals without signed agreements
- LLC operating agreements

Employment Contracts or Deals Without Signed Contracts

Some PTFs offer employment by hiring you to trade their firm's capital and paying you a salary, which is reported on a W-2. As a legal employee, you are eligible to participate in the firm's employee benefit programs including health insurance plans, retirement plans, and other fringe benefit programs. Because you get these benefits and a salary, employment prop trading deals offer significantly lower payout percentages from the trading gains you generate. Some employment deals require deposits, while others do not. Most offset future payouts with prior losses, so you are responsible for losses in a sense. Few employment deals require you indemnify the firm for losses.

For tax purposes, you have employment tax status. You have the following taxes withheld from your paychecks: payroll taxes (social security and Medicare taxes) and federal and state income taxes, based on your number of W-4 allowances. The firm pays 50 percent of the payroll taxes and you pay the other 50 percent through withholding. Employee tax status is inferior to trader tax status, independent contractor tax status, or LLC member (partner) tax status. All these other statuses have business treatment, which means they can deduct all possible business expenses from gross income without limitation. Employees don't have business tax breaks, but may deduct nonreimbursed employee business expenses on Form 2106. These miscellaneous itemized deductions are only deductible in excess of 2 percent of your adjusted gross income (AGI). Plus, these deductions are added back when computing alternative minimum tax (AMT). Home office expenses are not allowed unless your home office is required by your employer under strict conditions, which are rarely the case.

For legal purposes, don't just rest on the laurels of figuring you are an employee and therefore have no risk. Read the fine print of your agreement. The firm may require you to indemnify them for losses, which is rare, but possible. It's always wise to consult with an attorney before signing any important agreement.

The PTFs maintain a subtrading account for your trading activity, and your W-2 compensation is usually calculated as a percentage of your net trader profits (after the PTF charges you for various fees and expenses). Compensation percentages vary by firm, but 60 percent is probably average.

Independent Contractor Agreements or Deals Without Signed Agreements

Many firms that offer employment deals also offer independent contractor (IC) deals as well. Independent contractors are similar to employees in that they perform work for a company, but they are different in tax and legal ways.

A company is responsible for its employees, but not for its ICs. Many large companies try to save on employee benefit costs by using ICs since the company is not responsible to pay payroll taxes for ICs. But the IRS and state unemployment divisions challenge companies on the "20-part test" to determine whether the ICs really are not disguised employees. States are hungry to collect more unemployment insurance and workmens' compensation. ICs are not entitled to unemploment insurance, whereas employees are.

Ask your prop trading firm if your IC terms and conditions and actual fact pattern will pass these tests. If you don't have any other trading accounts outside of the firm, or any other work besides this job trading for the firm, and you report to work at the firm's office, and they supervise and direct your trading efforts closely, you may fail the independent contractor tests. To learn more, see Employees vs. Independent Contractors at www.irs.gov.

Independent contractors are responsible to pay their own taxes. Read the fine print in your IC agreements. IC agreements are similar to employment agreements, except you may be asked to deposit higher amounts of money and you should be granted higher payouts versus employees. IC agreements usually don't provide for advances, and you are just paid from your trading gains generated. Many firms will hold back reserves. IC agreements usually provide for full loss responsibility with the firm recouping your losses and expenses before they pay out new high net profit gains.

Watch Out: Some firms may require indemnification for losses even if you don't generate future gains, meaning the replenishment of deposits to cover losses or a promissory note to pay back losses over your deposit amounts. As an IC, you are engaged to trade the firm's capital, and you are paid for your work. You have earned income from management services, not a share of trading gains. So you owe SE taxes and you can contribute to tax deductible retirement plans and deduct your health insurance premiums. See the tax section for IC proprietary traders in Chapter 1 to learn about some ways to possibly avoid SE taxes.

LLC Operating Agreements

Many PTFs are organized as limited liability companies (LLCs). Some of these firms previously hired traders as ICs and provided their tax information on a Form 1099-Misc, but the SEC and exchanges forced broker-dealer PTFs to change their business model to become LLCs. The SEC and exchanges also required that all proprietary trader members of these LLCs organized as broker-dealers be registered with the SEC (Series 7 or other).

These PTF LLCs usually require LLC members to pay a minimum deposit of $25,000 to the LLC. This $25,000 may be related to the $25,000 required for the pattern day trader rules. When you read the fine print of the LLC operating agreement, you see similar provisions to those mentioned on IC deposit accounts. The LLC member proprietary trader must maintain his or her deposit account at $25,000. All the losses and expenses incurred by the trader are first charged against the LLC member's capital account and ultimately charged against their deposit account. The proprietary traders are usually a different type of LLC member from the member-managers, the real owners who manage the company and share in a portion of the LLC proprietary traders gains, as well as firm-wide profits (from commissions, etc.). Unless a proprietary trader receives commission overrides from recruiting other proprietary traders for the firm, in general proprietary traders don't receive a share of commissions.

Most LLC operating agreements are written in favor of the Class A true owner/managing members. These agreements tend to be one-sided, and much of what these firms say you are entitled to is actually stated as "at the managing members discretion" in the agreement. In other words, management can make any changes they like at year-end or otherwise.

With an LLC operating agreement, you are signing up and committing yourself in connection with your deposit and capital. It is a serious legal agreement, and you should consult with a lawyer, who represents you alone and not the company, to avoid a conflict of interest.

IMPORTANT TAX MATTERS FOR PROPRIETARY TRADERS

Some proprietary traders are treated as independent contractors (who receive Form 1099-Misc), others are LLC members (who receive Form K-1s), and still others are employees (who receive a W-2). Proprietary traders need to understand their underlying agreements and utilize taxwise strategies that match their facts and circumstances. Not all proprietary traders and firms are alike, and different tax planning and reporting strategies are warranted.

Proprietary trading firm agreements are complex, and the entire industry is in a state of flux. Our firm is following several new developments that may significantly affect proprietary traders. You should follow these developments in the book's free update area (see Introduction).

Independent Contractors Receiving a Form 1099-Misc

In most cases, these independent contractor (IC) proprietary traders work for a broker-dealer and get paid by them as individual sole proprietors to manage a subtrading account within the firm. For tax purposes at year-end, the firm reports their compensation on Form 1099-Misc (nonemployee compensation). The proprietary trader is considered a sole proprietor and required to report this income on their individual tax return Schedule C (Business Profit and Loss, line 1, Gross Receipts).

An IC proprietary trader should deduct any trading business expenses on that same Schedule C, including but not limited to (qualified) home office deductions (from Form 8829) and travel if he or she has a home office (otherwise commuting is not deductible), meals and entertainment, (qualified) education expenses, supplies, Internet, research, and much more. For a list of many possible trading business expenses, see our trader tax return examples earlier in this book. Proprietary traders have similar business deductions as retail business traders.

The main difference between IC prop traders and retail "customer" traders, who are also sole proprietors, is that an IC prop trader's net income is deemed earned income and therefore subject to self-employment taxes on Schedule SE. Trading gains for retail traders are not earned income and not subject to SE taxes. Per the IRS website, the total self-employment tax rate is 15.3 percent of net earnings from self-employment. The tax is made up of two parts. The maximum amount subject to the social security part for tax years beginning in 2004 is $87,900. All net earnings of at least $400 are subject to the Medicare part, 2.9 percent.

SE taxes are costly, but benefits also come in connection with "earned income." You may contribute to a tax-deductible retirement plan based on earned income, whereas retail traders may not, unless they form an entity. You may also deduct 100 percent of your health insurance premiums from AGI up to the amount of your earned income, whereas retail traders may not, unless they form an entity.

Some tax credits are also based on earned income, such as the child tax credit. Retail traders, using entities, have flexibility in declaring how much earned income they have, and they declare only enough to drive their desired deductions and credits, whereas IC prop traders owe SE taxes on all their net income (without any flexibility). In some cases, it is possible to argue IC income is "other income"—not earned income—thereby saving on self-employment taxes. Of course, without earned income, you can't set up a tax-deductible retirement plan contribution or deduct health insurance premiums from AGI. You should consult a trader tax expert on this issue.

LLC Members Receiving a Form K-1

These traders usually become an LLC member in a broker-dealer entity by contributing a certain amount (usually about $25,000) to the firm as a separate deposit account. In most cases, the proprietary trader is assigned a subtrading account based on his or her own deposit paid into the firm, and the trader keeps a high percentage of the trading gains. If the trader loses money, the firm usually charges expenses and losses to their LLC member capital account and ultimately those losses to the trader's deposit account.

In almost all cases, LLCs are taxed as partnerships and the firm files an annual Form 1065 partnership tax return. The firm gives each LLC member (a partner for tax purposes) a Form K-1 at year-end. Technically, some LLCs can choose to be taxed as C-corporations. However, they would rarely do so because it is not tax-beneficial.

Although the proprietary trader is an LLC member and partner in the partnership tax return, in most cases, the proprietary trader does not share in any of the other partners' income or the firm's overall gains and losses. This arrangement is contrary to what happens in most partnerships, where partners do share in firmwide gains and losses. Most proprietary trading firm LLCs are structured so that the Class A members (i.e., the owner/managing members) share in the gains and losses of the firm (including but not limited to their share of the proprietary trader's gains and commissions).

The proprietary trader is usually a different type of class member (like Class B, C, or D) and only shares subtrading account gains and losses (the trading gains that he or she generate). Sharing agreements vary widely from firm to firm and among individual traders within each firm. Different classes of LLC equity are designed for these purposes.

The key point for tax purposes is that the allocation of gains and losses must follow "substantial economic effect." Therefore, K-1 tax reporting must "follow the money."

It is odd that one LLC member may report a $1 million gain and another a loss, but the IRS should accept this tax reporting as proper because it does have substantial economic effect.

Most proprietary trading firms elect to use IRC § 475 mark-to-market accounting in connection with their proprietary trading activity in securities only (not commodities so they retain 60/40 treatment benefits). A few firms do not elect IRC § 475 and therefore have capital gains and loss treatment.

The key point to understand is that all tax status, elections and character of income, loss, and expense are determined on the entity level, not the individual level.

As a partner in a partnership for tax purposes, you are required to use the tax elections made on the entity level. You do not have to elect IRC § 475 MTM on your individual level, but you may want to if you have trading accounts outside of the firm on your own account.

The proprietary trading firm K-1 passes through the gains, income, losses, and expenses to the proprietary trader. Most firms won't pass through net losses, because the Class A members will take them on their tax returns—a tax benefit to Class A members—even though they may have charged those losses against your deposit.

Note: Trading gains are not earned income and pass through to your individual return on Schedule E (if MTM) or Schedule D (if capital gains without MTM). Only earned income is subject to self-employment taxes. LLC members therefore don't have to pay self-employment taxes as independent contracts and employee traders do (payroll taxes are the equivalent).

The good part of earned income is that you can set up a tax-deductible retirement plan and also deduct your health insurance premiums. LLC-member propriety traders can't form retirement plans and deduct health insurance premiums on their trading gains from the firm. Some proprietary trader LLC members do have earned income if they get mentor fees for training other traders, or commission overrides on recruited traders (make sure that is legitimate). If that is your case, ask your firm to break down earned income versus trading gains on your Form K-1.

Most LLC firms do not reimburse traders for their trading business expenses outside of the firm, including but not limited to home office expenses, meals, travel, supplies, Internet services, and other trading expenses.

Some firms have accountable plans for reimbursing prop traders expenses outside of the firm. Make sure to use or lose these benefits before year-end.

If your firm does not have an accountable plan, then you can deduct all nonreimbursed expenses directly on your Schedule E, under where you report your ordinary income from MTM trading gains. You can also deduct home office expenses on Schedule E. These deductions are valuable.

Proprietary trading firms using the LLC model are only permitted by the SEC to allow individuals to join as LLC members. A firm may not permit another LLC or entity to join as a member; proprietary traders can't use entities like retail "customer" business traders for added tax benefits including retirement plans and health insurance plan deductions.

Note: Employee and independent contractor prop traders also may utilize retirement and health insurance plans. In this case, the LLC proprietary trader comes up short on some benefits.

Employees Receiving W-2s

These jobs are the real jobs. Employees are rarely asked to put up any money, so they are truly risking a firm's money and none of their own money. There are a few firms that offer "hybrid" jobs, which also require a deposit.

True employment jobs without requiring a deposit are rare. Only the best firms offer them, and they only offer them to proven traders with good performance records. They are not "come-ons" designed to lure new traders.

Although they have a good job, when it comes to taxes, employees get reduced tax benefits versus the independent contractor using Schedule C and the LLC member using Schedule E.

Try to get the firm to reimburse you for your trading expenses outside the firm. Report your remaining "unreimbursed employee business expenses" on Form 2106. The problem is that Form 2106 expenses are miscellaneous deductions subject to a 2 percent AGI limitation and additional itemized deduction limitations and not deductible for alternative minimum tax (AMT).

Deposits and How to Write Them Off on Tax Returns

Most proprietary trading firms require traders to put up a deposit when they join a firm. Most broker dealer prop firms require $25,000 or more, similar to the account size needed for a pattern day trading retail customer account. Nonbroker-dealer smaller proprietary trading firms allow smaller deposits and do not require brokerage licenses.

The proprietary trading firms claim that these deposits are segregated from capital accounts (for LLC members) or the subtrading accounts of independent contractors and employees. They claim that the leverage provided the trader is unrelated to the deposit amount. When we look closely, however, we think it is fairly related. It's a technical issue for the regulators.

Traders are usually required to replenish their deposits after the firms take the deposits to cover trader's losses on the firm's trading accounts. The question that often comes up is how to report (on tax returns) lost deposits that are not returned. A deposit can be lost in two ways:

1. When you leave a firm and the firm does not pay you back part or all of your deposit, usually because the firm applied your deposit against your losses in the firm, in accordance with your agreement. It can also happen if your firm goes out of business or simply chooses not to pay you back. Maybe, they just don't have the money.
2. You stay with the firm but you lose part of your deposit (the firm applies it to losses) and the firm requires you to replenish your deposit account to the original amount. The firm only gives you a deposit credit on their books for the original amount, not the replenished extra amount, which then is lost.

For example, if you deposit $25,000, lose money, and the firm takes that $25,000 entirely and you replenish it with another $25,000. To date you have paid $50,000 of deposits and the firm gives you credit on their books for a deposit of $25,000 only. How do you report the lost $25,000 deposit?

First determine if your firm allocated these losses to you on your Form K-1. As stated earlier, some firms do not allocate losses to proprietary trader LLC members and instead take the tax deduction themselves. If this happens, the good news is that in most cases you can take a business bad debt, an ordinary business loss. With this option, you can avoid the capital loss limitations of $3,000 on an individual tax return. So as soon as you pay in more then you are credited for on the firm's books, or you leave and don't get paid back the deposit on the books (or a portion thereof), that deposit loss can be a business bad debt if it's not a Form K-1 loss. LLC members report that business bad debt on Schedule E, when it's officially lost. Independent contractor prop traders report that business bad debt on Schedule C, when it's officially lost. You should consult with a proprietary trader tax expert first.

Nonresident Proprietary Traders

If you are not a U.S. citizen or resident (a nonresident) and are an LLC member of a U.S.-based prop trading firm, you owe U.S. taxes, whether you spend time in the U.S. or not. Your U.S. K-1 income is U.S.-source income on which you owe U.S. taxes. These same rules exist for investing in a U.S. hedge fund with trader tax status organized as a pass-through entity (LLC or LP). Nonresident proprietary traders in U.S. proprietary trading firms are subject to U.S. income taxation and withholding solely on the earnings reported by the U.S. proprietary firm and not on any other direct-access customer accounts or other types of income.

Most U.S. proprietary trading firms are organized as LLCs, and they file a U.S. partnership income tax return. Each LLC member, including nonresident aliens, is given a Form K-1 to report the member's share of gains, losses, income, and expense. In effect, your Form K-1 represents what you earned at the firm. You owe U.S. taxes based on the earnings, not cash distributions. So, even if the firm did not pay you all your earnings, you still owe taxes in the United States.

If a firm does not comply with these rules and fails to withhold taxes, the firm faces penalties. Some firms are rushing to set up international firms outside the United States for their nonresident members to join instead of their U.S. firms in order to avoid these tax withholding issues. International tax planning in this regard is complex, and some firms may not carefully address all tax treaty provisions.

It is important to note a key difference in U.S. tax treatment. Traders outside the United States have tax benefits in trading direct-access (or otherwise) versus being a member of a U.S. proprietary trading firm that files a partnership tax return. The direct-access trader does not owe U.S. taxes on trading gains, whereas the proprietary trader member of a U.S. LLC does owe U.S. taxes. Learn more about tax issues for nonresident traders in Chapter 1.

STATE RULES FOR
REGISTERED INVESTMENT ADVISORS

Do independent contractor prop traders need to be concerned with state rules for registered investment advisors? The answer may be Yes, but this issue is widely overlooked. A proprietary trader is engaged by a proprietary trading firm as an independent contractor and paid nonemployee compensation for money management advice. How is this arrangement any different from what a money manager does, and should the registered investment advisor rules apply? The SEC and states have rules for registered investment advisors (RIAs). California rules for investment advisors require registration if you have even just one money management client who pays for your advice.

This situation begs an important question. Many proprietary trading firms are organized or operate branch offices in California. These California-based proprietary trading firms engage individuals who are residents of California to be independent contractor traders for their firm. Should those independent contractor proprietary traders in California register with the state of California as RIAs? What about all California proprietary trader independent contractors trading with any proprietary trading firm around the country, it may not matter if the proprietary trading firm is organized in California or has a branch office of presence in California. For California RIA purposes, it really only matters where the investment advisor lives and works. Thousands of proprietary traders live in California, so is this situation a new problem?

No one on the Internet or within these firms is currently addressing questions, but the conservative course would be to register with California as an investment advisor. LLC members may or may not face this same issue—employees do not.

CHAPTER SUMMARY

Proprietary trading firms (PTFs) offer traders a few different types of deals—employment, independent contractors, and LLC members. Each deal has different tax and legal pluses and minuses, and they vary greatly among the PTFs. A few terms and conditions are common. You usually are required to maintain significant deposits in a PTF before having access to trade the firm's capital—with far greater leverage than you could arrange as a retail pattern day trader. Your deposits are usually at risk for all your losses and expenses, and most tax and legal matters are stacked in favor of the firm. Yes, you have greater leverage, but you also have a big brother telling you what to do. That works great for some and not so good for others. At least you have some nice choices in the trading business thanks to the efforts of entrepreneurs in the PTFs.

A Word of Caution: There are rumors flying about the SEC and other regulatory bodies reviewing the practices of PTFs, and the consequences, if any, can hurt proprietary traders in these firms. You don't want to wake up one day and find out you no longer can trade and lost your deposit. Follow the stories at http://www.greencompany.com/Prop-Traders/Traders.shtml and in the free update website section for this book.

CHAPTER 10

IRS Exams

TURNING UP THE HEAT ON TAXPAYERS

Recently, the IRS has started to examine more traders, as well as other types of taxpayers. The IRS has a new blessing from Congress to get tough on tax cheats, and Congress needs to raise revenue quickly to balance new budget deficits. Better compliance and enforcement are a key part of the strategy.

The IRS is auditing more trader tax returns and attempting to deny tax loss deductions (expenses and trading losses) for money-losing traders and some part-time traders. Many traders made a fortune in the markets before 2000, and they paid their fair share of taxes on those gains. The IRS was happy to look upon them in those years as good tax-paying customers. The markets crashed in early 2000, and the majority of traders gave back all their prior years' gains.

Many traders set up their sole proprietor businesses properly with trader tax status and mark-to-market accounting, allowing them by law to carry back their net operating losses to prior tax years. These traders filed Form 1045 NOL refund claim tax returns, and some are still expecting to receive large refund checks, plus interest, from the IRS.

Now it seems that some traders are receiving tax notices and tax exams instead of tax refund checks. The IRS is unable to attack the tax law concepts of trader tax status, mark-to-market accounting, and net operating loss tax laws. Instead, the IRS is interested in making sure that a taxpayer claiming a large NOL or regular refund is fully entitled by law to use trader tax status and mark-to-market accounting. For example, the IRS may want to make sure a trader reaches the threshold of qualifying for trader tax status (being in the trading business) versus merely being an active investor. Investors are not entitled to business deduction treatment and ordinary loss treatment with mark-to-market accounting. In order to use mark-to-market accounting, which converts capital losses into ordinary losses, a trader must first qualify for trader tax status. Then, the trader must duly elect MTM on time (by April 15 of the tax year) and also file a timely and proper Form 3115 (Change of Accounting Method). Some traders elected MTM too late and/or filed a late or improper Form 3115.

One problem is that the IRS itself has generated little useful guidance on the qualification issue.

To accommodate the growing number of questions received from traders, on November 19, 2001, the IRS added a new section to its IRS Publication "Investment Income and Expenses—(Including Capital Gains and Losses)—For Use in Preparing 2001 Returns" titled "Special Rules for Traders in Securities." Unfortunately, this guidance is still vague and does not offer concrete objective standards.

Another problem for the IRS is the fact that online trading is basically a virtual business that sole proprietors may operate from their home, office, or on the road.

The IRS seems to be having a hard time understanding the business and respecting it as a real business. The trading business is not a retail store that an IRS agent can visit to see proof of business activity. An active investor may have the same computer and home office setup as someone in the business of trading, and it is difficult for the IRS to tell the difference.

Lastly, the IRS seems bent on classifying the buying and selling of securities as an investment activity rather than a business activity. Perhaps, for the IRS, it seems too good to be true that someone can quit his or her job or have a second job at home, trading for a personal account. The IRS figures if you lost money, you don't have a profit-making intent, which is the key to overcoming the hobby loss rules.

The fact is that anyone with capital and computer savvy can put themselves in the same position as professional traders on Wall Street, which are well respected by the IRS as being in the business of trading. The IRS is catching up fast on e-commerce, so it's time for their agents to understand new business opportunities on the Internet. Online trading businesses are probably the biggest new Internet businesses.

The Bottom Line: The IRS has few guidelines for traders, and those that exist are quite vague. Moreover, the IRS has a motive to balk on paying refunds, and it seems bent on not respecting trading as a bona fide business activity. At every step of the way, we disagree with the IRS in this context. But the IRS has the power to examine traders, and many agents around the country are not experienced in trader tax laws and exams. This combination can lead to trouble for traders being examined. The IRS can make your life difficult, but don't back away from your rights to use trader tax status, mark-to-market accounting, and net operating losses, which would be unfair to you.

Some actual examples of IRS exams that have been resolved in favor of the taxpayer follow in the next sections:

Case 1: NYC Trader Exam

Facts

A NYC money-losing trader filed his 2001 Form 1045, Application for Tentative Refund, in order to carry back his 2001 net operating loss and recoup prior taxes paid in the preceding two years of $115,500.

In 2001 the trader reported trading losses of $346,680 and trader expenses of $2,239. Total trading proceeds were more than $729,000,000 with thousands of short-term intraday trades made during the year. Taxpayer was trading full-time with no other sources of income except for some interest income.

The trader filed his carryback claim in early summer 2002. Normally it takes ninety days for the IRS to process this form. Some problems with the originally submitted Form 1045 included the option in 2001 of carry-backing two years or five years. The accountant who prepared the carry-back claim did not indicate that the taxpayer was waiving the five-year carryback and carrying back two years instead.

The taxpayer and his accountant straightened out this issue with the IRS and submitted the election to waive the five-year carryback. Despite these delays, the trader received his refund checks in November.

Then about five months later in March 2003 the taxpayer received a letter from the IRS stating his 2001 return was selected for examination and to call and schedule an appointment. The trader handled the exam on his own. He told the agent a mistake must have been made in selecting his return for audit.

The agent responded that his return was indeed being selected for examination. The trader explained he submitted all the documents and paid all his prior taxes in order to claim those refunds. The taxpayer explained what he did for a living being a full-time trader.

The agent disallowed his trading losses as ordinary, converting them to capital losses, and changed his carryback return requesting the entire $115,500 in refunds back plus penalties and interest. The agent verbally told the taxpayer only broker-dealers (and not traders) could use mark-to-market accounting treatment as the reason for the disallowance. After the agent made his changes on Form 4549 Income Tax Examination Changes, the trader came to us for help.

Exam Process

The taxpayer represented to us that he had duly filed his 2001 mark-to-market election on time with his 2000 tax return by April 15, 2001. His account-ant sent us a copy of the 2001 Form 3115, Change in Accounting Method, that was also filed on time with his 2001 tax return as well as a copy sent to the IRS National Office. Once we were satisfied that the trader did have mark-to-market accounting, the next step was educating the agent about IRC § 475(f).

The IRS agent initially would not listen to reason and was hostile with us at first. He wanted us to go directly to appeals. We told him that was unnecessary because we could resolve the case at this level. In fact we were trying to save the agent from embarrassment with his supervisor. The agent denied ever telling the taxpayer that only broker-dealers could make the mark-to-market election.

The agent claimed he had tax research to support his position that mark-to-market trading losses belonged on Schedule D as capital losses and not Form 4797 Part II as ordinary losses. We knew this was completely wrong. We sent a detailed explanation of the facts and circumstances of the taxpayer as well as trader tax law to educate the agent. We faxed over to the agent a copy of the special rules for traders in Chapter Four of IRS Publication 550 and FAQs about traders from the IRS's own website.

Finally, the agent came around after being educated about trader tax law and mark-to-market accounting treatment and section 475(f) by phone, fax, and correspondence from us.

He realized that his conclusions were wrong and that the taxpayer's 2001 Form 1045 as submitted was correct as filed.

Lesson: Don't approach every IRS exam as a full-fledged exam. First, find out what the IRS focus is, and win on those points early. You may be able to close the case at that point.

Exam Results

The agent went back and revised his Form 4549 as a no change showing zero due the IRS. The trader's 2001 Form 1045 was upheld and his refunds allowed. This particular examination did not take long for us to resolve. We got involved in the case in April and by May had closed the case in favor of the trader. Not all examinations get resolved that quickly, but the agent was clearly misinformed about trader tax law and was willing to concede once the overwhelming evidence was presented. If we had not persisted with the agent and gone to appeals instead, it would have taken much longer to resolve. Notice that this agent was not interested in checking the underlying income, losses, and expenses. Rather it was solely a question of IRC § 475 MTM application.

Case 2: Part-Time Trader Exam

Facts

This real-life example describes how we won without going through a formal examination. In August 2003 the taxpayer received an IRS letter stating his 2000 trader tax return had been selected for examination. What was unique about this particular letter was that the IRS was only interested in examining every single line item on his trader Schedule C. This request was a new line of attack by the IRS toward sole proprietor taxpayers.

Normally in a request for examination, the IRS will not ask for supporting documentation for every single line item on a particular form or schedule.

They typically focus on a couple of areas such as travel and entertainment where historically the IRS has found weakness in taxpayers not having enough substantiation to support those types of deductions.

We prepared this taxpayer's 2000 tax return, and the client came to us immediately as soon as he received the IRS notice. We reviewed the trading facts again with the client. In 2000 the taxpayer traded part-time while working a full-time job. Because the taxpayer lived on the West Coast and took advantage of the time differential, the taxpayer was able to conduct activities of trading in the morning, going to his regular job, and then doing market analysis and trading research at night.

According to the taxpayer's trading fact sheet, he would start his day about 5:30 A.M. PST by reading and watching business news. Then he would make trades and watch the markets from 6:30 A.M. to 1:00 P.M. PST. From 1 to 7 P.M. PST he would go to work either in the office or hold meetings with clients with respect to his job in sales. Then he would go back to his trading business from 8 to 10 P.M., reviewing the market news and preparing for the next day's trading.

Total round-trip trades were 470 with average holding period of one day. The taxpayer averaged two trades a day and traded all year long. Total trading proceeds were more than $1 million dollars. Our conclusion was all these facts, including his trading expenses of $21,871 and time spent, were sufficient for qualifying for trader status in 2000. The taxpayer did not elect mark-to-market for 2000 and was a cash basis trader, meaning he could report his trader expenses on Schedule C but not treat his trading losses as ordinary. Trading gains and losses were reported on Schedule D.

Exam Process

After reviewing the facts again with our client, we discussed our approach to his examination. The IRS was focusing in on trader expenses totaling $21,871, which were deducted on his 2000 return and helped offset income from other sources such as his wages. If the IRS disallowed his trader status and corresponding trader expenses, our client would be looking at an additional tax bill of $6,739 plus penalties and interest.

We discussed a particular strategy that had worked in the past and that we wanted to try again for this exam. We decided to correspond with the IRS to ask for a retraction of their examination. The IRS calls it a reconsideration, or recon procedure. We believed the facts and circumstances warranted such a request; the IRS lacked sufficient reason to conduct a full-blown examination, wasting valuable IRS resources not to mention the costs to the client for our time spent dealing with an exam.

We drafted and submitted a detailed letter explaining the taxpayer's facts and circumstances, trader tax law, why the taxpayer qualified as a trader, and why those trader expenses were ordinary and necessary business expenses under IRC section 162. We explained that we believe the taxpayer was selected for examination in error because of the unique way traders report their trading income on either Schedule D (for cash basis) or Form 4797 Part II (for mark-to-market) with trading expenses reported elsewhere on Schedule C.

When the IRS sees just expenses on Schedule C, it raises eyebrows and invites further scrutiny, but money-losing traders have no choice because it is the proper way to report their trading business on two separate schedules. We've seen many tax preparer mistakes where trading losses are erroneously reported on Schedule C. Trading gains or losses belong on Schedule D or Form 4797 Part II and the instructions are quite clear about it.

We do suggest a strategy of transferring gains from Schedule D or Form 4797 to Schedule C to reduce the chance at IRS questions and for other reasons. More on this follows.

Exam Results

After faxing our letter to the IRS district office, we received a phone call from an IRS supervisor. We went over the facts again, and the supervisor agreed with us that no good reason existed for them to conduct an exam. She realized it would wind up being a no-change audit, which the IRS prefers not to do. The IRS is not in the examination business to waste valuable resources chasing after taxpayers that will result in no audit adjustments or additional monies the government can assess or collect from taxpayers.

The next step was sending our request to the IRS's Area Compliance Director for final approval. By mid-September 2003 it was approved. The IRS response stated the following:

> We are pleased to tell you that after further review of your tax returns for the above periods, we have accepted them as filed. Do not consider this as an examination that resulted in no change in your tax liabilities. You were not examined for these years.

This case is an example of a win without going through hoops defending trader status and spending hours with an agent educating them on trader tax law and going over receipts and cancelled checks for all those trader expenses. Again, we were able to resolve this exam quickly in less than two months because of the facts and circumstances and the fact that the client came to us first rather than dealing with this exam on his own, which would have been a big mistake. Could the IRS come back later you ask? No, the statue of limitations ran out. Any reexamination of a 2000 trader return had to be made before April 15, 2004.

Case 3: Full-Time California Trader Exam

Facts

In July 2003, the taxpayer received an IRS letter stating his 2001 trader tax return had been selected for examination. Again, it was another letter indicating the IRS was only interested in examining every single line item on his trader Schedule C and nothing else. We noticed these unique examination letters coming out in July 2003. We talked to revenue agents who confirmed this approach is something new the National IRS office in Washington, D.C., came up with and that all IRS service centers started following last year. It's a particularly burdensome request. The IRS claimed they needed to conduct this type of audit to develop statistics to assist them in coming up with computerized red flags. Because of the uproar, those TCM exams (initiated in the late 1980s, which examined every single line of taxpayers' Form 1040) were put on the back burner until recently. The IRS was supposed to start up these TCM exams sometime in 2003 with 20,000 unlucky taxpayers.

We did not prepare this taxpayer's 2001 tax return. The client heard about us through *Active Trader* magazine and contacted us to help him with this exam. He was not in the mist of a full-blown examination, which made our job much easier and allowed us to use our retraction strategy from the beginning. Once an examination gets underway, it is too late to ask the IRS to reconsider because they've already assigned an agent to the case who started work on the exam.

We started by reviewing the taxpayer's 2001 tax return, paying particular attention to the trader portions of the return. We went over the following facts with the client: In 2001 the taxpayer was a full-time trader who traded all year long. Total trades were more than 4,400 with an average holding period of one day. The taxpayer averaged 20 to 30 trades a day. Total trading proceeds were more than $46 million. Our conclusion was all the facts, including his trading expenses of $17,561 and time spent, were sufficient for qualifying for trader tax status in 2001. The taxpayer did not elect mark-to-market for 2001 and was a cash basis trader, meaning he could report his trader expenses on Schedule C but not treat his trading losses as ordinary. Trading gains and losses were reported on Schedule D. We did notice an error in the way his trading losses were reported on Schedule D, which might have precluded an exam had it been prepared right in the first place. The accountant failed to report total trading proceeds on one of his trading accounts. Looking at the Schedule D itself, you would not see trading proceeds in the millions, which was evident when reviewing the 1099s.

Exam Process

After reviewing the facts with the client, we discussed our approach to his examination. The IRS was focusing in on business expenses totaling $17,561, which were deducted on his 2001 return and helped to offset income from other sources. If the IRS disallowed his trader tax status and corresponding trader business expenses, our client would be looking at an additional tax bill of $3,000 plus penalties and interest.

We discussed our retraction strategy. We believed the facts and circumstances warranted such a request.

We submitted a detailed letter explaining the taxpayer's facts and circumstances, trader tax law, why the taxpayer qualified as a trader, and why those trader expenses were ordinary and necessary business expenses under IRC section 162. We again explained that we believed the taxpayer was selected for examination in error because of the unique way traders report their trading income on either Schedule D (if cash basis) or Form 4797 Part II (if mark-to-market) with trading expenses reported elsewhere on Schedule C. When the IRS sees just expenses on Schedule C, it may invite further scrutiny.

Exam Results

After faxing our letter to the IRS district office, we called them. The supervisor agreed with us and sent our request for reconsideration or a "survey" as she called it to the area compliance director for final approval. In this particular case after waiting several weeks, we received a fax on IRS letterhead in mid-September 2003 stating the following: "This is written confirmation that, according to our records, the audit for the taxpayer's 2001 return has been surveyed and the administrative file is back at the Service Center. As we discussed, this action took place on 8/19/03 and there should have been a formal letter sent at that time. We apologize for any inconvenience this may have caused. This fax will serve as your written confirmation for your files."

This case is another example of a win without a big exam with the IRS. The retraction or reconsideration strategy works, and we have proof based on our own exam experience with two recent cases. IRS resources are spread thin and they are understaffed. They do not have time to waste with honest traders who are only following the law.

We were able to resolve this exam quickly in three months because of the facts and circumstances and because the client came to us first rather than dealing with this exam on his own. An IRS reexamination of this client's 2001 trader return must be initiated before April 15, 2005, according to the statute of limitations. We highly doubt this client will get another notice, but a remote possibility means we will continue monitoring the situation.

DO SCHEDULE Cs CAUSE
IRS TROUBLES FOR TRADERS?

After reading the above exam case section, it is apparent that the IRS targets Schedule C business losses for tax exams for all taxpayers including traders. Schedule C has historically been considered a red flag by tax preparers and care should be taken.

Sole proprietor or unincorporated businesses report their business activity including revenues, expenses, and net income on Schedule C (Profit or Loss From Business), which is part of their individual tax return Form 1040. Other businesses form separate legal entities, many of which must file separate entity tax returns.

Most small business owners prefer pass-through entities, which pass-through items of income and expense to the taxpayer's individual tax return. Traders who choose entities (for retirement plans and health insurance premium deductions) prefer pass through entities, and that means that all business activity still winds up on their individual tax return.

The question often comes up, should a business trader remain unincorporated and file a Schedule C or should they form a multimember LLC, partnership, or S-corporation and report their trading activity on Schedule E?

The IRS has announced new plans to increase their exams of pass through entities and individuals who report that income or loss on Schedule E. The IRS also has a matching program to compare pass-through entities returns with Schedule E, to make sure the pass-through is properly reported.

If a trader has trading losses and large trading business expenses, their individual tax return has the same results whether they are unincorporated with a Schedule C or have a pass-through entity with losses on Schedule E.

If a trader has trading gains and business expenses, here is how GTT suggests they file under both scenarios (unincorporated versus incorporated).

For an unincorporated business trader, trading expenses are reported on Schedule C and trading gains are reported on Schedule D (cash method) or Form 4797 (MTM method). A key GTT trader tax return filing strategy is to transfer sufficient trading gains from Schedule D or Form 4797 to Schedule C to zero out Schedule C, thereby not reporting a Schedule C loss. This strategy serves to prevent most IRS questions or exams.

For an incorporated multimember LLC, partnership, or S-corporation, trading expenses are reported on line 1 of the Form K-1 (ordinary gain or loss). If the entity uses MTM, trading gains are also reported on line 1 of Form K-1, reducing expenses or generating net income if gains exceed expenses. MTM trading losses add to the size of the Form K-1 line

1 ordinary loss, which is reported on Schedule E. If the entity uses the cash method, capital gains and losses are reported on different Form K-1 lines and pass through to Schedule D.

The Bottom Line: Both unincorporated and incorporated pass-through entity traders report business expenses and trading gains and losses on their individual tax returns, and both can cause equal attraction to the IRS audit systems.

Whether you incorporate or not, what's most important is to follow the GTT strategies on transferring trading gains to offset trading expenses to reduce your red flags. It is also key to include tax return footnotes to explain trader tax status, MTM, and how you handle your tax reporting.

As pointed out in our IRS exam cases, you should try to get a recon of your exam before it even starts. If that is not successful, then focus the exam on proving your trader tax status and explain that you have a low level of expenses versus other businesses, and they are at reasonable and believable levels. Query the IRS agent or supervisor. Why waste your valuable time and energy on my small trading business? There is no hidden cash income—the main focus of Schedule C exams—and all trading transactions go through highly regulated broker dealers.

CHAPTER SUMMARY

The first key to winning IRS exams is to prevent them from happening in the first place. Don't raise red flags on your trader tax return; report everything properly and explain it all in well written footnotes. This entire book is dedicated to making this happen. If you do receive an IRS notice or question, don't panic but also don't reply to it on your own. First engage a trader tax expert with good IRS exam experience on trader exams and have that expert reply to the IRS on your behalf. A good expert will first try for a recon and if that does not work, they should try for a quick win by focusing on trader tax status, the trader tax laws, your MTM status, and the general aspects, but not line-by-line documentation. Only as a last resort should you get into line-by-line documentation. If the agent still wants changes, so be it, go to the next level in appeals. An appeals officer has a different focus; they want to prevent tax court cases that the IRS may lose. If you lose in appeals and owe tens of thousands or more, consider tax court. Again, at every step of the way, you need a proven expert.

A Cautionary Tale: A recent tax court case was recently decided in favor of the IRS (Chen vs. IRS). Chen tried to defraud the IRS with a phony MTM claim, and he was also a part time trader in business for only one quarter of the year. He hurt his own cause and the cause of all traders by representing himself in his exam and trying to fool the IRS. To follow the latest in tax court cases and more news on the Chen case, see the free update section for this book at www.greencompany.com (see Introduction for details).

CHAPTER 11

Tax Law
Changes for Traders

Congress and the White House are always tinkering or suggesting drastic change to the income tax code. Business traders benefit from having most of their benefits occur "above the line" as part of gross income. We address new tax legislation passed and on the agenda.

HOW THE 2003 TAX ACT
AFFECTS BUSINESS TRADERS

Section 179 depreciation (which allows for 100 percent first-year depreciation) now includes off-the-shelf computer software. Before, software was not an eligible deduction.

The 50 percent bonus depreciation has many special dates for phase-in and phase-out. This classification means that taxpayers should not do their returns manually, instead, they should rely on tax software for these items.

Dividends

Brokers will be required to have their 1099s report qualifying dividends versus nonqualifying (or, 15 percent rate dividends versus ordinary dividends).

So, this change should reduce some complexity for taxpayers and their tax preparers. However, notice some complexities are all dependent on the taxpayer and will not be sought out on the Form 1099.

The holding period for qualifying dividends is changed to 60 of 120 days before the ex-dividend date (raised from 45 of 90). This change essentially ruins things for business traders, and they won't have qualifying dividends on their trading positions.

If you owe dividends on short positions, the owe part is ordinary. Therefore, the offsetting dividends on the long side of positions are nonqualifying.

The theory of the new tax act is clear. It makes sure that if you have offsetting ordinary (higher tax rate) tax deductions, you convert an otherwise qualifying dividend into a nonqualifying dividend. So, it eliminates arbitrage opportunities to deduct short dividends or other items at ordinary rates and get 15 percent rates on gains.

You can borrow money to buy dividend stocks as investment positions and deduct ordinary interest as an offset to 15 percent rate qualifying dividends. However, notice the next rule on investment income, which may limit some of this strategy.

Investment Income

This rule appears to mean that if you use qualifying dividends as part of your investment income for purposes of deducting investment interest expenses at ordinary rates (investment interest expenses are limited to investment income), your qualifying dividends become nonqualifying. It's not possible for a broker to report this investment income on a Form 1099, because every taxpayer's return is different. Tax software should handle this issue.

Many provisions distinguish between what is and what is not a qualifying dividend (REITs, foreign corps, regulated investment companies, etc.). On the other hand, most of the act is straightforward on rate acceleration, bigger and better depreciation, the child credit increase, and the complex rules on dividends.

The Bottom Line: Business traders and investors will benefit greatly from reduced tax rates. Ordinary rate reduction helps everyone. Business securities traders don't have many long-term capital gains, so this rate reduction won't help them much. Business and investor commodities traders will benefit from the long-term capital gains rate reduction, because they have 60/40 treatment and the 60 is the long-term part. All traders should consider segregating some investments to generate long-term capital gains and qualifying dividends. Buy-and-hold at low market values may be a good strategy now (if you think the market is trending higher).

Business traders and investors will benefit from increased depreciation; it is a subsidy to buy more computers and other equipment. This strategy is no giveaway, though, because it allows you to deduct what you spend a little faster. Big deal!

Business traders will rarely have qualifying dividends, because few will meet the 60-of-120-day holding period rule.

The dreaded alternative minimum tax (AMT) is reduced with higher exemptions. This change helps most middle and upper income taxpayers, especially those in higher-taxing states (state taxes are not deductible for AMT). Most business treatment with trader tax status is beyond the tangles of AMT.

All in all, the 2003 Tax Act is a helpful tax act. It's too bad all the dividend hoopla doesn't help business traders.

MISCELLANEOUS
RULES FOR TRADERS

Short-Sale Expenses and
Substitute Payments in Lieu of Dividends

If you short stocks as part of your trading program (certainly a profitable activity the past few years), you need to know how short-sale expenses and substitute payments in lieu of dividends are handled on your tax returns.

Short-Sale Expenses

While you are short a security, you might be responsible for paying a dividend to the true owner of the stock (the person or entity you borrowed it from). Your payment of this dividend is considered a short-sale expense.

According to IRS Publication 550, if your short sale is open for forty-six days or more, the short-sale expense is considered interest expense. Qualified traders deduct interest expenses on Schedule C (individuals) or as ordinary deductions on entities. Investors deduct investment interest expense as an itemized deduction on Schedule A.

According to IRS Publication 550, if your short sale is open for less than forty-six days, then the short-sale expense should be added to the cost basis of the securities purchased to close the short sale.

For this reason, all short sellers should elect and use mark-to-market accounting, which will ensure that your trading losses are ordinary in nature. You don't want to convert short-sale expenses into unutilized capital losses.

With MTM, you are in the best position to be a short seller. An investor ends up with limitation on capital losses or investment interest expenses. A business trader without MTM ends up with capital losses and ordinary trading business expenses. An MTM business trader ends up with ordinary losses and ordinary trading business expenses. If that's the case, you don't need to bother with the forty-six-day rule.

Most traders close short sales in less than forty-six days, so they will end up with their short-sale expenses reducing their trading gains and losses.

Substitute Payments in Lieu of Dividends

The flip side of short-sale expenses is substitute payments in lieu of dividends. Consider the case of person A, who lends a security to person B, who then sells it short to person C.

Person C receives the true dividend and has simple tax matters. In fact, he or she doesn't even know a short sale occurred. Person C receives a Form 1099-Dividend at the end of the year and reports their dividend on Schedule B (Interest and Dividend Income). Person B is the short seller and has short-sale expenses.

Person A is the one who has substitute payments in lieu of dividends. In a sense, person A is receiving a dividend. For tax purposes, though, only person C is allowed dividend tax treatment (because corporations get special advantages and the IRS does not want double dipping on these benefits).

Person A receives a Form 1099-Misc. A business trader should report this amount on Schedule C on the Other income line. This income is not subject to self-employment taxation. An investor should report this income on Form 1040, line 21, Other income, which is also not subject to self-employment taxation.

Tax treatment for a business trader versus an investor does not differ here. The only difference is using Schedule C versus page 1 of Form 1040. One benefit is the trader has more income, which comes in handy when using section 179 depreciation and home office expenses. Person A does not get qualified dividends treatment.

Conclusion

Congratulations—you made it to the end of my tax book, and tax books are not the most fun to read.

If you jumped ahead to this conclusion, that's okay, as long as you absorbed most of the book and plan to use it as a road map going forward. If you already read it cover to cover, we applaud you for making an excellent investment of your time. You have what it takes to save significantly more in taxes—patience, time and foresight. Now comes the good part— it's time to collect your rewards in the form of tax breaks, reduced tax payments, and/or big refunds. That part is on everyone's best-buy list.

You should now be fully informed about all the special tax breaks for traders. You also understand that knowledge alone doesn't deliver tax savings. You must execute these trader tax strategies on a timely basis and remember to not sell yourself short. These strategies are battle tested, and they work whether or not your friends know about them. Don't count on getting good second opinions from other accountants—they are still in the dark about this subject. Most traders and professionals still don't know how to turn a trader's garbage (losses and expenses) into gold. *The Tax Guide for Traders* not only shows you how to get huge refunds on trading expenses and losses, it shows you how to reduce your taxes on gains (with expenses, retirement plans, and much more).

Reading may have been beneficial, but only timely concerted action on your part will deliver these trader tax savings. Here is a summary of your steps to take:

First, determine whether or not you qualify for trader tax status, which is business treatment. This first step is actually the hardest and most crucial. If you qualify, all the trader tax breaks are unlocked, and you can collect them in further steps. But if you don't qualify, you will miss out on most of these benefits.

Don't make this qualification decision lightly. As pointed out, the laws are vague and unclear, and you may need to consult with a proven trader tax expert to make the right determination. If you don't qualify when you study the situation, consider that by trading a little more actively in the future, you may qualify later on, or even for the entire year.

Qualification for business treatment converts all your trading-related expenses to business deductions, which will save you a large amount in taxes (figure between several thousand to tens of thousands, depending on your level of expenses, including home office deductions). This savings alone is worth the price of *The Tax Guide for Traders* and the time you took to read it.

Now for the big bucks! A key golden strategy in this book is the concept of tax-loss insurance. If your trading house burns down (i.e., you lose lots of trading capital), you get an insurance reimbursement check (i.e., a tax-refund check based on ordinary tax-loss deductions). Investors lacking trader tax status can't get this type of insurance; they are stuck with onerous rules for capital loss limitations, wash sales, and straddle losses. Business traders are entitled to elect IRC Section 475 mark-to-market accounting (MTM) by April 15 of the current tax year (April 15, 2005, for 2005) to get this ordinary gain or loss treatment. MTM is the saving grace for traders who lose lots of money. It also exempts profitable traders from wash sales, thereby reducing their tax bills.

Securities, commodities, Forex, options, ETFs, E-minis—there are a bevy of new financial products to trade. Many products may trade alike, but they are taxed differently. The IRS breaks all these new products down into two camps—securities or commodities. You learned all the differences in this book and now know what are taxed as securities versus commodities. You learned you may save 12 percent in taxes by trading a commodity such as an E-mini rather than an ETF, a security. This is one case where you may want the tax tail to wag the dog. Commodities (including futures, broad-based indices such as the E-minis, and Forex—if you elect out of IRC 988) are taxed at 60/40, and the blended maximum 2004 tax rate is 23 percent. Securities (stocks, stock options, bonds, mutual funds, ETFs, narrow-based indices, and single-stock futures) are taxed at ordinary 2004 income tax rates up to 35 percent.

Mark-to-market accounting is recommended for all securities business traders, but not for profitable commodities traders. Securities traders pay the same 35-percent tax rate on gains with or without IRC Section 475 MTM, but with MTM they unlock ordinary loss treatment—a chance to get huge refunds faster. Commodities traders skip IRC Section 475 because why should they pay a 12-percent higher tax rate just to get ordinary loss treatment? From now on, when someone mentions IRC Section 475 (MTM), 1256 (commodities/futures), or 988 (currencies), you know exactly what they are talking about and what's good for you.

After you get the basics down, it's time to consider forming your own separate legal entity. The main benefits are creating earned income in order to have tax-deductible retirement plans, health-insurance premiums, and late-year MTM elections. You now have a good idea about which type of entity is best suited to your needs. If you are single, perhaps you want a single-member LLC or an S-corp. If you are married, maybe a husband-wife general partnership or a multimember LLC is best. Consider a consultation with an expert to find out if an entity is advantageous for you and exactly what the stealth taxes are in your home state.

Retirement plans are your ticket to a golden retirement. You learned about the best types of retirement plans for traders—mini 401(k) plans, SEP IRAs and Roth IRAs. You also learned how to avoid taxes and penalties from taking early withdrawals from your retirement plans. We showed you a few clever ways to trade your retirement funds directly, staying clear of ERISA, DOT, and the IRS. It's not easy or always prudent to trade your retirement funds.

Tax savings are great, but you also have potential accounting nightmares as an active trader. Commodities traders have it easy—their brokers give them a single profit or loss number on a Form 1099. All other traders face a potential nightmare if they try to figure out each trade-by-trade gain or loss manually, as they may have thousands or hundreds of thousands of trades. Consumer accounting software may be okay for investors, but it's not robust enough for hyperactive traders. Our GTT TradeLog family of software programs is designed for all levels of traders and is highly rated by the leading magazines. Download your trades and simply press a button for your tax reports, including all necessary adjustments (wash sales, MTM, 481 adjustments, and more). Your last—and maybe best—resort for accounting is our inventory approach or performance method approach accounting formulas. Rather than do your accounting trade by trade, you are able to come up with excellent results on an annual basis. It's like counting the entire forest rather than each tree in the forest.

You learned that you can claim business tax status after the fact, but you must elect MTM accounting benefits in advance of year-end. That's just one of many trader tax benefits that require advance planning (tax planning). For example, should or shouldn't you generate a wash sale at year-end? In one case it's smart; in another it's unwise. Should you pay your taxes on time with quarterly estimated tax payments or take a "margin loan" from the IRS to leave your money in the markets? You learned all the ins and outs of good trader tax planning in *The Tax Guide for Traders*, so now plan ahead!

You also learned about extensions. Too bad you couldn't use them at school or at work. The majority of people in the know use this hidden gem from the IRS. You also learned that it's only an extension of time to file, not to pay. The IRS and the states want their money on time. You learned how to navigate around the "safe harbors" and to be aggressive with returns and conservative with tax payments.

Proprietary trading gives you the chance to trade "other people's money." It sounds fantastic until you read all the fine print. In most cases, proprietary trading firms require deposits from you to cover part of your risks, and all your losses and expenses. Is that really other people's money? At a minimum, you do get other people's leverage, more than you could get as a retail trader. However, leverage is a double-edged sword: it can lead to faster profits or a faster demise. There are plenty of complications and nuances in various types of proprietary trading firms and their agreements, and they lead to different tax issues and business risks. Use the information in this book to avoid trouble and tap the benefits.

All is great until the IRS wakes up and selects your return for exam (audit). Expect the IRS agent to go on the attack, most likely because he doesn't have a proper trader tax education. Use *The Tax Guide for Traders* to turn your case around early and win. Educate the IRS agent and push to have your exam closed, even before it starts (with a recon). You will need a proven CPA or attorney to represent you. Don't become cannon fodder for the IRS without first getting help.

Tax laws change with the fierce political winds, but few significant changes are expected for business traders. Will 60/40 tax rates for commodities traders be repealed for commodities traders or extended to securities traders? Obviously, the latter is preferred. Tax rates may go up or down, but rates are applied on net income, the end result of business tax treatment. So, a trader's business deductions and losses are on safe ground, even with the far-reaching discussion of a flat tax.

Keep it simple and execute all our simple tax strategies. Trade, make money, pay lower taxes on income and, if you lose, get big refunds to replenish your trading accounts. Save for your retirement with tax advantages. Taxes are like trading—simulated trading does not make you any money, only actual trading does. Make the trades and execute your tax strategies.

Please join our GTT Alliance for Traders. Learn about the alliance and loads more on our website at www.greentradertax.com.

Thank you to all the fine CPAs and attorneys at GreenTraderTax.com and GreenTraderLaw.com for helping me with this book. Also thanks to Jeff Ponczak of *Active Trader* magazine for being my fine editor on our site, in our guides, and in this book. Thank you McGraw-Hill for sharing our vision to educate the big trader class on these (so far) hidden tax breaks. It's nice to be associated with the leading publisher for traders.

Happy trading and taxes.

Index